MW01201788

INSURANCE
Smart:

How to Buy
the Right Insurance
at the Right Price

Jeff O'Donnell

John Wiley & Sons, Inc.

New York • Chichester • Brisbane • Toronto • Singapore

Recognizing the importance of preserving what has been written, it is
a policy of John Wiley & Sons, Inc., to have books of enduring value
published in the United States printed on acid-free paper, and we exert
our best efforts to that end.

This publication is designed to provide accurate and authoritative
information in regard to the subject matter covered. It is sold with the
understanding that the publisher is not engaged in rendering legal,
accounting, or other professional service. If legal advice or other expert
assistance is required, the services of a competent professional person
should be sought. FROM A DECLARATION OF PRINCIPLES
JOINTLY ADOPTED BY A COMMITTEE OF THE AMERICAN
BAR ASSOCIATION AND A COMMITTEE OF PUBLISHERS.

Copyright © 1991 by Jeff O'Donnell

Published by John Wiley & Sons, Inc.

All rights reserved. Published simultaneously in Canada.

Reproduction or translation of any part of this work beyond that
permitted by section 107 or 108 of the 1976 United States Copyright
Act without the permission of the copyright owner is unlawful. Requests
for permission or further information should be addressed to the
Permission Department, John Wiley & Sons, Inc.

Library of Congress Cataloging-in-Publication Data

O'Donnell, Jeff, 1953–
   Insurance smart : how to buy the right insurance at the right
price / Jeff O'Donnell.
     p. cm.
   Includes bibliographical references and index.
   ISBN 0-471-52710-6 — ISBN 0-471-52711-4 (pbk.)
   1. Insurance—United States—Handbooks, manuals, etc.
2. Insurance—United States—Adjustment of claims—Handbooks,
manuals, etc. 3. Consumer education—United States—Handbooks,
manuals, etc. I. Title.
HG8531.O36 1991
368'.00973—dc20   90-44826

Printed in the United States of America

91 92 10 9 8 7 6 5 4 3 2 1

Contents

Insurance Awareness Test

WHAT DO YOU KNOW—OR THINK YOU KNOW—ABOUT INSURANCE?

This test will give you a good feel for what you can gain by reading this book. Please check YES or NO where indicated. You will find the answers at the end of the Introduction.

1. Your sewer backs up and ruins your downstairs carpet. Are you covered under your homeowners policy?
☐ **YES**   ☐ **NO**

2. Your car is hit by an uninsured driver. Will the damage be covered if you don't have collision coverage?
☐ **YES**   ☐ **NO**

3. You have a "stated value" of $3,000 on your 1965 Ford Mustang. If it's totaled in an accident, are you guaranteed a settlement of $3,000?
☐ **YES**   ☐ **NO**

4. You accidentally hit a deer on the highway and your car is a total loss. Is this covered under your collision coverage?
☐ **YES**   ☐ **NO**

5. You leave the window of your house open and your lawn sprinkler ruins your drapes. Is this covered under your homeowners policy?

☐ **YES**   ☐ **NO**

6. Do you think that term life insurance is cheap and will remain so even as you get older?

☐ **YES**   ☐ **NO**

7. A power surge blows out the $7,000 telephone system at the motel you own. Is this loss covered?

☐ **YES**   ☐ **NO**

8. When you turn age 65, can you automatically qualify for the majority of Medicare Supplement Insurance or Medigap policies regardless of your health?

☐ **YES**   ☐ **NO**

9. Your son accidentally breaks a lamp at your neighbor's house. Will your homeowners policy pay for it?

☐ **YES**   ☐ **NO**

10. Your garage burns down with your 750cc Yamaha motorcycle in it. Does your homeowners policy cover the bike?

☐ **YES**   ☐ **NO**

(Answers on page 5)

Introduction

Why should you buy and read this book? It's quite simple. Most consumers don't know anything about what their insurance will or will not do for them. Let me rephrase that just a little. Most consumers know just enough about insurance to make assumptions as to what's covered and what's not. This passing knowledge, usually gathered at the coffee shop, leads to a great many misunderstandings and potential disappointments.

I've never seen a subject in which so many people have an opinion as to what's covered or how much certain coverages cost. Here's a good example of how speculating about coverages can cost you money.

Most consumers think uninsured-motorist coverage on their car policy means that if an uninsured driver (and there are tons of them on the road) hits their vehicle, the damage will be paid for. Isn't that what "Uninsured Motorist" means? If that's the case, I should drop the collision coverage on my 1987 Chevrolet Impala and save some money, right? Wrong!

Uninsured-motorist coverage only pays "legally collectible damages if you or any person riding in your car is killed or injured by an uninsured vehicle." It doesn't say anything about your car.

If you removed the collision coverage from your Impala and were hit by a driver who had no insurance, you'd stand the loss of repairing the damage to your car or replacing it. You could sue the uninsured driver in Small Claims Court, but so what? If he doesn't have any car insurance, nine times out of ten he doesn't have any money either. Let's face it, you're out the dough.

Let me give you another example of why you should read this book. One of my clients, while preparing to leave for a vacation, accidentally unplugged her freezer. When she and her husband returned a week later, all of their meat was spoiled. When removing the meat (not a fun job), the wife tearfully asked her angry husband if they should write down what was ruined for the insurance company. He yelled that it would make little difference because the insurance company surely wouldn't pay for her carelessness! They never called me.

Several months later, the husband happened to mention this incident in passing. I knew right away they had the proper coverage to handle just this situation. In fact, their policy allowed me to pay them up to $500 with no deductible taken. Needless to say, they were very happy with the settlement.

The point is they had no idea this type of loss would be covered. I wonder how many times this occurs across the country, where money could be paid out if the people insured only knew. My rule is, "Always send it in! The claims department will decide what's covered and what's not."

I don't say you need to become an insurance expert. What I say is that by reading this book, you will become "insurance smart." You will shop much better for companies, agents, and coverages. You will know more about what is and what is not covered on a policy. You will also know whether to add optional coverage to better suit your specific needs.

I have included the questions my clients most frequently ask me. I have tried to explain and answer these questions in language that is easy to understand. Consumers today are sick and tired of "double talk."

Most people perceive insurance agents and their companies as "takers" in society. The consumer pays premium after premium. Some have claims that are paid, some have claims that aren't paid, and some have no claims at all. You never know what's in store for you. I will try to let you know what your insurance will do and what it won't do. I will let you know how to get the best insurance "buys" and how we quote each line of insurance for home, auto, etc. As you can see, this book will be most beneficial to anyone interested in buying insurance.

Answers to Insurance Awareness Test

1. No. There is no automatic coverage for sewer backup on a home-owners policy. However, some companies allow this coverage to be added on.
2. No. Uninsured-motorist coverage only pays for bodily injuries in an accident, not physical damage to your vehicle.
3. No. Having a stated value on a vehicle only means the insurance company won't pay *more* than what is stated on the policy. They will try to find out the true market value of the damaged vehicle.
4. No. If you strike a deer, it's considered a comprehensive loss, not a collision.
5. Yes, if the policy you have is a Special Form 3.
6. No. Term life insurance increases as you get older in most cases.
7. Yes, if you have a Business Owners Policy Package policy.
8. Yes.
9. Yes, if it's a Broad Form 2 or Special Form 3 policy.
10. No.

CHAPTER ONE

Home Sweet Home:
Homeowners Insurance

*F*or many people who buy homes, the purchase cost may be the largest single investment they'll make. Mortgage payments amount to a significant percentage of their income.

Almost all homeowners carry insurance, but many know little about it—until they file a claim. Only after the house is burglarized or burns to the ground does the buyer find out whether the insurance company provides prompt and fair settlements. Until then, homeowners typically pay the premium and hope for the best.

WHAT ARE THE MAJOR HOMEOWNERS CONTRACTS?

The main way standard residential policies differ is in the number of **perils** they cover. A "peril" is the cause of a loss that is covered on the policy. Fire, wind, and hail are just a few examples. The more perils your property is covered for, the more expensive the policy.

Generally, you can select either **named-perils** or **all-risks** policies. A "named-perils" policy is one in which the perils are specifically listed in the policy, while an "all-risks" policy is one in which everything is covered except the perils that are excluded. The consumer may find it less confusing to know what is *not* covered instead of what *is* covered.

THE SEVEN BASIC POLICIES

There are seven basic types of homeowners policies, called HO-1, HO-2, HO-3, HO-4, HO-5, HO-6, and HO-8, among which are policies for renters and for condominium and co-op owners (HO-4 and HO-6, respectively). Nearly 95 percent of homeowners are protected by such insurance; the figure falls to about 25 percent for renters.

The HO-1 and HO-2 are named-perils policies. The least expensive policy, the HO-1, covers eleven perils; the HO-2 policy adds 6 more, for a total of 17 perils.

The more expensive policies—the HO-3 and HO-5—are all risks policies, covering everything except the few perils that are specifically excluded from the policy. (See Tables 1.1 and 1.2.)

HO-1

The HO-1 policy offers basic protection against eleven specified perils known as fire, theft, and what are commonly referred to as **extended coverages**. "Extended coverages" are windstorm and hail, explosion, riot or civil commotion, aircraft damage, vehicle damage, smoke, vandalism, glass breakage, and malicious mischief.

HO-2

The HO-2 policy, called a broad form, is similar to the HO-1 but includes six more named perils. These are as follows:

- Sudden and accidental damage from artificially generated electrical current
- Falling objects, including trees
- Weight of ice, sleet, and snow
- Sudden and accidental tearing apart of a heating system
- Accidental discharge or overflow of water or steam
- Freezing

The HO-2 costs from 5 percent to 10 percent more than the HO-1.

HO-3

The HO-3 policy is decidedly the one being sold the most in today's market. Instead of stating what it covers, it tells you what it excludes. The HO-3 and HO-5 exclude damage from flood, earthquake (except in California, where the insurers are required to offer earthquake insurance on their policies), war, and nuclear accident.

Perils against Which Properties Are Insured under the Various Homeowners Policies

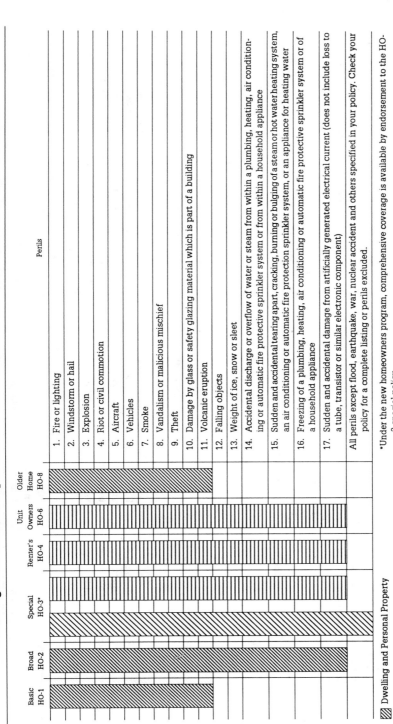

Columns: Basic HO-1 | Broad HO-2 | Special HO-3* | Renter's HO-4 | Unit Owners HO-6 | Older Home HO-8 | Perils

Perils:

1. Fire or lighting
2. Windstorm or hail
3. Explosion
4. Riot or civil commotion
5. Aircraft
6. Vehicles
7. Smoke
8. Vandalism or malicious mischief
9. Theft
10. Damage by glass or safety glazing material which is part of a building
11. Volcanic eruption
12. Falling objects
13. Weight of ice, snow or sleet
14. Accidental discharge or overflow of water or steam from within a plumbing, heating, air conditioning or automatic fire protective sprinkler system or from within a household appliance
15. Sudden and accidental tearing apart, cracking, burning or bulging of a steam or hot water heating system, an air conditioning or automatic fire protection sprinkler system, or an appliance for heating water
16. Freezing of a plumbing, heating, air conditioning or automatic fire protective sprinkler system or of a household appliance
17. Sudden and accidental damage from artificially generated electrical current (does not include loss to a tube, transistor or similar electronic component)

All perils except flood, earthquake, war, nuclear accident and others specified in your policy. Check your policy for a complete listing or perils excluded.

*Under the new homeowners program, comprehensive coverage is available by endorsement to the HO-3 special policy.

Legend:
- Dwelling and Personal Property
- Dwelling only
- Personal Property only

SOURCE: Sharing the Risk, published by the Insurance Information Institute. Copyright © 1989 Insurance Information Institute. Reprinted by permission.

Table 1.2 Guide to Homeowners Policies

These are the principal features of standard homeowners policies. The policies of some companies differ in a few respects from the standard ones. Policy conditions may also vary according to state requirements.

You can usually increase coverage for some items by paying an additional premium. The special limits of liability refer to the maximum amounts the policy will pay for the types of property listed. Usually, jewelry, furs, boats and other items subject to special limits have to be insured separately if you want greater coverage.

	HO-1 *(basic form)*	HO-2 *(broad form)*	HO-3 *(special form)*	HO-4 *(renters' contents broad form)*	HO-6 *(units or condominiums)*	HO-8 *(older homes)*
PERILS COVERED (see key)	1 to 11	1 to 17	1 to 17 on personal property except glass breakage; all risks, except those specifically excluded, on buildings	1 to 17	1 to 17	1 to 11
STANDARD AMOUNT OF INSURANCE ON house and attached structures	based on structure's replacement value	based on structure's replacement value	based on structure's replacement value	10% of personal insurance on additions and alterations to unit	$1,000 on owner's additions and alterations to unit	based on structure's market value
detached structures	10% of insurance on house	10% of insurance on house	10% of insurance on house	no coverage	no coverage	10% of insurance on house

trees, shrubs, plants	5% of insurance on house; $500 maximum per item	5% of insurance on house; $500 maximum per item	5% of insurance on house; $500 maximum per item	10% of personal property insurance; $500 maximum per item	10% of personal property insurance; $500 maximum per item	5% of insurance on house; $250 maximum per item
personal property	50% of insurance on house; 5% for property normally kept at another residence or $1,000, whichever is greater	50% of insurance on house; 5% for property normally kept at another residence or $1,000, whichever is greater	50% of insurance on house; 5% for property normally kept at another residence or $1,000, whichever is greater	based on value of property; 10% of that amount for property normally kept at another residence or $1,000, whichever is greater	based on value of property; 10% of that amount for property normally kept at another residence or $1,000, whichever is greater	50% of insurance on house; 5% for property normally kept at another residence or $1,000, whichever is greater
loss of use, additional living expenses; loss of rent if rental unit uninhabitable	10% of insurance on house	20% of insurance on house	20% of insurance on house	20% of personal property insurance	40% of personal property insurance	10% of insurance on house
SPECIAL LIMITS OF LIABILITY	Money, bank notes, bullion, gold other than goldware, silver other than silverware, platinum, coins and medals—$200. Securities, accounts, deeds, manuscripts, passports, ticket stamps, etc.—$1,000. Watercraft, including their trailers, furnishings, equipment and outboard motors—$1,000. Trailer not used with watercraft—$1,000. Grave markers—$1,000. Theft of jewelry, watches, furs, precious and semiprecious stones—$1,000. Theft of silverware, silver-plated ware, goldware, gold-plated ware and pewterware—$2,500. Theft of guns—$2,000.					Theft on premises limited to $1,000. No coverage for theft of items named at left off premises.
CREDIT CARD, FORGERY, COUNTERFEIT MONEY, ELECTRONIC FUND TRANSFER	$500	$500	$500	$500	$500	$500

(continued)

Table 1.2 (continued)

	HO-1 (basic form)	HO-2 (broad form)	HO-3 (special form)	HO-4 (renters' contents broad form)	HO-6 (units or condominiums)	HO-8 (older homes)
COMPREHENSIVE PERSONAL LIABILITY	$100,000	$100,000	$100,000	$100,000	$100,000	$100,000
DAMAGE TO PROPERTY OF OTHERS	$500	$500	$500	$500	$500	$500
MEDICAL PAYMENTS	$1,000 per person	$1,000 per person	$1,000 per person	$1,000 per person	$1,000 per person	$1,000 per person

KEY TO PERILS COVERED

1. fire, lightning
2. windstorm, hail
3. explosion
4. riots or civil commotion
5. damage by aircraft
6. damage by vehicles not owned or operated by people covered by policy
7. damage from smoke
8. vandalism, malicious mischief
9. theft
10. glass breakage
11. volcanic eruption
12. falling objects
13. weight of ice, snow, sleet
14. leakage or overflow of water or steam from a plumbing, heating or air-conditioning system
15. bursting, cracking, burning or bulging of a steam- or hot-water heating system or of appliances for heating water
16. freezing of plumbing, heating and air-conditioning systems and domestic appliances
17. injury to electrical appliances, devices, fixtures and wiring (excluding tubes, transistors and similar electronic components) from short circuits or other accidentally generated currents

Reprinted by permission from *Changing Times*, The Kiplinger Magazine (April–June 1988 issue). Copyright 1988 by The Kiplinger Washington Editors, Inc.

The HO-3 was developed to add to the previous two options, and it packages them into a "comprehensive" program. The HO-3 costs about 30 percent more than the HO-1.

HO-4 (Renters)

Renter's policies, which are relatively inexpensive, allow you to purchase the same types of coverages available to homeowners, such as replacement cost for your possessions and liability protection. For $100, the average cost of a complete renter's policy, you can not only cover $10,000 worth of personal property, but you can also get $300,000 worth of liability coverage, which is the amount most experts recommend as a minimum.

Liability is very important protection for any one to have and is especially important for the renter. Let's say you are renting an apartment in a triplex and through your carelessness, the triplex burns down. No doubt, your landlord has the building insured, but after the insurance company settles the claim, they'll probably come looking for you, as it was *your* negligence that caused the fire. Well, you *are* protected for this liability up to the limits of the policy.

HO-5

The HO-5 is the Cadillac of the homeowners policies. It's offered on a limited basis depending upon the age and condition of your home. Normally, it is not offered on houses built before 1950 or on dwellings insured for less than $50,000.

This policy is a more comprehensive version of the HO-3. Some of the differences are as follows:

- Instead of 50 percent of the dwelling insurance being provided for personal-property coverage, you get 75 percent.
- Instead of the $100,000 liability and $1,000 medical coverage, you get $300,000 and $2,000, respectively.
- Instead of having to add the replacement cost for contents endorsement, it's included.
- Instead of the $500 that is built into the HO-3 for jewelry, watches, and furs on a named-peril basis, you get a $2,500-aggregate, $1,000-per-item, all-risk coverage.
- Instead of the $500 for property damage to others, it provides $1,000.
- It includes the endorsement to replace your home at today's prices regardless of the amount the house is insured for at the present time. This means that if your house goes up

in smoke and it costs $89,000 to rebuild, you will get that amount of money despite having a face amount on the policy of only $85,000.
- It includes lock replacement in case of theft of your house keys.
- It provides coverage of up to $500 on the contents of your freezer for power interruption.

The HO-5 can cost about 10 percent more than the HO-3, but with most companies it is actually a little cheaper. The insurance company packages it to be more attractive by offering more coverages at either the same or a lesser premium.

HO-6 (Condominium Owners)

The HO-6 policy is issued to owners of condominium units. All too often, condominium owners overlook the damage and liability risks for which they alone are responsible. The HO-6 protects your personal possessions and your personal liability, and it provides coverage on real property, which is your insurance responsibility under the governing rules of the association.

The condo unit must be the principal residence of the insured and must be used exclusively for residential purposes. The named-peril coverages are virtually the same as with the HO-3 and the HO-5.

The insurance company covers

- The items of real property (e.g., light fixtures, built-in dishwasher, carpeting, etc.—anything not considered personal property) that are your insurance responsibility under the governing rules of the association
- Any building additions and alterations, installations, or additions that comprise a part of the insured premises
- Any fixtures and appliances contained within the insured premises that are part of the building

Items not covered by this policy are

- Outdoor antennas, including lead-in wiring, accessories, masts, and towers
- Detachable building items
- Structures designed or used for business
- Land on which the condominium or other structures are located

Your coverage consists of

- Real property
- Family personal property on your premises, including loss from theft
- Loss of use in case of damage to your property
- Condominium-loss-assessment coverage
- Liability
- Damage to property of others similar to the HO-4

HO-8

This policy is written on older houses that do not qualify for an HO-2 or HO-3. It is a very basic policy, covering the same 11 perils as the HO-1 policy. In most cases, your claim on a roof will be settled on an actual cash value basis rather than a replacement-cost basis.

This is a good policy if you don't have any choice. The insurance company will say whether your house qualifies for an HO-5, and if it doesn't, an HO-8 is the next best thing. The price is generally lower than for an HO-3, and you still get coverages for other structures, personal property, and liability.

NAMED PERILS—EXACTLY WHAT IS COVERED?

Let's look at HO-3 coverage for the purpose of this explanation. The HO-3, you remember, combines and expands the HO-1 and HO-2 coverages.

Fire or Lightning

The thing to be alert for is the lightning peril. If your clocks are off after a storm and your freezer has quit or the TV won't work, you probably have a lightning loss. Make sure you call your agent and let him or her know what's happened. It's possible to have major damage when lightning strikes, and this is a claim not everyone thinks of making.

Windstorm or Hail (Including Tornado)

After a windstorm, if shingles are strewn across the yard, it's obvious that you should call your agent and put in a claim. After a hailstorm, you may not see any damage, but that doesn't mean there hasn't been any. Look to see if there's any loose gravel in your rain gutters. If there is, then you've had damage to the shingles. The extent of the damage depends upon the age of the roof, the slope of the roof, the size of the hail, and the direction the storm came from. If the hail is larger than a golf ball, you should certainly call your agent, as it's almost certain there's been damage.

If, after inspecting the roof, your adjuster claims that you don't have damage but a month later your shingles start to curl, something is wrong! In many instances, the hail hits the shingle and breaks the seal; after being rained on and dried out by the sun, the shingle starts to curl. You have the right to ask for another inspection. Fight for your rights!

Explosion

This is not too common an occurrence, but the coverage is there none the less.

Riot or Civil Commotion

This peril covers damages sustained during riots when mobs that have gotten out of control damage property.

Damage from Aircraft

This category includes damage not only from aircraft but also from self-propelled missiles or spacecraft. If you live close to an airport, make sure you have this coverage.

Smoke

One of the worst losses you can have is from a fire in your home. Not only are the flames a problem, but the smoke also causes considerable damage. The residue from smoke covers absolutely everything, and it is difficult and expensive to clean up. In most cases, experts must be hired to do such a job.

Vandalism and Malicious Mischief

You're sitting in your easy chair reading the paper when, all of a sudden, something hits the living-room window. You look, and sure enough, someone using a pellet or BB gun has left a nice little hole or crack. Make two phone calls: to your agent and to the police department.

This coverage doesn't apply if the house has been vacant for 30 consecutive days immediately before the loss, which is a problem if you've moved away and haven't been able to sell or rent your house. Here's a helpful tip: Spend a night at the old house before the 30 days runs out. This will give you another 30 days' worth of coverage for vandalism.

Theft from the Premises

If you suspect that a theft has occurred on your premises, even before calling the insurance company, call the police. This gives them the opportunity to write a report and set up a file on what happened. Many insurance companies won't pay a theft loss if you haven't reported the incident to the police.

What if you fail to discover the theft for sometime? Let's say you put all of your fishing poles, tackle, etc., in the garage on the first of September; the next spring, when you go to get the gear for the new season, it isn't there! Sometime during the winter, someone got into your garage and stole everything. You can still put in a claim. Your insurance company should handle it without a problem even though months have elapsed since the theft occured.

Some situations in which theft is not covered are (1) if a person living in your home on a regular basis commits the theft; (2) if you're swindled, defrauded, or tricked out of personal property; and (3) if you lose a precious or semiprecious stone from the setting in a ring.

Theft Away from the Premises

Suppose you absentmindedly leave a nice 35mm camera sitting in the back seat of your car. If someone steals it, you're covered, whether the door was locked or not! Or suppose you're vacationing and there's a fire in your motel room; all of your belongings are destroyed. You're covered—just call your agent.

Damage by a Vehicle

This situation usually happens while you're backing out of or going into your garage. If you hit the garage door, you've got coverage under your homeowners policy after the deductible is paid. The damage to the car is paid for under your auto policy.

Glass Breakage

If you have kids, you've probably already used this coverage once or twice. Let's say your children are playing ball in the front yard even after you've told them twice to go down the block to the vacant lot. One of them hits the ball, and it breaks one of your windows. The good news is that the window is covered; the bad news is that you have a deductible of anywhere from $100 to $500. If your slugger breaks the neighbor's window, the insurance company pays for all the damages—no deductible!

Falling Objects

Covered under this peril is a tree limb that falls and damages your roof. This policy does not cover damage by outdoor equipment or yard fixtures that accidentally hit your house. For example, if a swing comes loose from your child's swing set and hits the house, this isn't considered a falling object. Also the policy will cover a loss to the inside of the building only if the falling object first damages the outside of the building.

Weight of Ice, Sleet, and Snow

This named peril happens more than a person might think, especially in states like Minnesota, Michigan, and Wisconsin; if you live in the South, having this coverage won't mean much to you.

Here's what can happen: A wet, heavy snow comes along and before you can say "blizzard," there's a three-foot accumulation on the patio roof. The roof groans and finally collapses under the strain. (It probably won't happen to the roof of the house itself. Most roofs on homes are built to withstand a heavy, wet snow.)

This loss is covered, but losses to the following items are not: awnings and fences, pavements, patios, outdoor swimming pools, outdoor saunas, outdoor whirlpools or hot tubs, foundations, retaining walls, bulkheads, piers, wharves, or docks.

Bursting or Tearing of Heating System

Heating, air-conditioning, or sprinkler systems are the items covered under this peril. Remember, it's the damage caused by the bursting or tearing apart of these systems that's covered, *not* the system itself. In other words, if your water heater breaks and floods the basement, ruining the carpet, the carpet is covered, but the water heater is not.

Accidental Discharge or Overflow of Water or Steam System

As with the above, this covers only the damage caused by a problem with these systems—not the pipes or the steam radiator, etc. If the pipe under the kitchen sink comes loose, floods the kitchen, and damages the floor and various home furnishings, all of the damaged items are covered. The cost to fix and replace the pipe is not. Here are some other exclusions from this peril:

- Gutters and downspouts—they are not considered part of the plumbing system
- Losses due to continuous or repeated seepage or leakage occuring over a period of weeks, months, or years. There's

a good lesson to be learned here: Don't wait! Make sure
you tell your agent right away if these problems occur.
- Sewer backups—they are *not* automatically included with
  this policy! This is a common calamity for homeowners. A
  sewer backup has all sorts of ramifications, like ruining
  boxes full of personal property that you are storing, or
  ruining the improvements you've made to finish a basement. While most companies don't include this peril, several major insurance companies are starting to write this
  coverage as an "endorsement" to the policy, so call your
  agent if you're interested, and see what he or she can do.

Damage from Freezing of Plumbing

This peril is covered as long as the house isn't vacant and/or
unoccupied. If the house is vacant, to be assured of compensation,
you need to (1) maintain heat in the building, and (2) shut off the
water supply and drain the system and all appliances of water.

Suppose you're living in the house and one winter you forget
to turn off and drain the outside faucets. As a result, the outside
pipe freezes and breaks, causing considerable water damage to
your house or household possessions. Does the fact that you forgot
to do what you usually do preclude you from collecting on the
loss? No, you can still collect on the claim.

Damage from Electrical Current to Appliances

If there's a power surge in the electrical system that blows out the
TV, you've got coverage for the damage. (If lightning causes the
blowout, you're covered under the lightning peril.) *Not* covered:
damaged tubes, transistors, or electrical components; or accidental
erasure of recorded data in computer systems.

Damage from Rain Seepage

This is important coverage, as it is a rather common occurrence.
If rain seeps through your roof and ruins the drywall ceiling
beneath it, damage to your ceiling is covered.

Accidentally Chipped Sink

If you drop a metal pan while washing the dishes and you chip
the porcelain sink, there is coverage for the damage.

Accidentally Scorched Surface

If you set a hot pan on your countertop and it scorches the surface,
you have coverage.

Accidental Building Damage

If you're moving a refrigerator down to the basement and the dolly strap breaks, allowing the refrigerator to crash down the steps, you've got coverage for the damage it causes on its way down.

Siding Accidentally Damaged by Missiles

One of the neighbors, angered because you let your dog loose on his lawn, grabs a rock and throws it against the side of your house, putting a hole in the siding. He denies he threw the rock, so what do you do? You can turn in a claim to your insurance company.

Damage from Wild Animals

This coverage protects you from deer, elks, or bears who pass through your town, get confused, and try a shortcut right through your front window.

Rodents—including squirrels—are not considered to be wild animals. Consequently, the quite considerable damage they can cause is not covered.

What about those incidents that you do not fit under the named-perils category? Should you assume that it probably isn't covered, and just do nothing? No! Call your agent and ask him or her what to do. You never know when something will be covered.

WHAT OTHER COVERAGE FOR PERILS MIGHT I NEED?

Flood Insurance

The most important risk excluded from homeowners policies is flood insurance. You can obtain it only through the National Flood Insurance Program, administered by the Federal Emergency Management Agency (FEMA), but only if you live in a community that participates in the program.

Under the program, your home can be insured for up to $185,000 in structural damage and $60,000 in losses to the contents. Premiums vary according to FEMA's assessment of the risk of flooding for a particular home. Obviously, the higher the risk, the higher the cost. The national average is about $240 per year for $65,000 in coverage. For information about the National Flood Program, call FEMA at 1-800-638-6620; in Washington, DC, call 731-5300.

Earthquake Insurance

If you live in an earthquake-prone area (like San Francisco), earth-quake insurance should be added to your basic homeowners pol-icy. In California, companies offering the basic policy *must* offer earthquake coverage to you *in writing*.

WHAT ARE THE COMPONENTS OF THE HOMEOWNERS POLICY?

DWELLING

A key factor in your insurance policy is the amount that covers the house itself. Except in the case of an older home, this figure should be based on the replacement value of your house, which is what it would cost to rebuild the structure. You should buy enough insurance to cover this cost, excluding the value of the land and the cost of the foundation (which doesn't need insur-ance).

Replacement cost (what it would take to rebuild your house from scratch) is not the same as market value (what you can sell your house for). Let's say you own a 15-year-old ranch-style home, for which you paid $50,000 ten years ago. How much insurance should you put on the house?

If you have a good insurance agent, he or she can work some figures up for you. Make sure that the agent measures the square footage of the house, notes whether the basement is finished, counts the number of baths, checks for central air-conditioning and heating, and sees if there's a detached or attached garage. All this information goes into figuring what it would take to re-build the same house, given today's labor and material costs. That figure is known as the replacement cost of the house.

Another way to determine the replacement cost is to hire a professional appraiser or you can measure the square footage of usable floor space in your house and multiply this figure by the current construction cost per square foot for similar homes in your area. For example, if your house covers 1,500 square feet, and the going rate for residential construction in your area is $45 per square foot, you should use $67,500 ($45 × 1,500) as the replacement-cost figure.

Don't underinsure! You can elect to insure the house for the whole amount or for a minimum of 80 percent of that amount. If the replacement value is $100,000, you can insure it for any-where from $80,000 to $100,000. There is, however, a danger if you choose to insure it for less than 80 percent. For example, if you insure it for 50 percent of the replacement cost ($50,000) and you have a loss of $25,000, you would collect only half of the damages, or $12,500.

In the case of a house that is more than 30 or 40 years old, how much insurance to buy is a tougher question, and you have to make certain adjustments. If you own an 80-year-old two-story house, you can't just rebuild without spending a small fortune. In most cases, you'll insure the house for the market value, a more realistic figure.

The best way to avoid being underinsured is to buy a guaranteed-replacement-cost policy. Companies that offer this option usually require that you insure your house for its full replacement cost. The company will adjust the amount of the insurance each year based on the increases in construction costs in your area. For its part, the insurance company guarantees that you will receive full compensation on any claims, even if replacing your house turns out to cost much more than the face value of your policy.

Another way you can avoid being underinsured is to request an "inflation guard," although most companies today automatically include this on your policy. It means that the company adjusts the amount of coverage based on the annual rate of inflation. Some companies build this protection into the policy, while others charge $2 to $5 a year.

OTHER STRUCTURES

This category covers your metal storage shed and detached garage. Other items included are fences, driveways, sidewalks, and permanently installed yard fixtures.

The normal coverage for "other structures" is 10 percent of what the dwelling is insured for. On a house insured for $40,000, you would have $4,000 of coverage. Be careful here! If you have a brand-new, two-stall, detached garage on the premises and it's destroyed by a tornado or fire, you run the risk of coming up short on compensation.

Most companies allow you to increase the basic coverage at a nominal cost, possibly as low as $2 per $1,000 of coverage. Double-check this point with your agent.

PERSONAL PROPERTY

Under this category you are reimbursed for losses or damages to your personal property. Personal property refers to all of your belongings, such as clothes, appliances, and furniture. It includes window air conditioners, curtains and other window coverings, whether they're permanently installed or not, and outdoor equipment and yard fixtures not permanently installed. All of your tools and lawn equipment, like mowers, rakes, and water hoses are covered.

The HO-3 policy comes with 50 percent of the dwelling is coverage as personal-property coverage. If the house is insured for $75,000, you would have $37,500 for personal property. Studies indicate that the cost of increasing your personal-property coverage is about $1 per $1,000 across the country.

Limitations on Personal Property

The major companies that write house insurance policies nationwide report virtually the same basic limitations on their HO-3 policies. You should be aware of the following limits:

- $200 on money, bank notes, bullion, gold other than goldware, silver other than silverware, platinum, coins, and medals
- $1,000 on securities, accounts, deeds, evidences of debt, manuscripts, and passports
- $1,000 on jewelry, watches, precious and semiprecious stones, gems, and furs
- $5,000 for loss by theft of silverware and goldware
- $5,000 for loss by theft of firearms
- $5,000 on electronic data-processing equipment

These limitations can be surmounted by adding optional coverages and endorsements.

Endorsements or Schedules for Personal Property

If you feel that the basic coverage that comes with your policy isn't enough, it's possible to **endorse** or **schedule** more property onto the policy. A "schedule" is a list of individual items or groups of items covered under one policy. To "endorse" a policy is to alter its basic provisions by adding a schedule. The insurance company will ask you to include in your list details like make, model, serial number, and, of course, the appraisal of value.

Items that can be endorsed include jewelry, furs, cameras, musical instruments, silverware and goldware, guns, computers, postage stamps, and rare and current coins.

Most endorsements, or schedules, are reasonably priced, but the cost can vary depending upon where you live. A fine-arts schedule might cost $1.50 per $1,000 of valuation in Minneapolis and $2.50 per $1,000 in New York City. A schedule on a $10,000 painting might cost only $15 in Minneapolis but $25 in New York.

Insuring items with an endorsement can run into hundreds of dollars a year. Some companies instead offer customized insurance plans that provide standard levels of coverage, as well as broader coverage on what you need.

LOSS OF USE AND ADDITIONAL LIVING EXPENSE IN CASE OF DAMAGE TO YOUR HOME

Loss of use covers the necessary increase in living expenses incurred when you have to move out of the house because of a covered loss. Perhaps you had a fire in the kitchen and it will take four weeks before you can get back into the house. You will be reimbursed for the *extra* expense incurred while living away from home. That is, the insurance doesn't pay all expenses, just the difference.

For example, if your house is paid for and your family is forced to live in a motel for four weeks, then you'll be reimbursed the cost of the motel *in full*. If you have to eat out, you'll spend more than what you normally spend at the grocery store, so the difference will be refunded to you.

EXAMPLE:

The Smiths, a family of four, are forced to vacate their home after a small fire. They live in a motel that charges $40 a day, and their meals in restaurants have been running $100 a day. They're out of the house for six days, and their expenses total $240 for the motel and $600 for meals.

They have a house payment of $300 a month, and prior to the fire they were spending $100 a week for groceries. Breaking this down, we find that they spend about $10 a day for the house payment and $14 a day for groceries. For the six days they are out of the house, this totals $144. The insurance company will pay the difference between the $840 in actual expenses and the $144 that would have been their ordinary expenses. Thus, they will receive a check for $696.

WHAT OPTIONAL COVERAGES AND ENDORSEMENTS SHOULD I KNOW ABOUT?

Replacement Cost on the Contents

The insurance company will pay either to replace the item with an item of similar quality or to fix it, whichever is less, without deducting for depreciation (the current value of the item as compared with what you paid for it originally).

EXAMPLE:

Under the standard policy, if your six-year-old refrigerator (for which you paid $500 brand-new) is ruined by a bolt of lightning, the claims adjuster will do this: take the original cost of the item, subtract depreciation *and* the deductible, and then write a check for the difference. Assume that on a $500 original cost, the depreciation after six years is $300, and the deductible is $100; the check to you is for $100 ($500-[$300 + $100]).

Not only do you get next to nothing for the refrigerator, but you also have to go out and buy another one. What kind of refrigerator can you get for $100?

Now let's look at the same scenario using the replacement-cost method.

EXAMPLE:

The adjuster takes the brand new cost of the item you need to replace subtracts the deductible, and then writes a check. If a new refrigerator costs $700, after the $100 deductible is subtracted, you get a check for $600.

Here's a more dramatic example.

EXAMPLE:

You flush the toilet, and it just keeps flushing. The toilet overflows and ruins the upstairs carpeting, the downstairs carpeting, the ceiling in the living room, the carpeting in the basement, and several pieces of furniture. If the carpeting was 20 years old and it was depreciated, its value would be next to nothing. The same holds for ruined furniture. However, because you had the replacement-cost endorsement, you receive brand-new carpeting, brand-new furniture, and repaired ceilings at the estimated current amount. This could save you over $5,000.

The extra cost for this endorsement runs from $10 to $25 a year. Isn't it worth it? My experience has been that the people who spend the extra money are a lot happier than the ones who don't.

Personal Computer Endorsement

If you have a computer at home, you might want to look at this endorsement, but only if you have quite a bit of equipment. Most standard policies have a built-in coverage of $2,000 to $5,000. Just the same, don't take it for granted that your policy has this coverage without checking with your agent. Rates across the country average $5 to $10 per $1,000 of coverage.

Jewelry Endorsement

Most policies provide $500 to $1,000 to cover jewelry. It isn't an all-risks coverage, and that can be a problem. In other words, the built-in coverage is strictly for named-peril losses like fire, tornado, theft, etc. But the most common losses of jewelry aren't from these perils.

Suppose you take off your diamond ring to rake leaves and carefully place it on an outside window ledge. When you're done, you forget you left the ring outside and by the time you remember, it's gone. This is called a **mysterious disappearance**, and while not covered under the basic policy, it is covered if you have the jewelry endorsement. Rates average $10 to $20 per $1,000 of coverage.

WHAT LIABILITY AND MEDICAL-EXPENSE COVERAGE SHOULD I HAVE?

Although most liability coverages were recently raised to $100,000, that may not be enough in this litigious age. Indeed, liability coverage is increasingly becoming one of the most important sections of a homeowners insurance policy—and one of the best buys around.

The liability portion of the policy covers you for bodily-injury and property-damage claims when you're legally liable for an accident that happens on your premises.

If a visitor trips on a tear in your carpet, falls down the stairs, and is paralyzed, you're probably looking at a law suit. If you or any member of your household is responsible for someone's getting hurt or for someone's loss of property, you'll have protection.

WHAT ARE THE STANDARD COVERAGES?

Here are the coverages that are automatically included with your homeowners liability protection.

Claim and Defense Costs

If you are sued because of an accident that occurred on your premises, the insurance company will defend your rights in court and the following:

* Costs billed to you
* Expenses incurred by the insurance company
* Up to $50 per day for loss of earnings if you are required to testify
* Any prejudgment interest (this refers to the interest charged prior to the court date in a case you either win or lose
* Interest that accrues after entry of judgment

Examples of Liability Coverage

* Acts of children—Your child is responsible for another child's getting hurt and needing medical attention. Let's say your son throws the baseball a little too hard and the ball crashes into his buddy's mouth, splattering teeth in every direction. The expenses incurred to have the boy's mouth reconstructed are covered under the liability portion of your homeowners policy.
* Acts of your pet—The most common claim is the family dog's biting someone other than a member of your house-hold.
* Sports activities—While participating in sports activity, such as golf or softball, biking or skiing, you are responsible for injuring another person.
* Damage to property of others—This covers situations in which a member of your family accidentally damages some-one else's property. Let's say your daughter knocks over the neighbor's beautiful grandfather clock. The damage to the clock would be paid.

WHAT OPTIONAL LIABILITY COVERAGES MIGHT I NEED?

Here are some coverages you might want to add to your basic liability policy.

Office, School, and Studio Use

Most policies cover business equipment in the home for $2,500. If you have a home office, you should consider buying additional business protection. For about $20 to $30 a year, you can buy $5,000 worth of coverage for business equipment and furniture, plus $100,000 in liability coverage.

Waterbed Liability for Renters

You're renting a room in the upper level of a two-story duplex and your waterbed springs a leak and soaks down through the ceiling. Not only does it damage the ceiling, but it ruins the couch of the people who live below you!

With the waterbed-liability endorsement, you would be covered. You can add this to your HO-4 policy at a cost of approximately $25 to $30 a year. If you do have a waterbed, some apartment owners require proof of this coverage before they let you rent.

EXTENDING YOUR LIABILITY COVERAGE

If your policy provides only $100,000 in coverage, studies show that anywhere in the United States, you can raise your liability coverage to $300,000 for about $10 a year.

Umbrella Policy

You can purchase an **umbrella policy** that will extend your liability coverage to $1 million or more. "Umbrella policies" provide broader coverage than typical homeowners policies. In addition to bodily injury, an umbrella policy covers false arrest, wrongful eviction, libel, slander, defamation of character, and invasion of property. It usually costs about $100 to $175 a year for $1 million in coverage. Such a policy makes sense for a homeowner who has many assets to protect.

Liability Extension on a Rental Property

Don't get caught here! It happens frequently that landlords think they have liability coverage when they don't. If you own a rental or several rentals, double-check your policies. If they're called Fire and Extended Coverage policies, they don't include liability coverage!

In that case, ask the agent who insures your house to "extend" liability from your home to the rental properties. It's rather inexpensive, maybe $10 to $20 per rental, and it's easy to do.

MEDICAL EXPENSE

Medical-expense coverage is a little different from liability coverage. It pays up to the policy limit for injuries sustained on your premises by anyone other than you or a member of your imme-diate family, regardless of fault.

In other words, you don't have to be sued and proved neg-ligent in order for the insurance company to pay a claim. If a T.V. repairman slips and falls on your sidewalk and hurts his back, he doesn't have to sue you in order for your medical cov-erage to pay his bills up to the limit on the policy.

WHAT GOVERNS THE COST OF HOMEOWNERS INSURANCE?

WHY DO HOMEOWNERS RATES VARY?

Homeowners rates can vary by hundreds of dollars from company to company, as a survey conducted by *Changing Times* magazine shows. (See Table 1.3.) For example, if you own a house insured for $94,000 in Denver (not one of the cities surveyed), you could

Table 1.3   Rates Around the Country

Changing Times surveyed annual insurance rates in ten cities and in several cases found differences of more than $400. We asked the five largest national writers of homeowners insurance to give us the insurance costs for a $150,000 20-year-old frame house with a brick front in an established neighborhood. We specified that it had three bedrooms, two stories, 2,100 square feet, a deadbolt lock and smoke alarm and was within five miles of the nearest fire station. The policy we wanted was a standard HO-3, with a $250 deductible, $300,000 in liability coverage and replacement-cost coverage on the contents.

	State Farm*	Allstate	Aetna	Nationwide	Travelers
AKRON, OHIO	$356	$270	$ 514	$317	$ 532†
BOSTON	948	963	1,135**	903	1,062†
BROOKLYN, N.Y.	857	855	1,004	968	1,257†
FORT LAUDERDALE	712	644	651	506	687†
GRAND RAPIDS, MICH.	503	569	545	767	907
HARTFORD	521	510	538	524	590†
LOUISVILLE	483	521	684	455	527†
PORTLAND, ORE.	424	393	518	458	470†
SANTA MONICA, CAL.	533	471	603	572	699†
WASHINGTON, D.C.	637	565	715	773	640‡

*Includes credit for fire extinguisher. †Figures supplied by Phoenix Insurance Co., a Travelers subsidiary. **Up to $1,300 in some areas. ‡Does not include credit for smoke-alarm.

Reprinted by permission from *Changing Times*, The Kiplinger Magazine (April–June 1988 issue). Copyright 1988 by The Kiplinger Washington Editors, Inc.

spend as little as $257 a year on insurance or as much as $536 for the very same coverage.

All companies calculate a policy's cost in the same basic way. They look at the kind of house you want to insure and the kind of policy you want (both in terms of coverage and deductible). Entering into their calculations are several factors, including location, what the house is made of, fire-protection class, cost of replacement, and age.

Location

Where you live is critical to the price. All companies divide the territory they cover into cities, zip codes, or even neighborhoods. They base their prices on local loss statistics, which are influenced by such factors as the quality of police and fire protection.

Frame or Brick

Most companies charge about 5 percent to 10 percent more to insure wood (frame) houses than those made of brick or masonry. Why? Brick houses tend to suffer less damage in storms, fires, and other disasters.

Fire-Protection Class

Every neighborhood in the United States has been assigned a fire-protection class by the Insurance Services Offices (ISO), an industry group. The classification is based on the quality of the fire-protection services in your area, including whether there is a full-time fire department, the training of the firefighters, and the distance of your house from fire hydrants or other sources of water.

Cost of Replacement

Labor and materials cost more in some areas of the country than others. The higher the building costs in your area, the higher the price of insurance. That's why it costs more to insure a $150,000 two-bedroom cottage in Westchester County, New York, than a $150,000 five-bedroom colonial in Topeka, Kansas.

Age of the House

Many companies offer discounts of as much as 20 percent on new houses.

WHY DO THE PREMIUM AND COVERAGE ON MY HOUSE INCREASE EVERY YEAR?

Insurance companies introduced the practise of increasing premiums and coverage to make sure people would not be caught short on insurance in case of major loss. If you insured your house for $60,000 five years ago, its value might have inflated to $70,000 today. Agents' hands are usually tied on these points, because most insurance companies make these increases automatically.

Still, if you feel your house coverage has risen too high, call your agent. By figuring what it would take to rebuild your home, he or she may be able to reduce your coverage.

WHAT ARE RENTER'S RATES LIKE?

The price of renter's insurance also depends on several factors:

- The number of units in the building—the more living units there are, the cheaper the insurance is. Prices for a $20,000 policy average from $100 a year in the Midwest to $200–$250 on either coast.
- Whether the place where you live is a frame or a brick building—if it's brick, it's about 10 percent to 15 percent cheaper.
- The amount of deductible you have on the policy—the higher the deductible, the cheaper the insurance. The most common amounts are $100, $250, and $500. You can save anywhere from 15 percent to 25 percent in premiums by going from the $100 to the $500 deductible.

HOW CAN I CUT COSTS?

Because the prices of standard policies are adjusted not only to meet the demands of local laws and regulations, but also for the marketing strategies of each company, it pays to make sure that you're getting the most for your money.

Ten Tips for Cutting Costs

1. Shop around. Prices can vary even within a single community. For example, with a $150,000 wood-frame house in northern New Jersey, the rate charged by Hartford and Camden is $614. Allstate offers the same policy for $525, and State Farm has it for $478.

2. Shop within the same company. You have to be streetwise to make sure your agent is doing a good job for you. The parent company may lower its rates, but your agent may renew you at the old rate, so check around with other agents and compare rates every few years. If there's only a 5 percent difference and you're happy with your agent's service, there's probably no reason to switch. But if there's a 20 percent difference, you'll want to think about it.

3. Buy all your polices from one agent or company. Many companies that write auto, homeowners, and umbrella policies offer discounts of 5 percent to 20 percent to customers who agree to keep all their business with them.

4. Install smoke alarms and deadbolt locks and buy a fire extinguisher. Most companies offer discounts of 2 percent to 5 percent for homes with these systems. The more effective the system, the higher the discount. Homes with in-house sprinklers and burglar-alarm systems can qualify for discounts of as much as 20 percent.

5. Don't smoke. A few companies offer discounts to policyholders who do not smoke. Hanover gives a 10 percent nonsmoker discount, and Farmers Insurance, a 4 percent discount.

6. Use fire-resistant materials in building. Allstate offers a 15 percent discount on homes made of fire-resistant materials.

7. Get a high deductible. All companies offer discounts for deductibles higher than the basic $250. You can usually get a 10 percent discount for selecting a $500 deductible, a 15 percent discount for a $1,000 deductible, and a 25 percent discount for a $2,500 deductible.

8. Ask about a mature-homeowners discount. Some companies, like Farmers and Metropolitan, offer discounts of up to 10 percent for homeowners who are at least 55 years old or retired.

9. Ask about a discount for long-time policyholders. Several companies offer discounts to homeowners who keep their policies for several years. For example, State Farm offers a 5 percent discount for people who stay with the company for three to five years and a 10 percent discount for those who stay for six years.

10. Check out the company's claims reputation. A survey conducted in 1989 by a leading consumer magazine named the top 10 insurance companies according to how they satisfied their claim customers. The four criteria for the survey were speed of handling, speed of payment, ease of access, and amount of final payment.

The top 10 companies were Amica Mutual Insurance, USAA, Erie Insurance Exchange, State Farm and Casualty, California

State Automobile Association, Continental Insurance, United
States Fidelity and Guaranty, American Family Mutual, Aetna
Casualty and Surety, and Horace Mann Insurance.

Homeowners Shopping List

As you shop around for insurance, be sure to compare apples to
apples. Make a list of the things you want covered, with amounts,
and keep this information in front of you when you go to the
phone. You'll want to compare companies on the following items:

- The amount for which you want to insure your house, and
  the cost of a replacement-cost endorsement for the structure.
- The price of replacement-cost coverage versus actual cash
  value on the contents. In most cases, you should get replacement-cost coverage.

Table 1.4 Residential Insurance Price Comparison Checklist

| | | Cost | |
| | | Policy A | Policy B |
Type of Insurance	Limit	Company Name	Company Name
Dwelling Insurance	$_____		
$_____deductible		HO-____ ____	HO-____ ____
$_____deductible		HO-____ ____	HO-____ ____
$_____deductible		HO-____ ____	HO-____ ____
$_____deductible		HO-____ ____	HO-____ ____
Other Structures	$_____	$_____	$_____
Personal Property	$_____	$_____	$_____
Replacement Cost	$_____	$_____	$_____
Valuable Items			
Jewelry	$_____	$_____	$_____
Other	$_____	$_____	$_____
	$_____	$_____	$_____
	$_____	$_____	$_____
	$_____	$_____	$_____
	$_____	$_____	$_____
	$_____	$_____	$_____
	$_____	$_____	$_____
Loss of Use	$_____	$_____	$_____
Liability	$_____	$_____	$_____
Medical Expense	$_____	$_____	$_____
Total Premium		$_____	$_____

- The amount of the deductible. As a general rule, don't ask for a deductible lower than $250—it's too expensive.
- The cost of any endorsements you may need for art, antiques, jewelry, coins, stamps, computer software, guns, or wine.
- The liability limits. The standard is $100,000 but $300,000 is better, and it isn't that costly because of the infrequency of large claims. If settlements of $300,000 were common, the price for this increased limit would increase.

See the sample form in Table 1.4.

HOMEOWNERS INSURANCE CHECKLIST

If you own a home, take a look at your insurance policy or call your agent.

Your House and Other Structures

☐ Check to see what type of house policy you have. Is it a Basic Form 1, a Broad Form 2, a Special Form 3, or a Deluxe Form 5? Remember, the number of perils your house is insured for depends on the type of policy you have. A Special Form 3 covers more than the Form 1.

☐ Do you want to insure the house for 80 percent or 100 percent of the value?

☐ Do you want to be covered for all risks or just named perils?

☐ Is there enough insurance on the dwelling itself?

☐ Are there any outbuildings, such as storage sheds or detached garages, and are they adequately covered?

Your Personal Belongings

☐ Do you have enough coverage on your personal property, such as furniture, appliances, clothing, etc.?

☐ Will you be reimbursed for a loss to your personal property at today's prices, or will the company deduct for depreciation before paying the claim?

☐ Do you have any *extra* items such as guns, jewelry, or computers that need to be endorsed?

☐ Are there any endorsements available, not currently on the policy, that might be of use to you?

Your Liability Coverage

☐ Do you need to raise or lower the amount of liability on the policy?

☐ Do you own any rental houses that need liability coverage extended to them from your home?

Miscellaneous

☐ Are you happy with the deductible? Have you priced it with different amounts?

☐ Is the inflation-protection clause increasing the face amount of the dwelling coverage beyond logical limits?

☐ Are you getting the most coverage for your premium dollar?

CHAPTER TWO

Bumper to Bumper:
Auto Insurance

More than 30 million auto accidents a year generate between 40,000 and 50,000 deaths and 5 million injuries—as well as economic losses that inflation pushes to increasing heights: $10.2 billion in 1960, $23.5 billion in 1970, $57 billion in 1980, $80 billion in 1986, $85 billion in 1987, and, in all likelihood, $100 billion by 1990.

Little wonder, then, that while the cost of living has increased by 4 percent over the past year or so, the cost of auto insurance has risen by 7 percent. Of every $10 that Americans spend for all property and casualty coverages, over $4 goes to pay the premiums for insuring motor vehicles. In some cities, it's possible to pay more over time to insure your car than to buy one! For a couple with a 17-year-old son and two cars, premiums of as much as $4,000 a year are not unusual in urban centers such as New York and San Francisco.

Given the potentially high cost, it makes sense to shop for auto insurance as carefully as you'd shop for your auto. Your goal should be to buy no more insurance than you need—but no less!

WHAT COVERAGES ARE INCLUDED IN AUTO INSURANCE?

An auto insurance policy is a package of six types of coverage, each with its own premium. The sum of these is the total price you pay for your policy. You can raise or lower the price tag by taking higher or lower limits of these coverages, and by eliminating some of them, although most states require that all vehicle owners carry at least bodily injury and property damage.

The six types, which will be covered in turn, are

- Bodily-Injury and Property-Damage Liability
- Medical-Expense
- Comprehensive
- Collision
- Uninsured-Motorist and Underinsured-Motorist
- Miscellaneous Optional Coverages

LIABILITY COVERAGE

In most states, the only coverage you *must* carry is for liability—insurance that protects others against damage you may cause by negligent driving. Together, the cost of bodily-injury and property-damage coverage makes up between 40 percent and 50 percent of the total insurance premium. Although it is a very expensive part of the policy, liability coverage is the most important.

In 1989, the only states that did not have one of these "compulsory" auto insurance laws were Alabama, Mississippi, New Hampshire, Rhode Island, Tennessee, Virginia, Washington, and Wisconsin. But even where ownership of automobile liability insurance is not compulsory, the existence of financial-responsibility laws, along with the ever-present threat of a financially crippling judgment in the event of an accident, has come to make the purchase of automobile liability insurance a virtual necessity for motorists.

The costs of insurance-claim settlements have risen steadily in recent years. From 1979 through 1988, the average paid bodily-injury claim rose 145.5 percent from $3,559 to $8,736.

What About No-Fault Insurance?

Despite years of effort to reform the insurance system, it's still more the rule than the exception that people seek legal redress, claiming that the other driver is at fault and demanding thousands of dollars in compensation for personal injury.

The **no-fault** movement that swept through half the states more than a decade ago was an attempt to hold down the cost of insurance and to speed financial compensation to those who suffered injury in accidents. However, in state after state, trial attorneys, who had the most to lose from this consumer-oriented initiative, succeeded in watering down no-fault laws to the point where the tort system (the system of laws and legal remedies for alleged wrongs) remained intact.

In plain terms, "no-fault" insurance denotes any auto program that allows the insured to recover losses for bodily injury from his or her own insurance company, regardless of who is at fault in the accident. No-fault states as of 1990 are Colorado, Connecticut, Georgia, Hawaii, Kansas, Kentucky, Massachusetts, Michigan, Minnesota, New Jersey, New York, North Dakota, Utah, Florida, Delaware, Maryland, Oregon, and Pennsylvania.

The most successful no-fault state is Michigan. The law there requires that insurance policies provide unlimited medical and rehabilitational benefits, three years' worth of wage-loss benefits (an injured person receives 80 percent of his or her gross income up to the current maximum of $2,670 per month), survivors' benefits, and a $20 daily benefit for replacement services.

No-fault also encompasses property damage. Insured motorists can buy collision coverage to pay for damage to their own cars and only enough property-damage-liability coverage to protect them when driving outside the state.

What Does Bodily-Injury Coverage Include?

Bodily-injury-liability coverage is what protects you in case you are at fault in an accident and someone is injured or killed. It pays for legal obligations to the parties involved; people you injure can collect against this coverage to pay for their medical expenses and lost wages.

This coverage also protects the liability of relatives and friends who drive your insured vehicles, as long as they have the owner's permission to do so. If your car is stolen and the person driving hits another car, your car insurance doesn't pay for the damage to the other party.

The coverage extends to trailers you might pull behind your car, so that if your pop-up camper comes loose on the interstate and crashes into another car, killing or injuring its occupant, you're protected. Liability *always* extends from the insured vehicle to the towed vehicle.

Bodily-injury coverage also pays for the following:

- First-aid costs to the other parties
- Investigation expenses
- Court costs

- Bail bond
- Attorney's fees
- Lost wages if you are needed in court
- Protection against fraudulent claims

What Does Property-Damage Coverage Include?

The property-damage portion of your policy, which is combined with the bodily-injury portion in your premium, pays if you damage someone else's property, usually another car. States require drivers to purchase minimal amounts of coverage, usually $5,000 or $10,000—not enough for an accident that totals a new car. An adult suburban driver would pay $90 a year for $10,000 worth of property-damage coverage from State Farm; increasing this coverage from $10,000 to $25,000 would add less than $10 to the premium.

What Liability Limits Are There?

Most states prescribe a minimum liability coverage that the drivers must carry. Judging by the size of some court settlements, however, these limits are too low. New York, for instance, requires minimum coverage that only pays up to $10,000 to each injured person, subject to a $20,000 maximum per accident.

According to a survey conducted in 1988 by a leading consumer magazine, most automobile owners carry more coverage than the state minimums, and properly so. People who own a house or other assets generally need minimums of at least $100,000 per person and $300,000 per accident in order to protect their assets from large court awards.

There are many different combinations of limits you can look at. Some of the most popular across the United States are the following:

- $25,000/$50,000/$25,000
- $50,000/$100,000/$50,000
- $100,000/$250,000/$100,000
- $250,000/$500,000/$100,000

In each of the combinations, the first figure is the protection you have in case you injure or kill one person in an "at-fault" accident, or when you're considered to be in the wrong. The middle figure is the protection you have if one *or more* persons are injured or killed in the accident. The last figure is the protection you have for all of the property damage you cause in the accident.

If you can afford to pick the limits you want, take at least the $50,000/$100,000/$50,000 limit, but even this can be too low, as the following example will show.

EXAMPLE:

Several years ago, I had a client who was transporting a center-pivot irrigation system on the highway from one farm location to another. The system was attached to his pickup truck and was properly flagged. He was traveling well within the speed limit. A refrigerated truck passed him, lost control, and crashed into the ditch. The truck was totaled, and the other driver accused my client of being over the center line and causing the accident.

The case went to court and the jury agreed with the other driver, so we paid $55,000 to the claimant under the property-damage portion of our policy. How could a truck, even a totaled one, cost $55,000? Easily: The award was not only for the truck, but also for the contents of the truck, the "down time," and lost sales.

Luckily, my client had limits of $100,000/$300,000/$100,000, or there could have been problems. If he had had only the state minimum limit for property damage, which is $25,000, he would have been forced to pay the other $35,000 himself.

In states with no-fault laws, injured parties are supposed to look to their own forms of coverage to pay for medical treatment, regardless of who is at fault. But an injured party has the right to bring a suit, and to include claims for pain and suffering, if damages exceed the threshold established by the law. Because the potential for high awards still exists in no-fault states, it is wise for the insured to carry bodily-injury limits comparable to what drivers carry in states without such laws.

What Is a Single-Limit Liability Policy?

Some insurance companies have what is called a "single limit of liability" coverage. You can tell what you have by looking at the cover sheet, or "deck" sheet, of the policy. This is the page that lists the vehicles insured, the serial numbers, coverages, etc.

A single-limit-liability policy pays one amount per accident, regardless of how many individuals are involved. Instead of saying $100,000/$300,000/$100,000, your policy would instead show the single limit of $300,000. This means that the most your insurance company will pay out for an accident is $300,000, whether it's for bodily injury or property damage.

This form of coverage is slightly more expensive than the equivalent amount of multiple-limit coverage, because it provides more benefits. If the driver carries $300,000 of single-limit coverage, one injured person can collect up to $300,000.

What About an Umbrella Policy?

You can supplement your liability coverage with an umbrella policy providing $1,000,000 of protection. Umbrella insurance "floats" above your other coverage—that is, you must carry the underlying liability coverage before you can buy the umbrella.

Umbrella policies are surprisingly inexpensive. For the $1,000,000 policy from American Family Mutual Insurance Company, a person who is a good risk will pay approximately $100 regardless of location (provided he or she has purchased the underlying policies from American Family). These policies are generally purchased by people who have assets worth far more than the limit of $300,000 liability coverage; such people need protection from big court awards.

MEDICAL-EXPENSE COVERAGE

Auto medical-expense coverage is not the same as liability; it is optional coverage to pay the medical expenses of you and your passengers. This coverage is not usually required in no-fault states. Many people who already have health insurance for themselves and their families forgo duplicate coverage in an automobile policy. Most people who do buy automobile medical insurance purchase coverage of $1,000 to $2,000 rather than large amounts like $50,000.

Medical coverage on your auto policy does the following:

- Pays medical expenses up to the policy limits for you or any persons injured "in, on, around, above, and below" your car, regardless of who's at fault.

  An example of "on, around, above, and below" is if you're lifting groceries out of the trunk of your car and sprain your back, or if you're stuck in a snowdrift and injure yourself while trying to push the car out. In both cases, your medical bills will be paid up to the limits of the policy.
- Pays medical expenses incurred up to one year from the date of the accident. Any bills generated after a year from the date of the accident will not be paid.

- Covers any relatives in your household who don't own a car if they are injured while riding in other cars, or are struck by another car.

Medical-expense coverage will also pay for an ambulance ride from the scene of an accident and for the funeral for an insured who is the victim of a fatal car accident.

What Is Personal-Injury Protection (PIP)?

States with no-fault laws stipulate that you must buy personal-injury protection, or PIP, a more comprehensive form of medical-payments coverage. PIP not only covers medical bills, but often it also covers lost wages while an injured person is unable to work, replacement services while a person is unable to perform routine tasks like caring for young children, and some funeral expenses.

Drivers in no-fault states generally can buy as much as $50,000 worth of PIP coverage, but most buy only $10,000. A few no-fault states require companies to provide unlimited PIP benefits, which will cover all of a person's medical and rehabilitation expenses. A few states make drivers buy a minimum amount, such as $5,000.

You might save on PIP premiums if your state's no-fault laws allow those insured to "coordinate benefits" with their health-insurance policy. You may elect to make your health insurance "primary"—that is, to seek reimbursements for medical expenses from your health insurer. That would shave as much as 40 percent from the premium for PIP.

If I Have Health Insurance, Why Do I Need Medical Coverage?

Remember, medical coverage is an option on the auto policy. It isn't required, but there are a couple of reasons why you might want to take it: First, it pays for you *or* anyone riding in your vehicle. If the passenger doesn't have any health insurance, this option could be important. Second, most health-insurance policies not only have a deductible for you to meet, but they also have *coinsurance*. "Coinsurance" is the amount of money you pay over and above your deductible. For example, in many plans the insurance company will pay 80 percent of the bills over the deductible, and you pay 20 percent up to a certain limit, such as $5,000. The insurance company then pays 100 percent of costs over that limit, up to a maximum. Therefore, if you have a $500 deductible, you would pay the $500 plus the next $1,000, or $1,500. You could use your automobile medical coverage to pay this deductible and coinsurance amount!

Does Medical Coverage Pay If I'm Disabled in an Accident?

Medical coverage doesn't include disability, but you can get a disability coverage added to your policy. Companies vary as to the limits they offer, but most companies pay a lump sum of $5,000, $10,000, or $20,000 if you become totally disabled due to an injury sustained in a car accident.

COMPREHENSIVE COVERAGE

As the name implies, this coverage is a catchall that pays for damages resulting from such events as vandalism, hailstorms, floods, and theft—just about every thing except collision with another car or a solid object, or upset. It also pays a transportation allowance if your car has been stolen. Coverage may be extended to CB radios, customized vans, and campers.

Comprehensive accounts for about 40 percent of the total premium, and it is carried by 70 percent to 80 percent of all policyholders. This coverage is usually subject to deductibles, which range from $50 to $500.

The specific coverages are

- Hail
- Vandalism
- Wind
- Falling Objects
- Fire
- Glass Breakage
- Riot
- Theft
- Flood
- Collision with Animals or Birds

Hail

The greatest losses are paid when a hailstorm ravages a town or city. A hailstorm can do a tremendous amount of damage to your car in a short period. On the other hand, if you have an old vehicle, don't worry about it.

Vandalism

If you have a newer car or pickup, this coverage is very important.

EXAMPLE:

One of my clients had a brand-new Buick that she drove to work. One day after work she noticed that someone had taken a sharp instrument and scraped the entire right side of the car. We paid for this damage under her comprehensive coverage.

Wind

High winds tend to blow gravel against cars and chip the paint. With comprehensive, you are covered for this peril.

Falling Objects

Although this peril isn't common, it does happen, as in the case of a tree branch or limb falling onto a vehicle.

> **EXAMPLE:**
>
> In a rather bizarre case I had, my insured had parked both his and his wife's cars in their driveway for the night. That evening a high wind came and blew over a pile of wood that he'd stacked right next to the driveway. The wood was blown against both vehicles, and we paid for the damages under their comprehensive coverage.

Fire

Usually, this involves an engine fire, and in most cases, the vehicle is totaled. The insurance company pays for the damages.

Glass Breakage

This is probably the most common claim in auto insurance. You're driving down the highway, minding your own business, when a truck passes you heading in the other direction and a rock flies out and hits your windshield. If the windshield is just pitted and not cracked, most companies will let you try a "repair" job on it. There is a method by which resin is forced into the pit under extremely high pressure, and when it's done you can hardly notice it.

The advantage of having a repair job done rather than putting in a whole new windshield is that the insurance company will waive your deductible and pay the complete repair bill. The insurance company would rather pay $40 for a repair job than $275 for a new windshield. If the repair job doesn't work out and later the windshield cracks anyway, your insurance company should pay for the new windshield less your deductible.

Riot

If your vehicle is damaged during a riot or civil commotion, you'll be reimbursed for the damages.

Theft

You are covered in case your car is stolen and never recovered, and in case it's recovered but has been damaged.

EXAMPLE:

I had a theft case in which the insured left her keys in the ignition, and when she returned from doing some shopping, the car was gone. A week later the car was found about a mile from where it was stolen. It was stripped and had been driven into the middle of the city on the wheel rims only. We paid for the damages.

Flood

Last summer, an insured tried to drive through a flooded underpass but couldn't make it. The water rose to such a level that it came in through her doors and up over the hood, "drowning" the engine. She had comprehensive coverage on the car, so we paid for all of the considerable damages.

Collision with Animals or Birds

Given the name of this coverage item, you would think that running into a cow, deer, or moose would be part of collision coverage instead of comprehensive. Not so. Damage to your car from such an accident will be paid for under the comprehensive part of the policy. If you run over someone's prize bull, the property damage part of your policy pays for the bull, and the comprehensive part of the policy pays for the damage to your vehicle. Either way, you're covered.

What Comprehensive Deductible Should I Have?

The normal comprehensive deductibles to pick from are

- no deductible
- $50
- $100
- $250
- $500
- $1,000

Most drivers are being forced into the higher deductibles because of high premiums, especially in metropolitan areas. You should probably consider the $250, $500, and $1,000 deductibles.

COLLISION COVERAGE

Collision coverage accounts for as much as 30 percent of the insurance premium on a new car or on an older model that has had many claims. This coverage is always limited by your deductible, which is separate from the comp deductible and usually higher. Collision coverage pays for any loss or damage to your vehicle caused by collision or upset, whether or not you're at fault, and whether or not another vehicle is involved. Therefore, if you either accidentally slide off the road into a telephone pole or run a red light and hit another car, you've got coverage to fix *your* car.

Other features of collision coverage:

- It covers hit-and-run accidents, including collision damage done to your car while it is parked. Someone nails your car and takes off. If you don't have collision coverage, you're stuck paying for the damage.
- It recovers your deductible if you're in an accident involving another car and you're not at fault. The way this works is as follows: You can use your collision coverage, less the deductible, to pay for the damage to your car and then let your insurance company try to get the money back from the other party.

The implications of not having collision coverage are that in all of the following situations, the insurance company will *not* pay the cost of fixing your car.

- Your car is sitting in a parking lot. Someone backs into it, leaves the scene, and never reports it. You have $500 worth of damage.
- You're broadsided by an uninsured motorist running a red light, and your 1985 Chevy gets totaled. You can sue, but in most cases you'll come up blank. If the party had enough money to pay you, he or she probably would have had at least the minimum amount of liability property-damage coverage.
- Driving home on an icy road, you lose control and hit a telephone pole. You get nothing for the car, although your company will pay for the telephone pole under the property-damage portion of the policy.
- While your car is parked on a steep hill, the brake disengages. Your car takes off and strikes several other parked vehicles on its way down the hill. The insurance company will pay for the other cars but not for yours.

What Collision Deductible Should I Have?

The deductibles available are $50, $100, $250, $500, and $1,000. One way to save is to take the highest deductible you can afford to pay in the event of an accident. The price of collision coverage with a $500 deductible is 15 percent to 25 percent less than the price for coverage with a $250 deductible. The savings can be significant in places where insurance rates are high. The difference in the price of coverage on a new car between a $250 and a $500 deductible is often over $100.

I advise dropping collision coverage entirely on an older car with a low resale value, since the resale, or "book," value of a car also represents the maximum insurance settlement possible in most cases. It usually pays to carry collision for cars less than three years old; for cars between three and seven years old, the decision about whether to carry collision coverage depends on how much risk you're willing to assume. Over seven years old, the car in most cases isn't worth enough to insure for collision.

UNINSURED AND UNDERINSURED-MOTORIST COVERAGE

What Is Uninsured-Motorist Coverage?

This must be the most misunderstood coverage in the field of car insurance. People usually assume that this coverage pays for the damage when their cars are struck by uninsured motorists. Not so. The coverage reimburses you for bodily injury but *not* for property damage in accidents caused by uninsured drivers.

Instead of looking to the motorist's policy for coverage, you look to your own.

Uninsured-motorist coverage pays legally collectible damages and medical expenses for you or anyone in your car in case of bodily injury or death caused by a hit-and-run driver, a driver of a stolen car, or a driver who has no insurance.

The minimum coverage that companies offer usually matches the minimum sums required by state law. Many people carry coverage comparable to the amounts carried for bodily-injury-liability coverage.

EXAMPLE:

You're changing a tire along the roadside when a car hits you and your car and leaves the scene unidentified. You suffer the loss of a leg as a result. Assuming you have a $100,000/ $300,000 limit for uninsured-motorist coverage, you're awarded a settlement of $100,000 by your own company. For the damage to the car itself you receive nothing unless you have collision coverage. If you don't have uninsured-motorist coverage, one can only hope you have a good health insurance policy.

In most states, uninsured-motorist coverage is part of every insurance policy. Although you may elect to reject the coverage, you would be well advised to keep it, except in states with good no-fault laws.

What Is Underinsured-Motorist Coverage?

This may be offered as a separate coverage with a separate premium, but it's usually sold as part of the uninsured-motorist coverage.

The difference from uninsured-motorist is simply that coverage is provided for bodily injury if the other driver doesn't have *enough* insurance to cover all of your bills.

This of course depends on the extent of your injury. If the other person's bodily-injury insurance is not adequate, your underinsured-motorist coverage will pay any balance subject to the limit on your policy.

EXAMPLE:

You're hit by a car whose driver is insured by XYZ insurance company. You suffer severe back and leg injuries and are forced to stay home from work for over a year. The other party has a $25,000 limit for bodily injury; your bills, however, total $89,000. If you have a $50,000/$100,000 limit for underinsured-motorist coverage, and if the judge rules that your injuries total at least that amount, you would collect $25,000 from XYZ and $50,000 from your company.

The coverage itself is usually quoted as follows (for both uninsured and underinsured motorist):

- $25,000/$50,000
- $50,000/$100,000
- $100,000/$300,000

In all three combinations, the first figure is what can be paid if you are the only one injured in the accident, and the second applies to cases that involve more than one person.

It is wise to have both uninsured- and underinsured-motorist coverage on your car policies. A typical premium around the country for both is $30 to $36 a year.

MISCELLANEOUS OPTIONAL COVERAGES

The optional coverages available vary from company to company, but most companies offer the following: emergency road service, auto rental reimbursement, and accidental-death-and-dismemberment reimbursement.

Emergency Road Service

This coverage pays the cost of towing your car to a repair shop, subject to the limitations of your policy. (It usually allows $25 to $50 in towing charges.) The premium runs around $5 to $10 per year. But some major companies go a little further and pay for

- Mechanical labor of up to one hour at the site of your breakdown
- Delivery cost (but not the cost of the items themselves) of gas, oil, tires, or battery to the site of the breakdown
- Towing to the nearest garage if all else fails

If you're a member of an auto club, you probably already have this coverage and don't need to duplicate it. Check your auto club membership provisions.

Auto Rental Reimbursement

This coverage usually pays $15 to $20 a day for a specified number of days while your car is being repaired. The cost for this coverage runs approximately $8 a year.

When can this coverage be useful? When you have an accident that is your fault and your car needs to go into the shop to be fixed. If the other party is at fault, you can get a rental car from their insurance company, and don't let anyone tell you otherwise! If you run into a problem, call your company and get them involved.

A lot of people think that they have this coverage, but they don't, and if the accident is their fault, they won't get reimbursed for the rental car. As with emergency road service, this is a good coverage for a single person or a one-car family, and if your agent doesn't offer it, you'll have to ask. Don't assume it's included in your auto insurance package.

Accidental-Death-and-Dismemberment Reimbursement

American Family Mutual describes this coverage as providing protection against "death, dismemberment, loss of sight, fractures, and dislocations which result accidentally while in or upon, entering or alighting from, or through being struck by an auto." It pays regardless of who's at fault and is quoted in the amounts of $5,000, $10,000, and $20,000. The cost is approximately $10 per year for the upper-limit coverage.

HOW ARE PREMIUMS CALCULATED?

What factors are taken into consideration in rating a policy? Who is a good risk? What are the procedures the agent uses to decide on a car rate for you?

To determine the premium you will pay, an insurance company sizes you up as a risk. Among other factors, it will take into account your record of accidents and traffic violations, and the make and model of your car. Then it will place you in one of three risk tiers: preferred, standard, or substandard.

Drivers with only one at-fault accident and, say, two traffic violations in the last three years will usually be placed in the substandard tier—at a premium that is approximately 20 percent higher than the preferred tier. A 20-year-old male (part of a high-risk group) with an at-fault accident and two violations could expect to pay anywhere from $150 to $275 for liability coverage— every three months!

Most companies reject all drivers who have drunk-driving convictions. Those people must buy insurance from companies specializing in substandard drivers, or from state-operated pools.

The specific factors that go into agents' calculations will be discussed first for the driver and second for the vehicle.

THE DRIVER

The person who drives the vehicle is the most important consideration. Insurance companies rate on age, sex, marital status, whether someone smokes, driving record, and prior insurance experience.

Age

In 1988, approximately 32.1 percent of motor-vehicle accidents involved drivers who were under the age of 25, and they represent only 18.6 percent of all motorists. Drivers in that age group also constitute 31.1 percent of drivers who have fatal accidents.

In 1986, drivers between the ages of 20 and 24 had the highest overall accident rate—37 accidents per 100 drivers, those between the ages of 55 and 64 had the lowest—13 per 100 drivers. Young drivers, therefore, pay higher insurance rates than older drivers.

With most companies, 25 is the magic age at which they are no longer considered "youthful drivers"—which means they qualify for a substantial reduction in their auto-insurance premiums. (Some companies extend that cut-off age to 30 for unmarried men or women who own or are the principal drivers of cars.)

Gender

Males comprise about 51.9 percent of the driving population, or just a little over half, but male drivers get into almost 68 percent more accidents than female drivers do. From 1978 to 1988, of the number of drivers in all accidents per 10,000,000 miles driven broken down by gender, 196 were males and 179, females. In the same time period, of the number of drivers in fatal accidents per 10,000,000 miles driven 46 were males and 21, females.

Parents with teenage boys who drive know how these statistics affect their car-insurance rates. How can you diminish the effect of the statistics, despite having teenage drivers? These are some answers:

1. Make your kids study hard, because getting good grades will enable you to qualify for good-student discounts. Insurers have found a correlation between good scholastic standing and safe driving, and a good-student discount can save as much as 25 percent on the premium with some companies!

    Discounts are also available to high school and college students under 25 getting insurance on their own, as long as they do one of the following:
    • Rank in the top fifth of the class
    • Maintain at least a B average, or a 3.0 average in a school using a 4.0 scale
    • Get on the Dean's List or Honor Roll
2. Insist that your children go through driver's education. Insurance companies have long been supporters of driver's ed, and many companies back their faith by offering

discounts, obtainable by presenting a certificate of completion from an approved course. Discounts vary from company to company but average 10 percent and are offered through age 20.

3. Emphasize how important a clean driving record is for lower car rates. A youth who acquires a bad record enters a high-risk category that is very expensive—insurance rates can almost double.

4. Get your young drivers a 1976 Chevy Impala and put only liability on it. This may be easier said than done, but your wallet won't take such a beating.

5. Make the kids pay the premium!

Marital Status

Single men under the age of 30 pay generally a little more than single females of the same age. A few states prohibit the use of sex and marital status to rate drivers and require companies to offer unisex rates.

Marriage seems to bring out the best in young drivers, if insurance records are a good indicator. Many companies charge young men less if they're married, and treat married young women (under 25) as though they've already moved out of the high-risk, youthful driver status.

Smoker or Nonsmoker

Many underwriters believe that smoking is linked with less careful driving behavior. "People who get the nonsmoker's discount seem to have fewer accidents," says James Nikolai, a vice president at Farmers Insurance Exchange, a company that uses smoking as a rating factor.

Driving Record

For many companies, an accident that results in death, bodily injury, or property damage in excess of $500 triggers a surcharge on your premium. The charge, which lasts for three years, varies from company to company and ranges from $10 to $75 every six months.

At State Farm, one at-fault accident results in a 10 percent surcharge. Two accidents add another 20 percent, and more than two increases the premium another 50 percent for each additional accident. At other companies, a single at-fault accident could bring a surcharge of 30 percent to 40 percent, and several accidents could add up to 200 percent.

Some companies have no surcharges. The California State Automobile Association Inter-Insurance Bureau does not add a surcharge for one at-fault accident once a policy is issued, but the company is choosy about who they accept originally. In other cases, this may depend on being insured with a company for several years. At Aetna, a policyholder who has one at-fault accident will not receive a surcharge if he or she has been with Aetna for at least five years and has been accident-free up to that point.

For the purposes of your driving record with an insurance company, here are some accidents that are *not* considered at-fault:

- Your car is struck while lawfully parked.
- You are reimbursed by or obtain a judgment against another person responsible for the accident.
- Your car is struck in the rear by another vehicle, and nobody in your household is convicted of a moving violation as a result.
- The other driver is convicted of a moving traffic violation, and the family member who is driving your car is not.
- Your car is damaged by a hit-and-run driver (note: you need to report the accident to the authorities within 24 hours).
- The accident is caused by contact with animals or fowl, or was caused by flying gravel, missiles, or falling objects.
- The accident results in a claim or payment under personal-injury-protection (no-fault) coverage and doesn't otherwise qualify for the assignment of a point.

THE VEHICLE

Use of the Vehicle

Part of the rating process and the premium depends on how often the vehicle is driven. These are the factors that the agent looks at when rating your car:

- Whether it is driven every day to work
- If so, how far it is driven to work
- How many miles it is driven per year
- Whether it is driven more for pleasure or for work
- Whether it is used by a person engaged in farming
- Whether it is driven solely for business purposes

The more the car is on the road, the higher the premium, because the risk of an accident is greater. Someone using a car for pleasure only, or who drives to a job that is less than three miles away, will pay about 25 percent less than someone like an insurance adjuster, who drives extensively for business.

Type of Vehicle

Most drivers are surprised at the precision of the records maintained by insurers on almost every make and model of car. Data on the price of the car, how easily it's damaged, how easily it's repaired, how "accident-prone" it is, and how popular it is with thieves are computed into an elaborate numbering system. The numbers usually run from 1 (least expensive vehicles) to as high as 50 (more expensive ones). Higher numbers translate into higher premiums. Numbers change from year to year once a company begins to gather new evidence on a model's damage, repair, and theft record. A poor record could trigger as much as a 15 percent increase in collision and comprehensive coverages (see Table 2.1).

Where the Vehicle Is Kept (Territory)

Insurance companies have data on the number of claims for each of their territories, often by zip-code location. They can single out problem neighborhoods and justify higher premiums for those areas.

> **EXAMPLE:**
>
> In New York City, Allstate charges the adult male owner of a 1987 Chevrolet Beretta Coupe who drives between four and nine miles to work each way $2,415 a year for full coverage if he lives in the Williamsburg section of Brooklyn. For someone driving the same car the same number of miles to work, the premium drops to $1,683 if he lives across the river in Manhattan.

It's interesting to note that in 1988 rural motor-vehicle accidents accounted for about 64 percent of all highway fatalities but only 38 percent of nonfatal injuries. About seven out of ten automobile accidents occur in urban locations. Likely reasons for these statistics would include the greater road mileage being traveled and higher speeds, poorer lighting, and perhaps fewer warning signs in rural than in urban areas.

More than One Vehicle

If you insure more than one car, you might get a discount of 20 percent to 25 percent. Companies say that families with several cars generally exhibit more stability and responsibility, which re-

Table 2.1 Relative Average Loss Payments per Insured Vehicle Year for 1989 Model Year Passenger Cars with the Best and Worst Collision Coverage Results*

	Best Results				Worst Results		
Make/Series	Body Style	Size	Result	Make/Series	Body Style	Size	Result
Plymouth Grand Voyager	P.V.	Large	46	Mercedes 300SE	Sp.	Large	235
Dodge Caravan	P.V.	Large	48	BMW 325i/iS 2D	Sp.	Midsize	217
Chevrolet Caprice	S.W.	Large	48	BMW 325i Conv.	Sp.	Midsize	200
Chevrolet Astro Van	P.V.	Large	49	BMW 325i 4D	Sp.	Midsize	190
Buick Century	Sp.	Midsize	49	Ford Mustang	Sp.	Midsize	182
Chevrolet Caprice	4Dr.	Large	50	BMW 500 Series	Sp.	Midsize	180
Dodge Spirit	4Dr.	Midsize	51	Nissan 240SX	2Dr.	Small	169
Dodge Grand Caravan	P.V.	Large	52	Pontiac Lemans	2Dr.	Small	168
Plymouth Acclaim	4Dr.	Midsize	52	Saab 900	2Dr.	Small	167
Ford Extended Aerostar	P.V.	Small	53	Lincoln Mark VII	Sp.	Midsize	162
Oldsmobile Cutlass Ciera	S.W.	Midsize	53	Mercedes SEL Series	Sp.	Large	160
Ford Crown Victoria	4Dr.	Large	55	Chevrolet Corvette	Sp.	Small	158
Ford Aerostar	P.V.	Large	59	Honda Civic CRX	Sp.	Small	156
Plymouth Voyager	P.V.	Large	60	Nissan Sentra	2Dr.	Small	155
Plymouth Reliant	4Dr.	Midsize	60	Geo Metro	2Dr.	Small	154
Dodge Dynasty	4Dr.	Midsize	60	Dodge Daytona	2Dr.	Small	154

P.V. = Passenger Van; S.W. = Station Wagon; Sp. = Sports or Specialty

*100 represents the average for all 1989 passenger cars ($214.7)

SOURCE: *1990 Property/Casualty Insurance Facts*, published by the Insurance Information Institute. Copyright © 1990 Insurance Information Institute. All rights reserved. Reprinted by permission.

sults in fewer accidents and traffic violations. Further, each car is driven less, which reduces its chances of being involved in an accident.

It might be useful to remember that, with all the above factors, the coverages you pick, whether full or for liability alone, dictate the premium. The quantity of coverage is the main thing.

HOW CAN I GET THE BEST RATE FOR MY VEHICLE?

The ways to save on your car insurance are to do some research on the various companies and to comparison shop. Also ask for discounts and get the right coverage.

WHICH COMPANIES OFFER LOWER PREMIUMS?

A few large insurers dominate the auto-insurance business. A well-known consumer magazine reviewed the premiums of the major insurers across several states, areas, and risks and found some interesting differences.

The magazine used one example of a husband and wife and their 17-year-old son, each with a clean traffic record. The hypothetical family owns a 1987 Buick LeSabre, which is used for commuting to work, and a 1985 Chevy Cavalier. Living in San Francisco, they might pay as much as $4,285 per year to insure their cars—or as little as $2,022 for identical coverage, depending on the company. In Manhattan, their premiums might be as high as $2,553 or as low as $1,853; in Chicago, as high as $2,976 or as low as $1,516.

The reason for these differences is not only that some insurance companies offer lower premiums than others, but also that two companies can come to different conclusions about the degree of risk presented by the applicants.

You can save a lot of dollars by comparison shopping for insurance. Make a list of the four or five highest-rated companies in your state, and then ask for a premium quote from each of them. You may be surprised to discover differences of hundreds of dollars a year in the annual premium for identical coverages.

In the above and other examples, the magazine specified the make and model of the car, the number of miles driven, and the various coverages each risk would buy. To pin down the differences in location, they asked for rates on each risk in three zip codes—urban, suburban, and rural—in each state.

The insurance companies with the lowest premiums overall were United Services Automobile Association (USAA), State Farm Mutual Auto, Auto Club Insurance Association, and Government Employees (GEICO).

Companies offering the middle level of premiums were American Family Mutual, California State Automobile Association, Nationwide Mutual, Aetna Casualty and Surety, Allstate, and Liberty Mutual Fire.

Companies with the highest premiums were Farmers Insurance Exchange and Travelers Indemnity.

Once you choose a company, it is still smart to price your program once a year to make sure your agent is still competitive.

DISCOUNTS

Ask about discounts. Here are a few of the common ones:

- Accident-free discount—if you're accident free for at least three years, you should qualify for this.
- Multiple-vehicle discount—the more vehicles you have insured, the more of a discount you can get.
- 50-plus discount—the older you are, the more discounts you should be able to get if your driving record is clean.
- Good-student discount—usually available if your child carries a B or better average, or 3.0 on a 4.0 grade scale.
- Package discount—more and more companies are offering a package discount if you have your house *and* car insurance with them.

COVERAGES

Analyze your coverage needs yearly. Look at different deductibles and have your agent price them out for you. Decide if you need full coverage (comp and collision) on a vehicle, or if the vehicle's age and value warrant dropping it. Make sure you don't have any frills on the policy that aren't worth the premium. To help you, use the form shown in Table 2.2.

OTHER COMMON QUESTIONS

WHO'S COVERED AND IN WHAT CAR?

All members of your family who live with you are generally covered under your auto-liability insurance. That includes your spouse and children, blood relatives, adopted children, in-laws,

Table 2.2 Auto-Insurance Buyer's Worksheet

	Company 1	Company 2
Minimum coverage your state requires for:		
Bodily injury liability	$_____ $_____	$_____
Property-damage liability	_____ _____	_____
Personal injury	_____ _____	_____
Subtotal A	$_____	$_____
Level of coverage you desire:		
Bodily injury liability	$_____ $_____	$_____
Property damage liability	_____ _____	_____
Medical payments	_____ _____	_____
Personal injury	_____ _____	_____
Collision		
$100 deductible	_____ _____	_____
$250 deductible	_____ _____	_____
$500 deductible	_____ _____	_____
Comprehensive, no deductible	_____ _____	_____
$100 deductible	_____ _____	_____
$250 deductible	_____ _____	_____
Subtotal B	$_____	$_____
Other coverages to look at:		
Emergency road service	$_____ $_____	$_____
Rental car reimbursement	_____ _____	_____
Death and disability	_____ _____	_____
Subtotal C	$_____	$_____
Do any other charges apply?		
Membership fee	$_____	$_____
Surcharges	_____	_____
Subtotal D	$_____	$_____
Total Premium	$_____	$_____

What's your choice? (Subtotal of A or B, plus C
and D)

wards, and foster children. They have the same protection as you,
as long as you give them permission to drive the car, because *car
insurance always follows the vehicle, not the driver.*

If you give permission to a friend to drive your car, he or
she will be covered by your liability insurance. The borrower could
also be covered by his or her own policy, but many states have
laws that hold the owner of the vehicle liable if a borrower's negligence causes an accident. Therefore, you should always be care-

ful about lending your car, because you can leave yourself wide open to a claim.

HOW EASY IS IT FOR MY INSURANCE COMPANY TO DROP ME?

Increasingly, consumers are becoming reluctant to report accidents to their insurance companies, leaving cars unrepaired or paying for repairs themselves, because they fear, and not unreasonably, that their insurance companies will raise their premiums or refuse to renew their policies at all. The complaints about auto insurance received most often by state insurance departments concern cancellation and nonrenewal.

Failing to report an accident can backfire on you. Weeks or even months later, the driver of the other car could sue you. Your insurance company, which you've paid to represent you, will not have heard of the accident. By the time it does, it may be too late to track down witnesses and other forms of evidence that could have helped your case.

You do have some reason to worry, however. As a result of consumers' concerns, however, many state insurance departments have established rules about when a company may cancel a policy or refuse to renew it. In Arizona, insurers must continue coverage unless the insured fails to pay the premiums or loses his or her license to drive.

With most companies, being at fault for one accident isn't enough to trigger a nonrenewal notice. But if the company believes the accident is the result of extreme negligence, carelessness, or drunk driving, the insured most likely will be dropped. Instead of dropping an insured outright, a company may offer coverage in one of its high-risk subsidiaries.

WHAT ABOUT A RENTED CAR?

You are protected under your own liability coverage for a rented car. However, you will probably need comprehensive and collision coverage on the rental vehicle. You have two options: (1) take the coverage they offer in the rental agreement, or (2) if a vehicle you are currently insuring has both of these coverages, most companies automatically cover you on the rental for a specified time period (usually 10 days) at no extra cost. Check with your insurance company.

SHOULD I INSURE MY CAR FOR A STATED VALUE?

Beware here! Once a client of mine wanted to insure a 1979 Pontiac specifically for $2,000. When I asked why he wanted to state the value like that, he said he wanted to make sure that if the car was totaled in an accident, he would get paid the full $2,000.

This common misconception can get you into trouble. To have a stated value placed on an auto policy doesn't mean you're guaranteed that amount if there's a total loss. "Stated value" merely means that the insurance company won't pay *more* than the amount stated, in this case the $2,000. The claims adjuster will come up with a "market value" for the car regardless of what the stated value is.

Also, what if the 1979 Pontiac is worth $2,500? You just cost yourself $500, not to mention the extra premium the company charges you for the stated-value endorsement.

WHY DOESN'T MY PREMIUM DECREASE AS MY CAR GETS OLDER?

I'm asked this all the time, and it's a good question. The car is getting older, true, but the labor it takes to fix a 1987 Chevy costs the same as labor for a 1990 Cadillac, and the same thing applies to the parts. The system just isn't set up for rate decreases as vehicles get older.

Of course if you do not have comprehensive or collision coverage on the vehicle, it makes no difference whether the car is new or old. The liability exposure is the same regardless.

HOW DO I INSURE MY CAMPER?

If the camper is a pull-behind type, the bodily-injury, property-damage, medical, and uninsured-motorist coverages extend from the towing vehicle to the camper automatically at no extra cost. The limits remain the same as the towing vehicle's.

If you want physical-damage coverage like comprehensive and collision, most companies allow you to add a "camper package" to the policy that includes these coverages. The premium is calculated on what you pay for the unit. The premium on the comp and collision package for, say, a 1989 pop-up camper for which you paid $3,500 would average about $100 a year.

IS MY INSURANCE GOOD IF I DRIVE OUTSIDE THE COUNTRY?

Virtually all auto policies issued in the United States cover accidents that occur anywhere in the country, plus U.S. territories and Canada. But if you're planning to travel extensively in Canada, you should (1) have insurance and (2) carry an insurance identification card that will serve as evidence.

If you're planning to drive into Mexico, talk to your insurance agent before you go, because your insurance is no good in Mexico! Under Mexican law you have to buy insurance from an authorized Mexican insurer. It's generally available at border crossing points.

AUTO INSURANCE CHECKLIST

If you currently have an insured vehicle, look at your policy.

☐ Do you have bodily-injury and property-damage? Do you have comp and collision? Do you have medical coverage? Do you have uninsured- and underinsured-motorist coverage?

☐ Do you have auto-rental reimbursement, death-and-disability, or emergency road service?

☐ Is your liability coverage adequate? Are the limits high enough? Do you have stated limits or is it a single-limit-liability policy?

☐ Do you live in a no-fault state?

☐ Are you satisfied with the level of your deductible?

☐ Are you getting all of the discounts for which you're eligible?

☐ If you have a camper, is it insured properly?

☐ Do you have any vehicles that are listed on a "stated-value" basis?

☐ If you're on a high-risk policy, do you know when you are eligible for preferred rates?

CHAPTER THREE

My Body, My Bills:
Health Insurance

*T*he principle behind health insurance is to protect you against the cost of medical care and supplies, so that, in theory, the more comprehensive the coverage you can get, the better off you will be. And yet, there seems to be a vicious circle of high-cost health care coupled with insurance-rate increases that threatens to break the backs of consumers in this country.

A single day in the hospital now averages more than $255, not including doctor's bills. Treatments that run up a tab exceeding $100,000 are becoming commonplace. Every year one out of five families faces medical bills that exceed the coverage limits of their insurance policies, or health programs that exceed 5 percent of their incomes, according to S.E. Berki and Leon Wyszewianski of the University of Michigan School of Public Health. The average monthly cost of health insurance in 1988 approached $100 for individual coverage and exceeded $200 for family coverage.

Approximately two-thirds of the country's population are covered under work-related health insurance. But as medical costs rise, employers are shifting more of the costs to the employees, who are asked to contribute a bigger chunk of the premium and to settle for a higher deductible.

Not only do policyholders pay larger shares, but they also lose control of the care they receive, as insurers try to hold down costs. With HMOs (health maintenance organizations), patients have little say in choosing the hospitals and even the doctors they use. With PPOs (preferred provider organizations), you *can* go outside the organization for services, but you will pay more. You might pay only $10 for a visit to a doctor in the network, as opposed to 80 percent of the regular fee of a doctor outside the network.

If you're fortunate enough to work for an employer who offers a large group-insurance plan, that's great! You have it easy. But if you're self-employed or own a business that employs 25 people or less, you may have a problem. This chapter will help you find the best health-insurance coverage for your money.

We'll look in depth at the options for (1) the small-business owner who wants to insure himself or herself and any employees, and (2) the individual or family who uses the fee-for-service contract, which is also known as individual health care.

HEALTH INSURANCE FOR THE SMALL-BUSINESS OWNER

The health-insurance industry, stunned by the rise in claim costs, is reducing its forms of coverage. Major insurance companies are bailing out of the business of covering individuals, associations, and small employee groups because, they say, their "losses are tremendous." It is clearly becoming very difficult to afford insurance premiums.

Between 1980 and 1990, the cost of group health benefits climbed nearly 350 percent, according to Noble Lowndes, a benefits consulting firm. And the biggest burden has fallen on the small-business owner. In the most recent round of premium hikes, manufacturing companies with less than 25 employees were hit with an average 33 percent boost, while the giants with 5,000 to 20,000 employees saw costs rise only 19 percent.

Noble Lowndes goes on to say that the small-business owner must spend 50 percent to 75 percent more to provide health insurance for a typical employee than corporate giants like Exxon or General Motors. Small firms don't have the muscle to negotiate lower rates and fees. In 1980, it cost approximately $710 to insure the average employee, which amounted to 4.9 percent of pay. Today, it costs $3,117 per employee—nearly 14 percent of pay.

In large companies, new employees enter into the health-insurance plan simply by filling out a sign-up card. But employees of small businesses are required to fill out health applications. They are also underwritten for their health status. That means that if they or their spouses are in bad health, they might be refused coverage. The entire business could also be turned down. A high-risk employee might then feel the need to withdraw voluntarily from a group, with a boss's promise to provide funds for individual coverage.

When an insurance company writes policies on a small business, it normally rules out preexisting conditions for at least a year and generally declines to accept employees or dependents who are costly health-care risks (like a worker with a heart condition). Therefore, during the first year, claims are few and premiums low. But in the second and third years, preexisting conditions are covered under the policy (see "Exclusions" below under individual health-care plan), and the effect of adding those conditions to unexpected new illnesses is that premiums tend to rise.

The potential for abuse is great, says North Dakota's Insurance Commissioner, Earl Pomeroy. A fly-by-night insurer can grab business from a more responsible company by insuring only the youngest and healthiest workers. In the first year they get a bargain price, but in the second year the premiums go up. So the small-business owner should really start out by looking for the right program.

WHAT HEALTH PROGRAMS CAN MY BUSINESS QUALIFY FOR?

Perhaps the most important change in the health insurance field in recent years has been the rapid expansion of **health maintenance organizations (HMOs)** and **preferred provider organizations (PPOs)**, which are part of the trend toward managed health care. According to Walter Bussewitz, CLU, and *Life Association News* contributing editor, HMOs and PPOs accounted for only 5 percent of all health care in a 1980 study. In 1990 they constitute approximately 30 percent of business done by commercial insurers.

According to a Health Insurance Association of America (HIAA) survey, 70 percent of the people in the country who had health insurance through their employers in 1987 were enrolled in HMOs, PPOs, or managed fee-for-service plans. Of this enrollment, 16 percent were in HMOs, 11 percent in PPOs, and 32 percent in managed fee-for-service and 41 percent in unmanaged fee-for-service plans. Some experts predict that within seven years, 95 percent of all health care will fall under some sort of managed-care plan.

For the small-business owner seeking group health-care coverage, it essentially boils down to three options: HMOs and PPOs in the prepaid health-care market, or individual health-care policies for each employee.

Health Maintenance Organizations (HMOs)

An HMO is an organization that provides a wide range of comprehensive health-care services for a specified group at a fixed-period payment. The HMO can be sponsored by the government, medical schools, hospitals, employers, labor unions, consumer groups, and insurance companies. Normally, the minimum number of people you need before you can use this service is five, but some organizations will take individuals.

This is a prepaid health-insurance plan. The subscriber pays a fixed amount in advance for his or her health care. With prepaid medical care, the premium covers doctor and hospital care without the bother of insurance forms. The trade-off is that you give up the right to select your own doctor, hospital, or clinic.

There are two main types: (1) staff/group HMOs, in which employees must go to specified clinics or practices; and (2) independent practice associations (IPAs), which offer a list of participating physicians and hospitals to choose from. Unlike individual health-care programs, HMOs cannot easily deny coverage for health reasons. Congress has also set higher limits to ensure that small employers pay no more than 10 percent above the HMO's community rate.

According to the Health Insurance Association of America, HMOs cost 12 percent less for individual coverage and 15 percent less for family coverage than conventional and PPO plans. In 1988, not only did HMO plans cost less, but their rate of cost increase (9 percent) was far lower than that for PPOs (17 percent) and conventional plans (20 percent).

The approach HMOs use is mainly preventative—providing physical exams, well-baby care, and diagnostics at no additional cost—services that are included in the monthly fee. However, the quality of HMO care can be problematic. In an HMO, care may be delivered in a cliniclike setting rather than in an office. A primary doctor will prescribe treatment or refer you to a staff specialist. Some members complain about the wait to see doctors, and in many cases, patients see a nurse practitioner before they see a doctor. Generally, a good way to get a feel for an HMO in your area is to ask some current members how they would rate the organization.

PPOs

The idea behind preferred provider organizations is that medical practitioners give discount rates in exchange for the insurer's sending patients to the PPO. Employees who go outside the preferred network for care may end up paying more because of having fewer expenses covered by insurance.

Unlike HMO members, PPO participants have the option to see any doctor outside of the PPO network, as long as they're willing to pay the extra cost. PPOs are considered to be a little more financially risky to consumers than HMOs, because they have to be concerned with profitability as well as quality of care.

WHICH ARE BETTER—HMOS OR PPOS?

During the spring of 1988, Westat, a Maryland-based survey firm, conducted 1,665 interviews with employers who offered health benefits to their employees, and 273 interviews with employers who did not. The following comparisons of the factors of cost, benefits, and regional differences are based on their results. (Note: Please keep in mind that HMO and PPO plans are influenced by geographic location, type of industry, employer size, and the health status of the covered employee. However, it is possible to get a general comparison.)

Cost

The average monthly cost for HMOs in 1988 was approximately $100 for individuals and $200 for families. The average monthly cost of a PPO plan was $103 for individuals and $233 for families.

Benefits

HMOs offered richer benefits than PPOs or conventional plans. (See Table 3.1.) For example, 98 percent of the employees in HMO plans had coverage for adult physical examinations, while only 39 percent of the PPO enrollees had this benefit.

About 98 percent of HMO plans offer well-baby care and preventative diagnostic procedures, compared with 62 percent and 72 percent respectively, of PPO plans.

Regional Differences

Despite considerable variation in percentages of HMO and PPO enrollment by region, there were few differences in overall premium increases from one region to another. For example, two-thirds of employees in the West were enrolled in either HMO or

Table 3.1 Employees Covered, by Type of Plan, 1988 (in percent)

Benefits	Conventional Plan	PPO Plan	HMO: IPA Plan	HMO: Staff Plan
Adult physical examinations	27	39	95	99
Well-baby care	45	62	99	97
Preventive diagnostic procedures	61	72	96	100
Prescription drugs	93	94	95	92
Home health care	84	90	90	86
Mental health: Outpatient	94	97	96	95
Inpatient	98	96	98	97
Treatment for substance abuse	87	93	98	98
General dental care	42	33	16	26
Orthodontia	30	26	8	18

SOURCE: *Research Bulletin—The Health Insurance Picture in 1988*, published by the Health Insurance Association of America (July 1989).

PPO plans as opposed to conventional plans, which was a considerably higher percentage than in other regions. Yet premium increases varied only from 13 percent in the West to 11 percent in the North Central region. The West is particularly interesting; lower HMO premium increases there were offset by higher conventional and PPO premium increases.

Health insurance tends to cost less in the South, where employers contribute smaller shares for the cost of coverage. In 1988, family coverage cost nearly 20 percent less in the South than in the Northeast.

Workers in the West were more likely to have coverage for preventative benefits in the form of physical exams, well-baby care, and diagnostic procedures than workers in other regions.

Analysis of Survey Findings

Overall, HMOs fared better in the survey than PPOs. For the same set of employers, they cost less than PPO and conventional plans, experienced lower rates of increase in premiums, and offered richer benefit packages. Yet business owners expressed higher levels of satisfaction with their PPO and conventional competitors. Why?

First, the lower rates of HMOs may be explained by the fact that HMOs tend to treat younger, healthier people, so that the poorer risks are relegated to the PPO and conventional plans. Second, the difference in levels of satisfaction may be due to quality of service. The majority of firms that canceled contracts with HMOs cited service as their primary reason for doing so. On the other hand, the majority of firms that canceled contracts with conventional or PPOs referred to cost as the primary reason for doing so.

HOW DO I KNOW IF IT'S A GOOD PLAN?

No two health plans are alike in every detail, but better-than-average plans have similar features. In the April 1988 issue of *Changing Times Magazine*, Philip Godwin spelled out what a typical HMO policy with good coverage is likely to have in benefits and other provisions. Based on a survey by the U.S. Bureau of Labor Statistics of medium and large employers in 1986, Godwin advises that you should look for the following types of coverage:

- Deductible—$100 each year per person (once two or three family members meet deductible, rest of family gets first-dollar coverage).
- Maximum benefit—$1,000,000 per lifetime.
- Limit on annual out-of-pocket expenses—$1,000 per year after deductible is met.
- Employee premium—$41 a month.
- Daily hospital room and board and doctors—100 percent of semiprivate hospital room and board, nursing services, medicines, and miscellaneous supplies for 365 days of confinement for each person.
- Surgical Fees—100 percent of reasonable and customary fees based on regional averages. Increasingly, plans cover inpatient surgery at 80 percent. Outpatient surgery is often reimbursed more liberally because insurers generally believe that it saves money. Second surgical opinion usually assures 100 percent of coverage.
- Outpatient Care—80 percent of lab fees, X-rays.
- Mental-Health services, including alcohol and drug-abuse treatment—100 percent for a maximum of 30 days of inpatient nursing and hospital services; 50 percent for a maximum of 30 days of outpatient therapy; no limit on out-of-pocket expenses; alcohol often has a 30-day limit on outpatient treatment.

- Dental—80 percent for accidental injury. Additional benefits are provided to 71% of employees in the form of exams, X-rays, fillings, and periodontal care at 80 percent to 100 percent; crowns and inlays are covered for 50 percent.
- Home Health Care—80 percent if supervised by a doctor.
- Private-duty nursing—80 percent.

Cautions

To find out which insurance companies are the safest, go to your local public library and consult an A.M. Best Insurance Reports. Only consider companies rated A or A$^+$ by Best. If the company has a rating lower than A, or is not listed, walk away.

When selecting the policy, watch out for a too-low price. If someone tries to sell you a package of benefits that is drastically cheaper than similar policies, something could be wrong. Remember to ask when you might expect to see a premium increase and what the percentage is likely to be—with or without large claims. You aren't likely to get a straight answer, but ask anyway because some companies try to entice you with low first-year rates and then jack up the price later to make up the difference.

Discounts for Life-style

Breaks on deductibles and premiums are available from some companies to employees who participate in programs aimed at pursuing a healthy life-style. The programs often emphasize giving up smoking and keeping blood pressure and cholesterol levels under control.

Cafeteria Plan

Another approach that might save on a premium is a **cafeteria plan**. Under this plan, the employee is allowed to choose among a range of benefits offered by his or her employer. The "cafeteria" concept doesn't always mean a plan will cost less, but it will allow you to choose the benefits that work best for you. If your company has this arrangement, you might choose to get more health insurance benefits and not take the life insurance, or you might choose to forgo a certain coverage and apply the money toward child care instead.

Incentives for Lowering Costs of Care

By choosing low-cost care, you can actually pick up extra cash in certain plans. Blue Cross and Blue Shield of Toledo, Ohio, will give a $100 check to mothers who stay in the hospital no more than two days for a normal delivery and no more than three days for an uncomplicated cesarean section. Under one health-insurance option, Eastman Kodak in Rochester, New York, will waive the 20 percent coinsurance charge if an employee avoids a hospital by using home health care, skilled nursing, or hospice care.

WHO CAN HELP ME FIND THE BEST PLAN FOR A SMALL GROUP?

Stalking the market for a new, better, or cheaper health-insurance policy for you and your employees is no small task. Quality, dependability, and service are the main goals, but when there are a number of options, along with many potential pitfalls, you may need an expert's help.

An available option is to work with an experienced health insurance **agent, broker, consultant**, or **financial planner**. These people—many of them independent business owners themselves—can spend the time you don't have to investigate alternatives, stay on top of developments, and compare rates and features. Ask friends for references and look in the yellow pages under Insurance for their service providers. They have become increasingly popular in the last five years, and it is easy to find them, especially if you live in a metropolitan area.

What are the differences among these professionals?

1. An "agent" represents a specific insurance carrier or group of carriers.
2. A "broker" is an independent who has access to a variety of plans, which he or she can sell.
3. A true "consultant" is an independent who does not sell products; he or she makes a profit by charging a fee for advice on what policy to select and where to find it. The most valuable of these is the "benefit specialist"—someone who is well versed in health insurance intricacies.
4. "Financial planners" can also be helpful, but they will most likely be generalists and not health specialists.

Employers are strongly advised to look for a health insurance professional who represents many products and who can quote prices on a variety of plans.

Once you've determined whom you might want as an agent, broker, etc., get client references. You need an agent who is trained and experienced.

INDIVIDUAL HEALTH INSURANCE

On an individual health-care policy from Empire Blue Cross and Blue Shield (New York), for a married couple under 25 the *quarterly* premium in 1989 went as high as $948! A similar insurance company in New York offers a policy with no deductibles or coinsurance for the quarterly cost of $538. Neither plan provides dental coverage.

If your employer doesn't offer a health-care package, or if you are self-employed and seek a health-care package, the cards are stacked against you—but it is not impossible to find a policy that fits your needs.

There are two parts to your protection in the traditional fee-for-service plan. The main policy is the basic coverage that pays hospital and doctor bills, imposing either a dollar or day limit for coverage. The other part is major medical coverage, which picks up where the basic coverage leaves off. In what follows, the key terms, the benefits, the exclusions, the rules, and the rates are outlined for the *basic* coverage in a typical fee-for-service, individual health-care plan.

WHAT DOES MAXIMUM BENEFIT MEAN?

Maximum benefit means the maximum amount of money an insurance company will pay out for covered injuries or sickness. There are several different limits to choose from—lifetime limit, per accident/per sickness limit, and no limit.

Lifetime Limit

The average limits set on this policy range from $500,000 to $2,000,000. This is the amount of insurance you have and can collect against for the rest of your life. If you have a car accident and the policy pays out $50,000, you have $450,000 left from the $500,000-maximum-limit plan. If your next illness or accident uses $200,000, you have $250,000 in your lifetime limit.

Which maximum limit should you get? The difference in premiums between the policy limits of $500,000 and $2,000,000 is so minute that it does not pay to take the lower lifetime benefit. Considering the spiraling costs of hospitals and other medical care, you should take the $2,000,000 maximum limit and not try to save on the premium.

Per Accident/Per Sickness Limit

Under this plan, the maximum benefit is applied *each* time you have a claim. Using a maximum benefit of $1,000,000 as an example, if you have a heart attack, you are covered up to $1,000,000; five months later, if you are diagnosed with cancer, you again have the $1,000,000 in coverage.

Your premium is much lower with this type of maximum payment, but the catch is that the insurance company will apply the deductible and coinsurance each time there is a claim. This increases the money you pay out of your pocket.

No Limit

There are companies that do not state *any* dollar figure as a maximum limit. The policy pays until you're cured or pass away. These policies cost an average of 5 percent to 10 percent more than the other two.

WHAT KINDS OF DEDUCTIBLES ARE THERE FOR INDIVIDUAL HEALTH INSURANCE?

You will be familiar with the term **deductible** from the previous two chapters: It is the amount you're obligated to pay before the insurance company starts paying the bills. If you have a $250 deductible and your bills come to $800, the insurance company will pay the amount over the $250, or $550. Do all insurance companies have deductibles? To my knowledge every health-insurance carrier has some form of a deductible. The most common are $250, $500, $1,000, and $2,000.

The higher the deductible you get, the lower the premium you will pay. It stands to reason that the insurance company will charge less premium if you're paying more of the bill.

> ### EXAMPLE:
>
> With a typical individual-health-care policy, assuming first a 25-year-old male and a 25-year-old female smoker, and second two 25-year-old nonsmokers, the 1990 monthly premium rates under four different deductibles vary as shown in Tables 3.2 and 3.3.
>
> Over a year's time, the savings for nonsmokers adds up, as Table 3.4 illustrates.

Premium rates obviously are affected by a number of factors besides the deductible, including gender, age, geographical location, and whether you smoke, to name a few of the most important ones. Age and gender are fixed—you can't change them—but smoking and the deductible are two variable factors, and the above tables show how they can make rates change.

Table 3.2 Monthly Premium Rates at Different Deductible
Amounts for 25-Year-Old Smokers

	Deductible Amount			
	$250	$500	$1,000	$2,000
Male	$56	$51	$44	$40
Female	81	77	72	63

The reason for the difference in rates because of gender is
because females historically account for a higher percentage in
claims than males.

EXAMPLE:

Now let's look at how the premium is affected by the deductible, assuming the same company and same geographical
location, for a hypothetical family of four—see Table 3.5.
There are a 35-year-old husband and a 34-year old wife (neither of whom smokes), and an 8-year-old daughter and 5-
year-old son.

In a year, this particular family could save $516 [the
difference between 12 × the $239 monthly payment for the
$250 deductible (or $2,868) and 12 × the $196 monthly pay-
ment for the $2,000 deductible (or $2352)]. This savings in
premium must be weighed against the prospect of having a
major claim. In a claim-free year, the $516 is pure savings,
but if you have a significant claim, the difference in actual
cost between a $250 deductible and one for $2,000 is $1,750!
Overall, you would lose $1,134 ($1,750 − 516).

If you start out with one deductible, it doesn't mean you have
to stay with it forever. You can request an increase or decrease

Table 3.3 Monthly Premium Rates at Different Deductible
Amounts for 25-Year-Old Nonsmokers

	Deductible Amount			
	$250	$500	$1,000	$2,000
Male	$48	$45	$39	$34
Female	70	67	62	55

Table 3.4 Annual Premium Rates at Different Deductible Amounts for 25-Year-Old Females

	Deductible Amount			
	$250	$500	$1,000	$2,000
Smoker	$972	$924	$864	$756
Nonsmoker	840	804	744	660
Difference	$132	$120	$120	$ 96

by contacting your agent. It's usually a simple process, especially if your health has not deteriorated. The company may require, however, that you wait until the anniversary date of your enrollment, or you may have to re-qualify in terms of the status of your health.

Deductibles are met in one of two ways, either (1) in a calendar or policy year, or (2) on a per accident/per sickness/per person basis.

Calendar-Year or Policy-Year Deductible

This is by far the most common type of deductible. What it means is that you accumulate all doctor bills and prescription bills incurred during the calendar year (January 1 to December 31) or policy year (one year from the date the policy was taken out), and when they total more than the deductible, the insurance company reimburses you for the amount over and above the deductible. If the bills are less than the deductible, your policy won't pay anything.

Table 3.5 Monthly Premium Rates at Different Deductible Amounts for a Family of Four (Nonsmokers)

	Deductible Amount			
Members	$250	$500	$1,000	$2,000
Husband (35)	$ 64	$ 59	$ 53	$ 46
Wife (34)	79	74	68	60
First child (8)	48	48	47	45
Second child (5)	48	48	47	45
Total	$239	$229	$215	$196

Let's say you have a $250 deductible and by the end of the year your bills total $400. You probably would have been sending each bill in as you have received it, so it should be very easy for the insurance company to reimburse you for the $150 left over after the deductible. If it looks like you won't exceed the deductible for that year, many insurance companies allow you to accumulate the bills for the last three months of the year and carry them over to the next year. This is a nice option, and you should definitely ask your agent about it.

Calendar-year or policy-year deductibles are excellent for married couples with young children. I don't have to tell someone who has small children how easy it is to run up big bills at the pediatrician's office. It's almost certain you'll go over the deductible, and after paying it once, you'll be done for the year. On the other hand, if your children have outgrown the phase of frequent coughs, colds, and ear infections, you may want to change to the per-incident type of deductible.

Per Accident/Per Sickness/Per Person Deductible

With this option, you must satisfy the deductible each time you make a claim. If you're in a car accident and have extensive injuries, you will have the deductible to satisfy. Four months later, if you have a heart attack, you have the deductible to satisfy again. It is obvious that this type of policy isn't very practical for someone who expects to have many small bills.

EXAMPLE:

Table 3.6 uses the same hypothetical nonsmoking family of four (father 35, mother 34, daughter 8, son 5). You can see the difference between the two *kinds* of deductibles at three different deductible rates:

By using the per-accident option for the deductible, your family can save $840 to $1,368 per year in premium (the difference between the calendar-year deductible and per-accident per sickness deductible at the $250 and $1,000 levels). That savings can be used to pay for office calls and prescriptions.

I speak from experience, having raised three kids on the per accident/per illness/per person program. While my family would have benefited from the kind of policy that allows you to accumulate bills over the space of a year and turn in the amounts over your deductible, the money we saved in premium dollars compensated for the expense. No two families' needs are exactly alike,

Table 3.6 Monthly Premium for Calendar-Year versus Per-Sickness Deductible at Different Deductible Amounts*

	Deductible Amount		
Policy Type	$250	$500	$1,000
Calendar year	$239	$229	$215
Per sickness	169	127	101
Difference	$ 70	$102	$114

*Assumes a family of four

however. You should weigh all the factors to determine the direction in which you should go.

WHAT IS COINSURANCE?

Agents usually find this term to be difficult for prospective clients. While most consumers know they have a deductible to satisfy on their health policy, 90 percent of them probably don't know what **coinsurance** is and how it works.

"Coinsurance" simply means "sharing the risk" with the insurance company. It is a provision by which both the insurer and the insured pay part of a covered loss in a specified ratio, typically 80/20, or 80 percent by the insurer and 20 percent by the insured. This means that after your deductible is satisfied, you're still responsible for a certain percentage of the total bill.

Most major medical policies limit the amount the insured must pay under the coinsurance provision by including a **stop-loss** provision. This specifies that the policy will cover 100 percent of the insured's eligible medical expenses after the insured has incurred a specified amount of out-of-pocket expenses—such as $1,000, or $2000, or $5000—under the coinsurance feature. (In a major-medical policy that covers a family, the stop-loss provision usually specifies that once any two family members have individually reached the stop-loss limit, then all deductibles and coinsurance requirements are waived for all other family members.)

> **EXAMPLE:**
>
> You have a $250 deductible and a $5,000, 80/20 coinsurance policy. Thus, you pay the first $250 of your claim and then 20 percent of the next $5,000 worth of bills, or $1,000. The insurance company pays the remaining 80 percent, or $4,000, and then 100 percent of the remaining bills up to the policy maximum limit.

When pricing health insurance, *always* ask the agent to state what the stop-loss limit is on the policy. You might say, "If I have a bill for $10,000 and my deductible is $250, how much will I have to pay out of my own pocket?" If the agent says $1,250, then it's a $5,000 stop-loss, or coinsurance (20 percent of $5,000 is $1,000, plus the $250 deductible); if the agent says $650, then it's a $2,000 coinsurance (20 percent of $2,000 is $400, plus the $250 deductible). If the agent can't explain coinsurance, find another agent!

Normally, the higher the coinsurance, the lower the premium. For a 30-year-old male nonsmoker, a policy with a coinsurance limit of $500 would have an annual premium of $581; at the higher limit of $2,000, the premium goes down to $465; and at a coinsurance limit of $10,000, the premium falls to $291.

WHAT ARE COMMON HOSPITAL BENEFITS?

Most health insurance policies carry the following hospital benefits:

Semiprivate Room Charges

According to a continuing survey conducted by the Health Insurance Association of America, the national average cost of a semiprivate room as of January 1988 was $254.87 per day—a 6.7 percent increase over January 1987. (See Table 3.7.) The highest regional daily average rate ($308) was in the West. The lowest rate ($207) was in the South. Coverage for the cost of a semiprivate room, which includes meals and general nursing care, is a standard benefit. Also included under room coverage is the cost for a hospital intensive-care unit, coronary-care unit, and isolation.

Doctors' Fees

This benefit pays **reasonable and customary** doctors' fees and related expenses for inpatient and outpatient surgical procedures.

"Reasonable and customary" refers to the going rate or change in a geographical area for services, procedures, and supplies identical to the ones you are claiming. It is applied commonly to surgeries, and you have to hope that if you have a broken nose repaired, the surgeon's bill will not be more than what is deemed reasonable and customary. What if it is? In most cases, you will have to pay the extra charge.

Some policies also pay 100 percent for consultation fees and second opinion charges.

Table 3.7 Comparison of Hospital Semiprivate Room Charges by State and Territory*

States and Territories	January 1987	January 1988	Percent change
Alabama	$176.11	$187.00	6.2%
Alaska	317.82	330.66	4.0
Arizona	232.88	251.22	7.9
Arkansas	154.81	158.94	2.7
California	328.21	360.54	9.9
Colorado	242.08	261.25	7.9
Connecticut	333.29	344.28	3.3
Delaware	305.00	325.00	6.6
District of Columbia	422.74	449.05	6.2
Florida	202.06	217.94	7.9
Georgia	151.89	161.91	6.6
Hawaii	241.72	257.25	6.4
Idaho	229.95	249.67	8.6
Illinois	265.24	275.55	3.9
Indiana	205.52	223.81	8.9
Iowa	192.79	201.96	4.8
Kansas	200.74	216.23	7.7
Kentucky	198.65	215.32	8.4
Louisiana	199.69	208.56	4.4
Maine	231.86	257.20	10.9
Maryland	213.25	231.69	8.6
Massachusetts	286.47	312.04	8.9
Michigan	279.67	293.78	5.0
Minnesota	223.31	243.59	9.1
Mississippi	124.80	140.50	12.6
Missouri	213.47	225.71	5.7
Montana	214.22	218.73	2.1
Nebraska	172.63	181.88	5.4
Nevada	223.39	223.92	0.2
New Hampshire	220.77	238.28	7.9
New Jersey	212.32	228.73	7.7
New Mexico	232.13	233.88	0.8
New York	254.19	265.69	4.5
North Carolina	156.68	174.45	11.3
North Dakota	183.97	195.04	6.0
Ohio	261.19	275.65	5.5
Oklahoma	178.49	187.72	5.2
Oregon	263.46	286.65	8.8
Pennsylvania	284.25	301.32	6.0
Puerto Rico	131.22	139.77	6.5
Rhode Island	244.20	274.86	12.6
South Carolina	145.23	159.48	9.8
South Dakota	174.67	181.85	4.1
Tennessee	161.83	172.62	6.7
Texas	183.40	198.78	8.4
Utah	234.23	242.48	3.5
Vermont	257.02	284.48	10.7
Virginia	180.99	195.01	7.7
Washington	268.39	281.04	4.7
West Virginia	180.70	196.00	8.5
Wisconsin	171.56	185.83	8.3
Wyoming	177.14	188.83	6.6
Average U.S.	$238.78	$254.87	6.7%

*Matching data only.

SOURCE: Health Insurance Association of America, *Source Book of Health Insurance Data 1989.*

Table 3.8 Total Cost of Having a Baby, 1986

	Usual birth			Cesarean		
	Average physicians' fees	Hospital and medical	Total cost	Average physicians' fees	Hospital and medical	Total cost
Northeast						
Metropolitan	$ 980	2,020	$3,000	$1,210	$3,070	$4,280
Nonmetropolitan	960	1,650	2,610	1,240	2,910	4,150
Total	980	1,900	2,880	1,220	2,980	4,200
South						
Metropolitan	840	1,670	2,510	1,100	2,920	4,020
Nonmetropolitan	760	1,560	2,320	1,010	2,860	3,870
Total	800	1,590	2,390	1,060	2,890	3,950
Midwest						
Metropolitan	760	1,970	2,730	1,020	3,520	4,540
Nonmetropolitan	640	1,610	2,250	880	3,100	3,980
Total	690	1,770	2,460	930	3,290	4,220
West						
Metropolitan	1,090	2,000	3,090	1,390	4,050	5,440
Nonmetropolitan	820	1,440	2,260	1,110	3,270	4,380
Total	950	1,780	2,730	1,250	3,680	4,930
US						
Metropolitan	900	1,900	2,800	1,110	3,340	4,450
Nonmetropolitan	760	1,580	2,340	970	3,070	4,040
Total	830	1,730	2,560	1,040	3,230	4,270

NOTE: Costs are based on birth in labor and delivery room in hospital and exclude pediatrician's routine, inhospital newborn care fee, circumcision fee and anesthesiologist's professional fee.

SOURCE: Health Insurance Association of America, *Source Book of Health Insurance Data 1989.*

Maternity

According to a national survey conducted by the Health Insurance Association of America in 1986, the average cost for a normal (not cesarean) hospital delivery was $2,560, which represented a 25 percent increase over the average cost in 1982. (See Table 3.8) Most births in this country are "normal deliveries," but the number of cesarean sections increased from 4.5 percent of all births in 1965 to 21.1 percent in 1984. The average cost of an uncomplicated cesarean in the United States in 1986 was $4,270.

Most policies cover pregnancy as a sickness. Some companies have very minimal pregnancy benefits, paying only $300 to $500, but the premiums are 25 percent lower than those of the companies with better coverage. Therefore, you can save some premium when looking for a health-insurance policy by choosing one of these companies—*if* you are not planning on having any children, or any more children.

CAUTION: Make sure you know whether your policy covers the newborn at birth. Why? The baby could be born with major health problems. Retardation, premature birth, or heart aberrations could put a family in a lot of financial stress if the newborn isn't covered at birth. Also check for coverage of well-baby nursery costs. If the mother has to stay in the hospital longer than the usual few days, will the newborn's stay also be covered? Be sure to discuss this with your agent.

Dependent Coverage

As a general rule, children can stay on your policy and receive all hospital benefits until (1) they graduate from college, (2) they reach the age of 19, or (3) they get married.

Organ Transplants

Given the new technologies in medicine that allow kidney transplants, heart transplants, and lung transplants, you need to investigate how your company handles this area. See if they cover organ transplants in general, and if they do, what restrictions there are on how much they pay.

Miscellaneous Expenses

This benefit pays for "reasonable and customary" (see above) miscellaneous expenses incurred for medication or drugs administered at the time of hospitalization, including laboratory fees, X-rays, ambulance service, and supplies. Specifically included in this category are the following:

- Services of a radiologist, pathologist, and anesthesiologist
- Drugs, lab fees, medicine, and dressings
- Oxygen and its administration
- Operating-room charges

Number of Days Covered

Some policies put restrictions on the number of days of coverage you're allowed in the hospital—for example, 365 consecutive days. Other policies state no restrictions on time spent in the hospital.

Outpatient Treatment

Outpatient treatment for a covered injury or covered sickness could include the following:

- Treatment by radium, radioactive isotopes, or chemotherapy
- Physical therapy
- Surgery done in an office or hospital without the patient's being admitted to a room

- Diagnostic work-ups, preadmission testing, and lab procedures

Specialized Equipment

Included under this category is equipment such as a hospital bed and wheelchair, required for your convalescence and treatment at home. Also covered would be the cost of any prosthetics, braces, canes, or other special equipment required for rehabilitation purposes.

Home Care

This coverage is for home-care services up to a certain number of days (usually 60) immediately following a period of at least seven days of hospitalization. This coverage is receiving more and more attention, as insurance companies try to reduce costs and get patients out of the hospital earlier.

Such services usually must be provided by state-licensed or medicare-certified health agents or hospital home-care service administrations in order for the insurance company to pay.

WHAT IS EXCLUDED FROM MY INDIVIDUAL HEALTH PLAN?

While not every agent tells you what's *not* covered in an individual health-care policy, the good ones always do. Here are nine standard items excluded from most policies:

1. Medical services, treatment, or supplies for injuries resulting from war or military service.
2. Elective medical care. An example of elective medical care is having your nose altered because of its size. The point here is that you have decided to have something done to your body that is not medically necessary or therapeutic.
3. Intentional, self-inflicted injury, and attempted suicide.
4. Preexisting conditions. A **preexisting condition** is a medical problem that was being covered by your previous health plan and that you didn't disclose to the new company. It is normally defined as an injury that occurred or a sickness that first manifested itself before the new policy was issued *and* that was not disclosed on the application.

   Any condition you disclose on the application is not considered to be a "preexisting condition"; insurance companies will pay benefits for the treatment of such a disclosed condition unless the policy excludes the condition from coverage (see #5). Usually, however, you will have to wait two years.

5. Waived conditions. An insurance **waiver** refers to the specifying of certain medical conditions you have at the time of application (preexisting condition) that will not be covered. For example, if you have recently had reconstructive knee surgery, there will be a "waiver" on that knee, so that the insurance company will not pay for any expense you incur if that knee is reinjured. Depending on the condition, waivers can be permanent or pertain to a limited time period.

6. Hospital-surgical procedures paid for by other coverages, such as worker's compensation, or that are provided free in government facilities.

7. Routine dental care. This is another tricky area in health policies. Most regular health policies do not pay for dental care unless it's due to an injury, such as being in a car accident and having several teeth knocked out. Then, unless you're treated by a doctor of oral surgery *in* the hospital, you won't get any coverage.

8. Plastic surgery for cosmetic purposes (see #2). But corrective surgery required because of accidental injury, or plastic surgery performed on a newborn to correct a birth defect is covered.

9. Treatment for alcoholism, drug abuse, or chemical dependency. Some policies pay for this and some don't. Thirty days of treatment for alcoholism in a hospital is very expensive! Check your policy to see how this area is handled.

GENERAL PROVISIONS OF AN INDIVIDUAL HEALTH POLICY

Time Limit on Certain Defenses

After two years from the effective date (date of issue), only fraudulent misstatements in the application may be used to void a currently paid-up policy or to deny a claim. Also after two years from the date of issue, no benefits will be reduced or denied because of a sickness or physical condition that existed before the date of issue. This does not apply if the sickness or physical condition is *specifically* excluded from the policy in writing—i.e., put in a waiver.

Grace Period

Most policies have a 31-day grace period. This means that if a renewal premium is not paid on or before the due date, it may be paid during the following 31 days. During the grace period, the policy stays in force. The grace period will not apply if you give advance, written notice to cancel the insurance.

Reinstatement

Your coverage ceases if you don't pay the premium within the time granted, but it may be reinstated if certain conditions are met:

- Usually, the insured must pay any overdue premiums and must complete a reinstatement application. The insurer has the right to evaluate the reinstatement application and to decline the policy on the basis of statements in that application. This can be a major problem if, in the meantime, you've developed a medical condition that could keep you from getting the insurance.
- If the insurer does not complete the evaluation within 45 days after receiving the reinstatement application, or if the insurer accepts an overdue premium without a reinstatement application, then the policy is automatically deemed to be reinstated.
- Coverage under a reinstated policy is limited only to accidents that occur after the date of reinstatement and to sicknesses that begin more than 10 days after the date of reinstatement.

Not all insurance companies have a reinstatement provision; you could be left out altogether.

Premium Rates

Most insurance companies have the right to raise rates on individual health policies as follows:

- Rates may be increased by class, so that every policyholder's rates are increased at the same time. A class consists of all policies of a particular type or all policies issued to a particular group of insureds—for example, all policies in force in a particular state, or all policies issued to insureds of a particular age or who fall into a specific risk category.

    To change a rate by class, the insurer must get the

approval of the state insurance department before the rates can go into effect. This may sound like a big obstacle, but most rate increases are approved with relative ease.

- In addition, some companies raise their rates by age, in five-year increments starting with 25 and extending through 60. This is usually done automatically, whether there has been a rate increase by class or not. Once you reach age 65, you are eligible for a Medicare supplement policy, which is much cheaper than health insurance. You should make arrangements to drop your health-care policy and get a Medicare supplement program. You should never be paying for a health-care policy at age 65 or over. (See Chapter 7.)

- Rates may also be raised in **rate-ups**. A "rate-up" is an increase in your premium due to a preexisting condition. The amount of the rate-up depends upon the severity of the condition. Although it costs more, a rate-up is still better than no coverage at all. Some of the conditions that warrant rate-ups are high blood pressure, obesity, and asthma.

Conversion Privilege
Most policies may be continued if you and your insured spouse get divorced, if the marriage is annulled, or if one of you dies.

Renewal Agreement
Although you can keep renewing policies up to age 65, the age of eligibility for Medicare, merely by paying the premium, check to make sure the company you're dealing with has this renewal agreement. If you move to a state in which your present company isn't licensed to sell health insurance, most carriers will let you keep your policy regardless.

SHOPPING TIPS
Whatever kind of policy you have, you don't want to pay more than necessary. If you're pricing policies, you should do the following:

1. Get quotes at different maximum-benefit amounts.
2. Ask for quotes at the same deductible from different companies, whether it be $100, $250, or $500, etc. Also, ask if it's a calendar-year, policy-year, or per accident/per person/per sickness deductible.

3. Look for a company that will pay a surgeon's bill that is higher than the reasonable and customary rate. Find out how much more than the going rate the company will pay, and who pays what, when.

4. Check on any requirement that you get a second opinion or permission from the insurance company before entering the hospital. Stay away from companies that have such a preadmission-approval rule and stick with those that say, "If your doctor says you have to go, that's okay with us."

5. Find out how a claim is handled: Who gets the bills, how long does it take to be reimbursed, and where do the checks go? Ask how often their rates have increased in the last five years and by what percentage.

HEALTH INSURANCE CHECKLIST

Small-Business Owners

☐ Check to see if there is an HMO or PPO close to your location. If so, call and gather as much information as you can regarding their programs.

☐ If you've found an HMO or PPO, how do its coverages compare with the models in this chapter?

☐ Have you found a broker, agent, or financial consultant you can call to get help choosing a good, affordable insurance plan?

☐ Have you called any of the local, regional, and national organizations that can provide information or possible assistance on health-insurance coverage for small-business owners? Here are a few:

- Health Insurance Association of America—HIAA can provide you with information on private insurance for individuals as well as small and large businesses. Address: Box 41445 Washington, D.C. 20018 Consumer Help Line: 1-800-942-4242.
- Blue Cross/Blue Shield Association—Address: 676 N. St. Clair Street Chicago, IL. 60611. Publications Office: (312)-440-6000.
- Group Health Association of America, Inc.—This organization is a source of information on HMOs. Address: 1129 20th St., N.W., Suite 600, Washington, DC 20036. Telephone: (202) 778-3200.
- American Association of Preferred Provider Organizations— Address: 111 E. Wacker Drive, Suite 600, Chicago, IL. 60601. Telephone: (312) 644-6610.

- Trade Associations—If you're not sure which ones you may be eligible to join, go to a library and check the *Encyclopedia of Associations*.
- A chamber of commerce in your area—See if they offer any group health plans or can make referrals for small business.

Individual Health-Care Purchasers

☐ Have you confirmed in your own mind whether your situation fits a calendar-year deductible or a per accident/per person deductible? The calendar-year deductible is generally recommended for the following subscribers:
- Young couples wanting to have children
- Married couples with children under eight years old
- Individuals or families with known medical conditions

The per accident/per sickness deductible is generally recommended for the following subscribers:
- Single males or females over the age of 23
- Married couples with children over the age of eight
- Married couples without children, or whose children have grown up and left the household

☐ Have you obtained comparative quotes on the different variables?

☐ Do you understand coinsurance? Did you ask how much each company's coinsurance is and how much it would be paying on a hypothetical $10,000 bill? From that example, you should be able to find out the coinsurance rate.

☐ Does your policy have a "schedule of benefits" that may limit the amount of money paid on a claim?

☐ Does your current company pay only "reasonable and customary" charges?

☐ Does your current company have a history of rate increases every year? Of over 20 percent to 30 percent?

CHAPTER FOUR

Protecting My Life's Work:
Business Owner's Insurance

OVERVIEW OF BUSINESS INSURANCE

WHAT IS COVERED?

There are three basic areas of business-insurance coverage: property insurance, liability insurance, and workers' compensation insurance.

- Property insurance, more commonly referred to as "fire" insurance, protects the small-business owner against the loss of assets, including buildings, business equipment, and inventory, aused by various perils: fire, smoke, tornado, windstorm, explosion, vandalism, and even riots.
- Liability insurance protects you in the case of law suits arising from injuries to others or to others' property, as a result of a problem with your premises, service, or product.
- Workers' compensation insurance provides benefits to the injured employee for lost or reduced wage-earning ability and medical and hospital expenses, plus survivors' benefits in the event of the employee's death.

In addition to these three essential coverages, special circumstances will sometimes mandate other types of protection. Commercial insurance can provide lines of coverage for many kinds of operational loss, such as loss of business income, loss of refrigeration, and employee dishonesty, to name just a few.

STANDARD AND PACKAGE POLICIES

Insurers make commercial coverages available as either standard-ized policies or package policies. Under the standard-form policy businesses are protected against the usual named perils, but there are special form policies that protect against multiple risks. The term **multiple-line**, or **multiple-peril**, is used to describe an in-surance policy that combines different lines of insurance in a package.

Business package policies may be grouped into two catego-ries: those for small businesses and those for larger firms. Two commonly used multiple-line policies are the business owner's policy (BOPP), used for small stores, offices, and apartment build-ings, and the commercial package policy (CPP), used for contract-ing businesses, older buildings, restaurants, larger businesses, and public institutions. While the CPP policy states what's *covered*, the BOPP states what's *not covered*, which tends to be easier to under-stand.

The CPP will be covered briefly, but the main focus of this chapter will be on the BOPP, which is 30 percent to 40 percent cheaper than the CPP in most cases.

In my dealings with business owners, I've found a consistent lack of knowledge regarding insurance packages, along with their various optional coverages. The danger of this lack of knowledge becomes evident when a disaster occurs such as a fire, tornado, or break-in. If you wait until then to find out what you do and, even more importantly, *don't* have, it may be too late. This chapter has been written with the small-business owner in mind: the woman who owns a dress shop, the husband and wife who own a bookstore, the beauty-parlor owner who employs a staff of three. You need to know exactly what kinds of coverage to get and how to get the best prices for what you need.

BUSINESS OWNER'S PACKAGE POLICY (BOPP)

This is a very popular business policy in today's market, because it provides a broad base of coverage that keeps the product simple and the rates competitive. You can tailor this policy to your busi-ness-risk requirements by using the various options available for coverage, but many of these coverages are already included.

The type of business you have will determine whether you qualify for the BOPP program. Major insurers such as Aetna, Kemper, St. Paul, American Family Mutual and State Farm usually make BOPP programs available for apartment complexes, motels, religious institutions, office complexes, and certain mercantile businesses.

Here is a partial list of businesses that should qualify for the BOPP:

Accountants	Dry cleaners
Art, craft, and hobby stores	Fabric shops
	Florists
Auto accessory stores	Gift shops
Barber shops	Ice cream shops
Beauty shops	Motels
Bookstores	Musical instrument stores
Camera shops	Offices
Card shops	Opticians
Churches	Photo studios
Clothing stores	Shoe stores
Dental clinics	Variety stores
Direct sales (Hoda, Tupperware, Mary Kay, etc.)	

PROPERTY COVERAGE UNDER BOPP

There are two components of property coverage under BOPP. They are (1) the building, and (2) business personal property, and they will be discussed in turn.

THE BUILDING

If you own the building in which your business is located, or if you own rental apartments or single-family rental units, you will probably want coverage for damages resulting from tornadoes, fires, etc.

Perils

The named perils on a BOPP are as follows:

- Fire
- Lightning
- Windstorm and hail
- Weight of ice, sleet, and snow
- Collapse
- Falling trees and objects
- Aircraft and vehicle damage

- Smoke
- Riot and civil commotion
- Sprinkler leakage
- Vandalism and malicious mischief
- Building glass breakage

If you'll notice, the named perils are exactly the same as the ones in the Homeowners section.

If there is a loss under the covered perils, note that your company should pay to tear out and replace that part of the building needing repair. This is important in situations where it is necessary to tear into a building to fix the original problem. Sometimes that expense is more than what it takes to fix the main problem.

How Much Insurance Does the Building Need?

The most important question regarding the building portion of property coverage is, "How much should I insure the building for?" You don't want to be overinsured, but you also don't want to be underinsured. That's why it's important to deal with an experienced insurance agent.

You do not have the option to insure your building for between 80 percent and 100 percent as you do in the homeowners program. Most companies that offer the BOPP require that you insure the building for as close to 100 percent of replacement cost as possible.

The Premium

As with a homeowners policy, the important factors in determining premium rates for the building are location, building material (frame or brick), and fire-protection class.

To give an idea of the variation by location, a leading commercial insurer in the United States rates a brick building in downtown Kansas City at $6 per $1,000 of coverage, while the same type of building runs $5.40 in other parts of the state. Rates for downtown St. Louis run $7.30 per $1,000 for property coverage, while in less populated areas of Missouri, they run $6.40 per $1,000 of coverage. For the same type of building in New York City or Los Angeles the rates would be almost double those of Kansas City or St. Louis.

Regarding building material, rates are much higher—around 33 percent—for wood-frame than for brick buildings. A frame building in St. Louis runs approximately $13 per $1,000 worth of coverage, while the same building made of brick runs $7 per $1,000 of coverage.

Fire-protection class means the same thing for businesses as for homes. The classification is based on the quality of services in your area, including whether there is a full-time, well-trained fire department and how close your business is to fire hydrants or other sources of water. This criterion means that you will pay more for a business located just outside of town than for one in town.

BUSINESS PERSONAL PROPERTY

This coverage is for your business property located on or in the building you own, rent, or lease, or that sits in the open within 100 feet of this same location. It generates the most premium by far on the BOPP policy, running about two-thirds as much as for the building component.

What Is Covered?

This coverage takes in the following:

- Your stock of merchandise, materials, and supplies.
- Furniture, fixtures, machinery, and equipment.
- Permanent attachment, to the building.
- All building glass, including the cost of boarding up damaged openings, installing temporary plates, and removing obstructions when necessary.
- Outdoor furniture and yard fixtures. One example would be the playground equipment you find at many fast-food restaurants.
- Your business property that is used for maintenance and service of your business. This includes fire extinguishers and appliances used for refrigerating, cooking, dishwashing, laundering, etc. If you own an apartment complex that furnishes washers and dryers for the tenants, are these appliances covered in the policy or do you have to list them separately?
- Personal property of other people you have in your care or custody if it is in your building or within 100 feet of it. If you borrow a floor scrubber from a friend and it's stolen from your place of business during a burglary, the policy will pay your friend for the stolen scrubber. It will *not* pay the replacement cost of the item, but it will pay the actual cash value or depreciated value.

- Your personal property while in transit in vehicles owned, rented, or controlled by you or by others for your benefit. Most policies cover your business personal property in transit up to $5,000. If you need more than that, call your agent.

  The term "property in transit" refers to goods or merchandise while they are being moved from the point where they were accepted for shipment, or while they are temporarily stored at an intermediary station awaiting shipment to the point of destination.
- Cash. Money used in business usually carries an internal policy limit of $10,000 if the business itself is robbed, and $1,000 if the money is taken while being transported to or from the bank, or is taken from the living quarters of the person who has custody of the funds. Check the policies of your company to find out what your limits are.

EXAMPLE:

One of my clients owned a restaurant that was robbed. The amount of the theft was almost $9,000, and, of course, the first thing my client wanted to know was "How much am I covered for?"

  When I originally took the application, I failed to ask him how much money he was likely to have on the premises at any one time. Now the pressure was on and I wasn't sure just what we would cover. I was relieved to find out that his policy (BOPP) had an internal limit of $10,000, so there was a happy ending to the story. If there *hadn't* been any coverage, or if there was coverage but it was limited to $5,000, my client would have been out a considerable amount of money, and I would have looked very foolish.

- Tenant's improvements. If you rent the building in which your business is located and you decide to put up an awning over the sidewalk, it's considered a tenant's improvement and is automatically covered.

How Much Insurance Do I Need For My Business Personal Property?

To answer this question, you have to find out exactly what business personal property you have in your establishment. Take your time. Most agents have forms that will help you calculate how much insurance you need. Go through this list carefully with your agent.

If the internal limit of $10,000 for on-premises coverage is too low, increase it! The cost to increase the amount averages from $15 to $20 per $1,000 of coverage. The cost to increase the off-premises coverage is considerably less—approximately $1 to $2 per $1,000 of protection. Make sure you analyze the amount of coverage you need in this area, because you don't want to pay any more premium than is necessary.

What Records Should I Keep for Insurance Purposes?

Whenever you have a loss, it's up to you to provide a list of the damaged items, proving in effect what you had. After a fire or theft, it's difficult to itemize everything that is missing and document what you paid for it. Here are some suggestions for easing the confusion in case of a loss:

- Keep the receipts of every item you purchase. If you depreciate business property for tax purposes, you probably already have this information.
- Make a visual record of your office, inventory, and possessions. There are many video-recording businesses that can make such a room-by-room visual record.
- Keep a written inventory. Try to list each item in the office, its date of purchase, its price, and its present value. Most insurance companies have booklets that can help you with this task.

IMPORTANT NOTE: Never take any coverage or lack of coverage for granted! If a question about your insurance pops into your mind, call your agent. If you wonder whether something is covered, call your agent. Make a record of the conversation, with the date (it can just be a note), and put it into your insurance file. If your agent confirms a coverage and there's a loss that turns out not to be covered, you can still get the money if your conversation was well documented.

WHAT OTHER PROPERTY COVERAGES ARE AVAILABLE?

Here are some coverages that come at *no* extra cost with the BOPP.

Arson Award

Many companies provide a reward as high as $5,000 for information leading to an arson conviction in connection with a covered fire loss.

Fire Extinguisher Recharge

Many insurance companies pay the expense to recharge your fire extinguishers after they have been used to combat a covered fire.

Inflation Protection

As with homeowners insurance, your coverage increases each year for your business building and specified personal property to allow for inflation.

Seasonal Variance on Business Personal Property

The limit of insurance for your inventory automatically increases by 25 percent at specified times. This is an excellent coverage for many retail businesses, as it allows for seasonal increases in the value of the property. If you normally have $50,000 in inventory but you increase it in November to prepare for the Christmas season, there is an extra $25,000 of coverage whether you tell your agent or not.

Temporary Locations

If you take a typewriter or a computer home from the office for the weekend, you have limited coverage on a loss. Most companies allow up to 10 percent of what the business-personal-property limit is but not more than $2,000. This coverage does not apply to (1) property that you rent or lease, (2) property that is being kept on someone else's premises while construction or installation work is being done at your place of business, or (3) newly acquired property.

Accounts Receivables

What happens if all your papers and records are burned in a fire? You can claim up to a specified dollar limit for damage by an insured peril to your records of accounts receivable. The coverage includes (1) all sums due from customers that you are unable to collect as the result of loss, (2) interest charges on any loan made to offset the money that is uncollectible, and (3) collection expenses in excess of normal because of the loss or damage.

Collapse

There's coverage if your building or the one you lease collapses if the event was caused by (1) a covered peril; (2) hidden decay, or hidden insect or vermin damage; (3) weight of contents or people; or (4) use of defective material or methods of construction if the collapse occurs during the course of construction, remodeling, or renovation.

Damage to Buildings from Theft

If someone breaks into one of your buildings, damaging it in the process, you may collect up to $5,000 for these damages.

Debris Removal

The policy will pay for the removal of debris following an *insured loss*.

HOW AM I REIMBURSED FOR A PROPERTY LOSS?

In case of a loss, the insurance company will determine the loss to your property on the basis of either **replacement cost** or **actual cash value**, depending upon what you chose when the policy was written up.

Replacement Cost

When replacement cost is the basis for valuation, the company will pay no more than the smaller of (1) the cost to repair or replace the damaged property at the same site and for similar use, using the same quality of material, without deduction for depreciation; or (2) the amount spent to repair or replace the damaged property.

The premium for this important coverage can be anywhere from $.30 to $.40 per $1,000 of coverage. If you have $50,000 worth of business personal property, the replacement-cost endorsement would run from $150 to $200 extra a year.

By having the replacement-cost endorsement, you're assured of getting the damaged item restored with only the deductible subtracted.

> #### <u>EXAMPLE:</u>
>
> If you have a loss in your store on an electric typewriter that cost $500 eight years ago, you'll be reimbursed for what the same type of typewriter will cost brand-new (less the deductible). In other words, no value or money will be subtracted from the item just because it's eight years old, no depreciation will be taken. If the electric typewriter costs $1,000 today, you will get $1,000, less your deductible.

Actual Cash Value

When actual cash value is the basis for valuation, the insurance company will pay the smaller of (1) the actual cash value at the time of the loss, or (2) the cost to repair or replace the damaged property with property of like kind and quality.

EXAMPLE:

Continuing the above example, if the typewriter that was $500 eight years ago and is valued at its worth today, there could be as much as 50 percent to 60 percent depreciation, or amount subtracted from the item's value. The insurance company will pay the actual-cash, or depreciated, value, which in this case would be $250 or $300, less the deductible. More than likely, you still have to go out and replace the item, and this is not a nice picture. If the typewriter costs $1,000 new, but the insurance check is for $300, less a $250 deductible, or $50, you will not be very happy.

Remember, having the replacement-cost option is *always* better for you, because it pays for a new item 99.99 percent of the time. If you can't afford this feature, remember that having actual-cash-value coverage is better than having no insurance at all. You can always add the replacement-cost endorsement when you're financially ready to do so.

As with everything else in insurance, if nothing ever happens, it seems as if you're wasting those premium dollars. On the other hand, if you have a major fire and all of your office furniture burns up, being able to go out and replace your losses with brand-new items makes you look like a genius. It is important that you weigh the risks to your business and protect yourself against losses that are distinct possibilities.

WHAT COVERAGES ARE EXCLUDED FROM MY BOPP?

Here are the items specifically not covered.

Acts of Persons and Governments

You will not get paid for a loss that is (1) caused by acts or decisions of any person, group, organization, or governmental body, (2) caused from seizure or destruction of property by order of governmental authority, or (3) considered contraband or property involved in illegal transportation or trade.

Earth Movement

"Earth movement" means an earthquake, a landslide, a mudslide, or the sinking or shifting of earth. You can endorse the BOPP for this coverage at different price structures depending upon where you live. In Nebraska it costs a mere 11 cents per thousand dollars of coverage, as opposed to California's coverage, which runs three times that much.

Also excluded under this category is any volcanic eruption, explosion, or effusion.

Faulty Planning, Workmanship, or Design

The company will not pay for loss that is caused by the following:

- Faulty planning, zoning, surveying, siting, grading, or compaction
- Flawed design, specifications, workmanship, construction, maintenance, repair, renovation, or remodeling
- Defective materials used in construction, repair, renovation, or remodeling.

This exclusion means that if your building collapses because of a design problem, the BOPP won't cover the damage. You would have to file suit against the architect or builder for this particular problem in order to be reimbursed for damages.

Power Failure

There is no coverage for loss resulting from the failure of power or other utility service if the failure occurs away from the insured premises. If some unlucky squirrel blows a city utilities transformer and you suffer damage from this loss of electricity to your business, there is no coverage automatically included in the BOPP.

Accounting Errors

If your accountant makes an error that costs you money for any reason, you are not insured.

Consequential Loss

This means loss of income from being unable to conduct business because of another loss. There is no automatic coverage for delay, loss of use, or loss of market.

Credit Sales Loss

There is no coverage for loss resulting from a default on payment by anyone who buys your goods or services.

Damage to Property in the Open

If you leave your business property out in the rain, snow, or sleet and it becomes ruined, there is no coverage.

Electrical Injury

There is no coverage for damage caused by artificially generated electric current, including arcing that disturbs electrical devices, appliances, or wires. But if a fire results from these occurrences, the company will pay!

Fraud or Dishonesty

The company won't pay damages resulting from fraudulent, dishonest, or criminal acts done at the instigation of the insured, partner, or director.

Interior Damage

You will not get paid for loss to the interior of your building caused by the entrance of water, rain, snow, ice, sleet, sand, or dust, whether wind driven or not, unless entry is the result of damage caused by a peril not excluded. Thus, if a high wind rips off your roof and rain comes in, you're protected, because wind is a covered peril. But if the roof leaks because it is worn out and rain comes in, there is no coverage. Wear, tear, and deterioration are not named perils (see below).

Inventory Shortage

There is no coverage for any unexplained loss or discrepancies discovered when inventory is taken.

Leakage or Seepage

There is no coverage for loss or damage resulting from leakage or overflow from plumbing, heating, air-conditioning, or other systems or appliances if the leak is due to freezing while the building is vacant or unoccupied. This exclusion doesn't apply if you use reasonable care to keep heat in the building, or turn off the water and drain the pipes if heat is not maintained during a permitted vacancy.

There is also no coverage for continuous or repeated seepage of water from a plumbing, heating, or air-conditioning system. If you know about a leak but don't take the time to fix it, and the problem eventually causes major damage, the insurance company can reject the claim because of your lack of response to the original problem. Make sure that if you're having a problem, you don't put off looking into it.

Mechanical Breakdown

There is no coverage for loss in the case of a mechanical breakdown, including rupture or bursting by centrifugal force; or because of an inherent defect, failure, or breakdown of machines.

Steam Explosion

If the steam boilers, steam pipes, steam engines, or steam turbines explode, there is no coverage. But if a fire results from the explosion, the BOPP pays for the damages.

Theft from Vehicle

If the vehicle you drive for business purposes is broken into and items are stolen from it, there is no coverage. In order to be covered for this type of loss, you would need to have a commercial-vehicle policy that includes comprehensive coverage.

Vandalism, Theft, or Attempted Theft

If your building is vacant for more than 60 consecutive days, there is no coverage for vandalism or theft. Vandalism and arson are just a few of the potential disasters that can befall a vacant building, which is why insurance companies are reluctant to extend coverage over 60 days.

Wear and Tear, Deterioration, or Defect

The company will not pay for a loss caused by the following:

- Wear and tear, marring, or scratching
- Deterioration, inherent or latent defect
- Rust or corrosion, mold, wet or dry rot, or contamination
- Occupancy by animals, birds, rodents, vermin, or insects
- Frost or condensation
- Smog
- Smoke, vapor, or gas from agricultural or industrial operations
- Settling, cracking, shrinking, or expansions

WHAT ADDITIONAL COVERAGES CAN I PURCHASE?

There are endorsements you can purchase to offset some of the above exclusions. The most important of them for business purposes is the protection against loss of business income. Other good options are exterior-sign coverage, loss-of-refrigeration coverage, and electronic data processing (EDP) insurance.

Loss-of-Business-Income Coverage

What happens if there's a fire and your retail business or apartment complex burns down? You can't sell anything or collect any rental income. Suppose the damage is such that you can't open the doors for three months. You may have a serious problem.

Your sales and income have stopped, but there are expenses you must continue to meet, such as the loan payment to the bank, payroll responsibilities, and inventory expenses. Without any money coming in, you could go bankrupt in a hurry.

Some businesses, such as dairies, newspapers, and health clinics, must continue operating regardless of the extent of damage to their property. Often, extra expenses are incurred to avoid or minimize the suspension of business and resume operations.

Other businesses, such as restaurants and taverns, experienced a slow-down even after they resume operations and need time to reattract a clientele. They can purchase an endorsement to cover lost profits until business is back to normal.

A business may be prevented from opening on schedule due to damage to buildings under construction. Coverage may be provided for loss of earnings from the originally planned opening date until the date the business actually opens.

Loss-of-business-income, or business-interruption, insurance, is designed to help in all these situations. The insurance company will cover your loss, either of income from sales or service, or from rents. Here is how this coverage works, first for earnings and second for rents.

Earnings refer to your actual net profit, plus payroll expenses, taxes, interest, rents, and other operating expenses *normally* charged in your business. The term covers only such expenses as are necessary during the time you are shut down.

When they try to figure the earnings lost, the adjusters will consider what the business was grossing before the loss and what it would be producing had no loss occurred. The insurance company assumes that you will try hard to reduce the loss, and most companies won't pay continuing losses due to your failure to resume complete or at least partial operations within a reasonable amount of time.

EXAMPLE:

Let's say your net profit and monthly expenses total $5,000. In the worst scenario, it will take six months to rebuild your place of business. Multiplying $5,000 by six months yields a figure of $30,000 of needed protection. If the rate is $2 per $1,000 of coverage (the average range is $1 to $4 per $1,000 of coverage), it will cost $60 a year for this endorsement—a bargain!

Most companies state this coverage as "actual loss sustained for up to 12 months." You aren't required to state a specific dollar figure as in the above example in order to be covered. Check out your company and see how they would handle this type of loss.

Rents refer to (1) your actual loss of rental income, whether the property is rented furnished or unfurnished, and (2) any expenses such as taxes that your tenants had agreed to pay.

The insurance company will cover your loss as long as it reasonably takes to resume normal operations (up to 12 months), but no longer than the time it takes to rebuild, repair, or replace the property that has been damaged.

Exterior-Sign Coverage

Most insurance companies don't automatically include detached signs under this policy. (We're talking here about signs that are free-standing, not those attached to the building, which are covered under the building's insurance.) Make sure you find out the cost to replace your sign at today's prices and talk to your agent about it. Signs can be very expensive, so don't slip up here. The cost to insure exterior signs can run from $35 to $50 per $1,000 of coverage, so that a $10,000 detached sign would cost between $350 and $500 extra each year to insure.

Loss-of-Refrigeration Coverage

The endorsement for loss of refrigeration provides coverage for loss of perishable stock on the premises due to temperature change. The loss must be a direct result of one of the following: electric power fluctuations, failure of power, mechanical breakdown of refrigeration equipment on the premises, or faulty operation of a breaker.

The endorsement only covers electrical failures due to a covered peril, such as a power surge through the system or being struck by lightning. It does not cover failure of a freezing unit due to wear, tear, or deterioration.

> **EXAMPLE:**
>
> The refrigeration unit in a yogurt shop I had insured blew out, causing all of the yogurt in the freezer to melt. We paid for this loss because it was caused by a power surge. When we wrote up the original policy, we decided that $2,000 of yogurt would be the most they would ever have in the unit at any one time, so we insured it for that amount.

The cost for loss-of-refrigeration coverage runs about $20 to $30 per thousand dollars of coverage; thus, if you have an inventory of $40,000 to protect, it can cost as much as $120 a year.

Electronic Data Processing (EDP) Insurance

Most business policies are very limited in their coverage for EDP equipment, if they offer any coverage at all. You can add the EDP endorsement, which pays for your computers, monitors, disks, software, etc., on a replacement-cost basis up to the limit you request. It covers these items whether you leave them at the office or take them elsewhere.

> **EXAMPLE:**
>
> One of my clients wanted to take her computer to a convention. She would be gone a full week and wanted to know if there would be coverage for theft. I found there was the same coverage away from the premises as on the premises.

Premiums run around $3 to $7 per $1,000 of coverage. If you have any EDP equipment in your business, talk to your agent about how to cover it effectively.

LIABILITY AND MEDICAL COVERAGE UNDER BOPP

Simply put, if you own a fast-food restaurant and one of your customers falls, breaks her neck, and becomes paralyzed, you may be obligated for liability damages.

You and your business need protection against claims resulting from injury to others or damage to others' property. If you're in business and you aren't adequately covered, look out! Today people are extremely liability-conscious; individuals are eager to sue a business or corporation, hoping to get rich in the process.

WHAT CONSTITUTES BODILY-INJURY AND PROPERTY-DAMAGE LIABILITY IN A BOPP?

Sources of Liability

Most liability situations arise from the following:

- Ownership of a premises. Those who own or lease a building may be held responsible in case of injury or property damage as a result of some unsafe condition of the business premises. Let's say you own a dress shop and neglect to have a faulty sidewalk repaired. If someone trips and falls as a result of that unsafe sidewalk, you are protected.
- The conduct of a business. This coverage also comes in

handy if you run a Day-Care Center, for example. If a child becomes ill because of the food you served, you may be sued by the parents. In this case, the liability part of your policy will protect you. A business may also be held liable for actions of employees away from the premises (e.g., while working at a job location, a roofing contractor drops a hammer and injures a bystander on the ground below).

- The manufacture, distribution, or selling of products. You can be held responsible for injuries or damages attributable to the product. Let's say you are a manufacturer of power tools and as a result of a defect in a tool, someone gets cut badly. Although some companies attempt to limit their liability by posting disclaimers, there is no way to guarantee that the disclaimer will be of any use in court. Make sure your lawyer is completely familiar with product-liability law.
- Completed operations. You are liable for damages that are caused by your faulty construction, installation, service, or repair work but that occur after the work has been completed. If you are a professional plumber and after some faulty work you do there is a leak, you are held responsible for the water damage.

Personal-Injury and Advertising-Injury Liability

Another source of liability is in personal and advertising injury, as in slander or infringement or false claims.

EXAMPLE:

A couple of years ago one of my clients was sued because the name of his motel sounded similar to another motel name. The parties settled out of court as a result of negotiations conducted by our claims department, and we paid $2,500 to the claimant with the promise that our insured would change the name of his motel.

Under the BOPP, the insurance company will cover those sums the insured becomes legally obligated to pay as damages because of personal injury or advertising injury within the policy limitations.

Insurance Company Responsibility and Limitations

In case of a claim, the insurance company will pay all monies for which the insured becomes legally obligated as a result of bodily injury or property damage. The insurance company will defend you in case of legal action, with the following limitations:

- The insurance company won't pay any more than the limit set forth on the policy, which is usually between $100,000 and $1,000,000. This figure is determined by you and the agent when the application is completed in the beginning.
- The insurance company has the right to investigate and settle any claim at its discretion.
- The insurance company's duty to defend you ends when the limit of insurance has been used up for payments to the claimant.

IMPORTANT POINT: For it to be a liability issue, you have to be proved negligent. Claimants must prove in a court of law that you did or did not do something that caused the conditions allowing them to be injured. If they can't establish negligence on your part, it's not a liability issue.

How Much Liability Coverage Should I Have?

Most BOPP policies come with $300,000 as the basic limit, but you may feel that isn't enough. You can raise your liability coverage to $500,000 or even $1,000,000 relatively inexpensively.

EXAMPLE:

My own office in a major East Coast city has 2,000 square feet. The rate for $1,000,000 liability coverage for an office averages $7 to $10 per 1,000 square feet. Thus, the total for the higher cost limit would be around $15 to $20. This is a very affordable price for increasing my liability coverage from $300,000 to $1,000,000.

In a fast-food restaurant or a roller-skating rink, it would certainly be higher, but the concept of affordable cost for increased liability limits runs true through all lines of insurance, including autos, homeowners, etc.

Liability Premiums

Premiums depend upon the type of business you have. The lower the risk, the lower the premium. In an office, where there is considerably less walk-in traffic than in a fast-food restaurant, there is lower liability exposure, which means lower premiums. Fast-food restaurants, candy shops, dry-cleaning stores, and gift shops are higher-rated businesses than offices and apartment complexes, and their rates can be 30 percent to 100 percent higher than those for the lower-rated operations.

EXCLUSIONS AND ENDORSEMENTS ON A BOPP

This insurance does not cover a number of situations, such as intentional injury, contractual liability, liquor liability, professional liability, pollution effects, and nonowned-auto liability. In some cases, endorsements are available that can be added onto your coverage.

Intentional Injury

There's no coverage if you intentionally hurt someone in your business. If you get into a fight with one of your customers and break his jaw, you're on your own.

Contractual Liability

If you assume a contract for a business that has a liability problem pending, your own insurance company will not assume the problem.

Liquor Liability

In states such as Colorado and Iowa, if you own a bar, liquor store, or restaurant that serves liquor, you may be held liable if one of your customers gets drunk and kills someone in a car accident. More and more states are passing legislation in this area. The basic BOPP policy won't pay any liability claims that arise by reason of (1) causing or contributing to the intoxication of any person; (2) the furnishing of alcoholic beverages to a person under the legal drinking age or already under the influence of alcohol; or (3) the violation of any statute, ordinance, or regulation relating to the sale, gift, distribution, selling, serving, or furnishing of alcoholic beverages.

The BOPP policy *will* protect you, however, if you have a liquor-related problem and you are not in the business of serving liquor.

> ### EXAMPLE:
> As a manufacturer of nurse's uniforms, each year you host an awards banquet with an open bar for your sales representatives. After this year's banquet, an intoxicated guest is involved in an auto accident in which the guest and several others are seriously injured. If someone sues you as a result of this accident, the company will not apply the liquor-liability exclusion because you're not in the business of serving liquor. In this situation, you would be protected.

If you do serve liquor as part of your business, you can apply for a liquor liability policy written separately from the BOPP that gives you all the protection you need.

Professional Liability

The insurance company will not pay for damages due to bodily injury or property damage arising out of the improper rendering of services by the following professionals:

- Accountant or attorney
- Architect or engineer
- Beautician or barber
- Clergyman or clergywoman
- Cosmetologist
- Dentist, physician, surgeon, or oral surgeon
- Druggist or pharmacist
- Health-care practitioner of any kind
- Insurance agent or real estate agent
- Mortician or funeral director
- Nurse
- Optician or optometrist
- Psychologist or social worker
- Veterinarian
- X-ray or other medical technician

Many professionals already have liability coverage through a group within their profession. For example, insurance agents have what is referred to as an errors-and-omissions policy, which protects them in case they make a mistake that costs the insured money. If this is true for your profession, you do not need to pay for extra coverage on your BOPP.

Some of the professional coverages you can endorse onto the BOPP are the beauticians and barbers professional liability; counseling and professional liability endorsement (for clergy); and druggists, pharmacists, and opticians professional liability. If you purchase one of these options, you are covered for bodily injury or property damage arising out of malpractice of your profession or an accident.

EXAMPLE:

In a beauty shop I have as an insured, one of the beauticians accidentally spilled some dye on the blouse of the client she was working on, ruining the garment. We paid for a new blouse because it was a property-damage loss and the beautician was at fault. The same principle would apply in the case of a beautician's accidentally turning a customer's hair green or causing it to fall out. Items not covered under this endorsement are illegal services or preparations, face lifting, plastic surgery, and flammable shampoo.

To give an idea of the rates for a professional-liability endorsement, a beautician, mortician, or optician would pay $40 a year under a $300,000 policy; $44 a year under a $500,000 policy; and $52 a year under a $1,000,000 policy. A pharmacist's coverage would be slightly higher, costing $60, $66, and $78 for the three policy amounts. Check with your agent to see what professional coverages are offered that you could benefit from.

Pollution Effects

There is no coverage on a basic policy for damage to the environment or for bodily injury arising out of the contamination by pollutants that are at any time introduced by you into or upon the land, the atmosphere, or any watercourse or body of water.

You are also not covered for contaminating the environment through a gradual emission, discharge, release, or escape of pollutants from any source. Contamination includes any unclean, unsafe, or unhealthful condition, whether permanent or transient that is caused by pollutants. These pollutants include smoke, vapor, soot, fumes, acids, alkalis, chemicals, liquids, gases, and thermal pollutants. Gradual emissions include leaks, drips, seepages, oozing, leaching, diffusion, infiltration and permeation.

This means there is no coverage if you own a business such as a gas station and its underground gas tanks leak. However, just because the protection doesn't come with the policy doesn't mean you can't get it. Call your agent to find out.

Nonowned-Auto Liability

This has become a very sticky issue for business owners who either (1) have delivery trucks or (2) allow employees to deliver products in their own vehicles.

The insurance company won't pay for bodily injuries or property damage arising out of the use of any nonowned auto in your business driven by a person other than yourself. This means that if your business delivers a product, and someone other than you is the driver, there is no coverage!

A good example of a business with this problem is a pizzeria. The drivers who deliver the pizzas are often 16, 17, or 18 years old and don't have a great amount of driving experience. In addition, many pizza parlors pride themselves on getting a piping hot pizza to your front door, so the drivers are pressured to deliver the pizzas as fast as possible, which leads to accidents.

The insurance industry not only balks at insuring your delivery vehicles, but companies also don't want the liability exposure when the employees use their *own* cars for deliveries. If a person making a delivery for you runs a red light and kills someone, his or her car insurance is the primary carrier, but since the driver was working for you at the time of the accident, your business can be sued and drawn into the mess.

If there is any delivery exposure in your business, it will be difficult to find nonowned auto coverage—but not impossible. If your agent digs a little, he or she should find something for you. Most states have what are called assigned-risk pools, in which the state assigns your risk to a company for coverage. The limits of coverage are lower, but you still get some protection.

What about a nondelivery situation in which an employee drives his or her own car to go get the mail for you, or to take some receipts to the bank? Most insurance companies cover this situation at no extra cost. If your employee has an at-fault accident on the way to the bank, his or her own auto coverage is the primary source of insurance, meaning the car insurance company would pay first, but the driver will also have protection from your business policy.

Call your agent and check this out. If a loss occurs in the liability area and you don't have the coverage, you could lose your business.

WHAT IS INCLUDED IN MEDICAL COVERAGE ON A BOPP?

The insurance company pays medical expenses up to a stated limit (usually $5,000) for bodily injury caused by an accident whether you are negligent or not.

If someone slips on a banana peel in front of your store, breaks his hip, and incurs $3,000 worth of medical bills, the medical-expense section of your BOPP will pay regardless of who was at fault. If the injured party's claim exceeds the normal $5,000 medical limit, it is then incumbent upon the claimant to prove negligence on your part.

Restrictions

There are some stipulations on your medical coverage, which are as follows:

- The accident must take place (1) on premises that you own or rent, (2) on passageways next to premises that you own or rent, or (3) because of your operations.
- The policy pays *reasonable* expenses for (1) first aid at the time of the accident; (2) necessary medical, surgical, X-ray, and dental services, including prosthetic devices, and (3) necessary ambulance, hospital, professional nursing, and funeral expenses.
- The insurance company will make payments regardless of fault, provided that (1) the expenses are reported within a year of the date of the accident, and (2) the injured person submits to an examination at the insurance company's expense by physicians of their choice as often as they require.

Exclusions

The company will not pay medical expenses to the following:

- Any insured
- A person hired to do work for or on behalf of any insured.
- A person injured while taking part in athletics on premises that you own or rent
- A person, whether an employee or not, if benefits are paid under workers' compensation or disability benefits

WORKERS' COMPENSATION INSURANCE

HISTORY

This insurance protects the employee from loss of income due to occupational disease or injury. Before the early 1900s, if an employee became disabled from a job-related disease or injury, the only recourse was to sue the employer. It was the *employee's* responsibility to prove the employer's negligence. This was a slow, costly, and uncertain process.

Then each state began creating specific worker's compensation and disease laws to protect the employee, which made the *employer* responsible for occupational disease or injury *without* regard to fault or negligence.

These laws provided for sure, prompt, and reasonable incomes and medical benefits for work-related accident victims, or else income benefits to their dependents, REGARDLESS OF FAULT. They provided a single remedy, thereby reducing court delays, costs, and work loads as well as fees to lawyers, arising out of personal-injury litigation. At the same time, they encouraged employers' maximum interest in establishing safe procedures and working conditions.

Over the years, the compensation insurance that employers provide their workers has expanded greatly. This protection is now compulsory for employees in all but three states, plus Puerto Rico, the U.S. Virgin Islands, American Samoa, and Guam. Even in the three states—New Jersey, Texas, and South Carolina—whose laws make coverage elective, nearly all businesses provide the coverage in order to limit their risk of negligence suits.

WHO IS COVERED, AND WHAT IS PROVIDED?

State workers' compensation laws protect employees in almost every occupation. The only employees for whom coverage is not provided occupy job classifications that are specifically exempted by law. Workers most commonly exempted include agricultural laborers, domestic workers, casual laborers, public employees, and employees of nonprofit groups and businesses that employ fewer than three to five persons, depending on the state.

In general, the following benefits are provided:

- Medical payments to hospitals, doctors, or for other medical expenses
- Disability—weekly payments for a portion of lost income
- Rehabilitation—therapy that will enable the worker to return to the job or to train for his or her new position
- Survivors' benefits—compensation in the event of death resulting from a work-related accident or disease

THE PREMIUM

The premium is calculated on the number of thousand dollars in your total estimated annual payroll times the rate charged for your business classification. There is a code that determines this rate.

EXAMPLE:

In Nebraska, the code for restaurant workers puts them at a premium rate of $17.30 per $1,000 of payroll. If the total payroll is $79,000, you multiply 79 by $17.30, to get $1,366.

An "expense constant" of $120 is added to this, with a total of $1,486 for the premium. In contrast with the high rate for restaurant workers, the rate for clerical employees is only $2.50 per $1,000 of payroll. The state obviously figures that if your work involves cutting, chopping, cooking, etc., it's far more dangerous than sitting at a desk typing.

All policies are issued with an estimated annual premium, not a final premium. To determine the final premium, the policy states that you must let the insurance company audit all records related to your payroll (ledgers, journals, vouchers, etc.) on an annual basis. If you owe more because your payroll increased during the year, you will be billed for the difference. If your payroll went down, the insurance company will refund the difference.

Even though the state sets the price, it may be possible to lower your premium through **experience modification**. An "experience modification" recognizes the record of past losses. In most cases a special formula is applied using your past three-year-loss experience, excluding the current year. If this formula shows that the risk of working in your business is better than average, your business earns a decrease in premium.

This is a nice incentive; there are companies that do a really good job in employee-safety training and save as much as 10 percent on their workers' comp rates.

Because the state in which your business is located sets the rates, and because each company uses the same figures, there isn't much advantage in bidding out the insurance. However, you should get an agent who's smart enough to see if you qualify for the experience modification. If he or she doesn't know what you're talking about, get an agent who does!

COMMON QUESTIONS ABOUT WORKERS' COMPENSATION

Are There Limits to the Money That Can Be Paid under a Workers' Compensation Policy?

There are limits, but not in all areas of coverage. Under Part One—Workers' Compensation in the standard policy, there is no limit of liability.

Under Employer's Liability, there are the following standard limits:

- Bodily injury by accident: $100,000 each accident

- Bodily injury by disease: $100,000 each employee
- Bodily injury by disease: $500,000 policy limit

What Should I Do If One of My Employees Is Injured?

Contact your insurance agent immediately! I can't stress this enough. The Workers' Compensation Court has made it very clear that it's your responsibility as a business owner to notify your agent immediately when an injury or illness occurs. Your insurance agent can follow up with the necessary forms so that the employee's case is handled as quickly as possible.

INSURANCE FOR A BUSINESS IN THE HOME

Many people today run businesses out of their homes. Child care, animal care, landscaping, bookkeeping, and different sales-related jobs are just a few that come to mind. Do you need a separate business policy, or does your homeowner's policy cover everything? If you need a separate policy, will the cost be prohibitive? These are questions that you need answered.

If you work at home, you can protect yourself from the normal risks for significantly less premium than if you were operating a business outside the home. The following are the areas you should know about:

BUSINESS PROPERTY

While your homeowners coverage protects your personal property from fire, tornado, and the other perils, it will *not* protect any property you use for business purposes, such as desks, chairs, file cabinets, typewriters, etc. Make sure you inventory the business property you have in the home thoroughly and cover the total amount as an endorsement. By the time you add up the value of a computer, a typewriter, telephone-answering machine, filing cabinets, desks, chairs, a copier, and a fax machine, you could have several thousands of dollars' worth of business property to protect.

There are many other concerns you must address if you work out of your home. What they are depends on what you do. If you are a painter, are your paintings covered, and if so, for how much? What if you are a bookkeeper—are your accounts receivable covered? Discuss your business with your agent and make sure you are adequately covered.

LIABILITY TO CUSTOMERS

While the standard homeowners policy protects you from personal liability if a guest is injured at your home, it does not protect you against bodily-injury liability if the visitor is there for business purposes. If you do tax work and a client slips on your icy steps and breaks a leg, your homeowners policy is not going to cover his or her bills. You need additional coverage.

This coverage is available for most occupations and businesses that are run out of the home simply by adding an endorsement to your homeowners policy. It costs around 5 percent to 8 percent of the total premium.

GENERAL LIABILITY

Insurance broker Toby Haynes of Pasadena, California, considers the risks of liability for home-based entrepreneurs to be as high when they're working away from their offices as when they're working at home. If you are in someone's home as a consultant and accidentally break a coffee table, you are liable. If you are running a training session at a hotel and someone is injured during the training, you are liable. General liability insurance will protect you from such risks for around $150 to $225 a year.

You may be thinking, "I'm not going to hurt someone or break anything, so why should I pay for the extra coverage?" This may be true, but you're not just guarding against your own clumsiness. You are protecting yourself against risks that you have no control over, like slick floors and fragile chairs. If you are self-employed and do any work away from the home, the coverage is a wise investment.

There are many other concerns you must address if you work out of your home. What they are depends on what you do. If you are a painter, are your paintings covered, and if so, for how much? What if you are a bookkeeper—are your accounts receivable covered? Discuss your business with your agent and make sure you are adequately covered.

COMMERCIAL PACKAGE POLICY (CPP)

If your agent determines that your business, apartment complex, or manufacturing concern doesn't qualify for the BOPP program, you will be forced to take a CPP policy. The CPP is used primarily for larger, more complex businesses and institutions.

The CPP is available for mercantile, office, apartment house, processing or service, motel and hotel, industrial, and contracting businesses. With the exception of workers' compensation insurance, all major risks are covered by the CPP policy or can be covered by endorsement to the policy.

The difference between the two is that while the BOPP comes in a self-contained program, requiring few endorsements, the CPP is a core policy with endorsements being routinely required. While the BOPP has a broad range of "automatic" coverages, the CPP is more flexible in terms of choices of coverages and the amounts of protection provided. The CPP is generally more expensive than the BOPP program.

WHAT COVERAGES ARE AVAILABLE UNDER THE CPP?

The CPP starts with the base coverage, and then you pick and choose as from a menu what you want to add. Here are the offerings:

Crime

This part of the policy includes protection against a wide range of crime perils:

- Employee dishonesty
- Forgery
- Theft, disappearance
- Burglary
- Computer fraud
- Extortion
- Theft and robbery outside the premises

General Liability

The commercial general liability policy (CGL) is a protection package for most insurable business-liability exposures. It is referred to as "general" liability to distinguish it from auto, professional, and personal liability insurance, which afford liability protection against exposures of a different nature and which may be purchased separately.

Under the CGL policy, insurers agree to cover all sums up to the policy limits for which the policyholder is found legally liable because of bodily injury and property damage arising out of the premises, operations, and products of the policyholder.

The CGL policy does not cover liabilities for which benefits are provided under worker's compensation, unemployment insurance, or disability benefits laws. Other excluded events are the following:

- Damage resulting from the release or escape of pollutants
- Damage to property of others that is in the policyholder's care, custody, or control

EXAMPLE:

If you are a locksmith and while installing a lock in a glass cabinet you accidentally break the glass, there's no coverage because the cabinet was in your care and custody. On the other hand, if you drop your hammer on a nearby counter by mistake, that counter is covered since it wasn't in your care or custody.

- Liability resulting from a product's failure to do what it is intended to do

In 1986, the Insurance Services Office, Inc., developed a new commercial general liability policy. It has two liability sub lines— one covering the policyholder's premises and ongoing operations, and the other covering the products or completed operations of the policyholder.

INLAND MARINE

Inland marine coverage is insurance that evolved from ocean marine insurance. In general, inland marine coverage provides protection for property in transit or to property that is movable in nature. Here are just a few examples:

- Dry cleaners goods that belong to customers
- College athletic equipment
- Contractors' shovels, compressors, loaders, etc.
- Builders' tools
- Department store merchandise

The policy itself is broken down into several component coverages, which include the following:

Bailee

Bailee means custody of the property of your customers while on your premises. What if there's a fire and your dry-cleaning plant is gutted? You are covered for all the losses your customers sustained to their clothes. What if one of your employees accidentally burns a hole in a blouse as it's being ironed? No problem, you have the coverage.

Commercial Articles

This endorsement covers collections of fine arts, musical instruments, or photographic equipment owned by businesses, educational institutions, or musical groups.

Contractors' Equipment

This endorsement is for mobile construction equipment such as graders, shovels, cranes, bulldozers, backhoes, trenchers, loaders, etc. It also covers smaller equipment such as air compressors, wheelbarrows, picks, etc.

Installation

Installation covers property that will become part of a building or other structure. If you're a contractor and have a load of wood delivered that may have to sit at a construction site for several weeks, the wood is covered in case of fire, theft, etc., until it's used.

For the full array of coverages, and to determine if the CPP is the program for you, talk to your agent.

SHOPPING FOR AN AGENT AND A PRICE

HOW CAN I FIND THE BEST AGENT?

Insurance agents do not charge you for their services; they are compensated by the insurance companies for which they write policies. Therefore, you're not only shopping for an individual.

Insurance is a *highly* competitive industry. Companies differ in their rates, premium-payment plans, and insurance packages, so it's important to find an agent who is willing to give you the best program for your money. In scouting agents, *do*:

- Talk to a **captive agent**—one who writes for one company alone—and get a quote. Then go to an **independent agent**—one who represents many different companies. That way, you should find someone who will give you the best price.
- Talk to your friends and business acquaintances and see if they are satisfied with their agents. Get referrals.
- Make sure to choose an agent who has experience in writing business insurance packages. It pays to look for an agent who is knowledgable and responsive to your needs.

HOW CAN I GET THE BEST COMPANY AND THE BEST PRICE?

The whole point of having insurance is to get exactly the right coverage for the dollars you can afford to spend. Here are six steps you can take to do that:

1. If you are just getting into business, ask several different companies to quote exactly the same coverages for you. Make sure that the quotes are from reputable agents and that the companies have a good history of paying claims. Call other people you know in the same business and see who they deal with. The people you talk to should give you a pretty good idea about a company's reliability.

2. If you have an existing policy, quote it out every year just to make sure the company is still competitive. Give your policy to your existing agent and maybe three others. Have them quote on exactly the same items—compare apples to apples.

3. Be suspicious of a company that seems to be tremendously cheaper. There is no free ride in insurance, and if the difference is as low as, say, 50 percent, something's rotten in Denmark. There are companies that go out and "buy" the business. In other words, they price it out very cheap the first year in order to get you to switch over, and then they sock it to you the next year with a huge price increase.

4. Establish good safety procedures both for your employees and for your customers. Make sure sidewalks in front of your store are in good repair, stairs in apartments are in good shape, etc. The fewer claims you have, the more insurable you are, which means you should command the best rates.

5. Make sure you are not paying for coverage you don't need. If you don't spend nights worrying in case your detached sign is destroyed, don't insure it. Figure the exact amount of business property you want to insure, as well as the amount you want on any buildings you may own, and buy only that coverage.

6. Work with your deductible options. Raising your deductible is an excellent way to lower your insurance premium. You can save around 10 percent by raising the deductible amount from $100 to $250; 13 percent by raising it to $500; and 15 percent by raising it to $1,000. Of course, the higher the deductible, the more you pay out of your

pocket in case of a loss, but you may go many years without a claim and in the process save a considerable amount of premium.

BUSINESS INSURANCE CHECKLIST

If you own a business, take a look now at your insurance policy.

☐ Check and see what type of business policy you have. Is it a BOPP program or a CPP policy?

☐ Do you have a replacement-cost policy or an actual-cash-value policy?

☐ Do you have enough insurance on the building you own?

☐ Do you have enough coverage on your business personal property, such as furniture, fixtures, and inventory?

☐ Are there any endorsements you should have that you don't have now? Do you have coverage for loss of business income?

☐ Do you have enough liability coverage on the policy?

☐ Have you addressed the nonowned-auto question if it relates to your business?

☐ Are the limits you currently have on coverage for money and negotiable instruments adequate in case of a robbery or burglary?

☐ Do you want your exterior sign covered?

☐ In case of an employee's sickness or accident, do you know what procedure to follow in notifying the proper people?

☐ Have you checked to see if you qualify for a premium-modification credit on your worker's compensation policy?

☐ Does your present policy cover all your needs at a fair, competitive price?

CHAPTER FIVE

I Know I Should, But . . .
Life Insurance

TALKING ABOUT LIFE INSURANCE

Talking about life insurance reminds me of a scene I saw on television: A man identified as a life insurance salesman is thrown into a cell with the prisoner-hero. The prisoner's sentence is to listen over and over to the salesman's spiel on why he should buy life insurance.

I'm sure it got a lot of laughs; even *I* thought it was funny. Most consumers today seem to view talking about life insurance with an agent as an unbearable torture. Why should that be?

It can't be because the product itself is rotten. When you think about it, there's really no other product on the market that guarantees thousands of dollars to a family or spouse with the mere stroke of a pen the way life insurance can. None!

So why do people cringe and head for the garage or basement when a call comes from the local life insurance salesperson wanting to "review their program"?

Why will you let someone "sell" you insurance for your car— a piece of metal that can be replaced—and yet tense up at the idea of talking life insurance? Why does this product get so different a response from car insurance or house insurance or health insurance?

WHY PEOPLE DON'T LIKE TO TALK ABOUT IT

In fact, there are several reasons for these negative attitudes toward life insurance:

First of all, many people either think they are not going to die or, maybe more to the point, don't like to talk about death. Let's face it, death is not a fun subject. If they don't want to talk about death, they're not going to want to talk about life insurance, which implies death. Dying is something that happens to other people, not to us! Right?

A second reason for not wanting to talk about life insurance is that most of us have not been brought up with the idea that we have to have it. We all *know* that we need auto insurance in case we're in an accident, or house insurance in case of a fire or tornado. But whose mom and dad sat them down and said, "Gee, Son and Daughter, we think you should plan on having $100,000 in life insurance. Why not call the life insurance agent tonight so you can learn all about protecting your future family." That never happened to me!

A third reason why people feel uncomfortable about this product is that life insurance is a concept. As products go, it's a nebulous one. It's a state of mind and doesn't denote something you can touch with your hands like a car or a house or a motorcycle. We have a hard time buying products we can't touch, especially one that only pays off if we die!

Fourth, there *are* agents out there who make life insurance overly complicated and who are pushy, obnoxious, and overbearing. Just as in any other business, the few bad agents make things harder for the good ones.

All too many people can imagine this scenario: A local agent comes to your house, spouts a bunch of facts and figures, and before you know it—Wham! You've bought a policy you may or may not think you need and probably don't understand. You have been "sold"; you didn't "buy"—there's a huge difference between the two!

The purpose of this chapter is to give you the basics of life insurance, so that *with* the help of a professional insurance agent—somebody you can trust—you will find a program that (1) you understand, (2) you can afford, and (3) you get plenty of benefits from.

WHAT IS LIFE INSURANCE AND WHY SHOULD I HAVE IT?

Life insurance is protection for your survivors against the loss of your ability to support them when you die. There are several kinds of life insurance, some paying dividends and increasing in value.

These provide "living benefits." Others are mainly for protection against the owner's death. The types that will be covered in this chapter are whole life, term life, universal life, variable life, and business life. Each has its unique features and its advantages and disadvantages. There is plenty of product variety to allow you to tailor a plan to your special needs. Nevertheless, some people aren't buying.

No, Thank You

There are many people today who absolutely, and for a variety of reasons, don't believe in life insurance—period. Sometimes there just isn't enough money left in the budget after the regular bills have been paid to spend on life insurance. Mom and Dad may not have believed in it, and their children follow their example. I've heard husbands say, maybe as they heard their fathers say, "I don't need any life insurance. If I die, my wife will get remarried anyway." There are also people who don't have families or obligations to protect that would require their taking out life insurance.

Thus, life insurance isn't a product everyone believes in, can afford, or needs. A life insurance agent will disagree with this, but it's what *you* think that really counts! The agent is not paying your premium.

Reasons for Having Life Insurance

It's your prerogative not to have life insurance, but if you think you *might* be interested in purchasing it, you might as well know something about it. Here are some reasons why you might be interested:

- If you have a large debt and are concerned about not passing it on to others in case you should die unexpectedly, you may be interested in a policy that would pay off the debt.
- If you want access to the funds required to educate your children without having to borrow from a bank, the federal government, or a private source, you might consider certain types of life insurance.
- If you would like to have funds that will supplement your retirement income (other than Social Security), you should investigate certain types of life insurance. Contrary to what some consumers think, you can enjoy the cash benefits of a life insurance program while you're alive.
- If you want the $3,000 to $10,000 needed for a decent burial to be available (it's not cheap to die these days),

outright without your family's having to pay them off on installments or taking the money from your savings account, you might consider a life policy.

- If you want to guarantee that your family is not evicted from their home for lack of funds and doesn't come to resent you in death for not providing for them, then life insurance is something to consider.

WHAT IS WHOLE LIFE INSURANCE?

The term **whole life** is used interchangeably with **cash-value** insurance, or permanent insurance. "Cash value," also called "cash-surrender value," refers to the amount available in cash if you voluntarily terminate a whole life policy before it becomes payable. The cash value is *not* the same as the face value of the policy, which is the dollar amount of insurance on the insured's life. (The face amount may or may not be the same as the death benefit—the amount of money the insurance company will pay to your beneficiary upon your death. This will be explained below.)

A whole life policy is one that gives you living benefits at a fixed premium rate and that grows over the long term. This type of policy combines a tax-deferred investment with insurance protection. It pays tax-free dividends, which the policyholder can borrow at any time and at no cost. The cash value, or principal, can also be borrowed at any time, but at a low interest rate (anywhere from 1 percent to 8 percent).

The availability of cheap credit is one of the most attractive features of whole life insurance, but it is no longer ubiquitous. Low fixed rates for borrowing against the cash value have given way to variable loan charges with many companies. Borrowers may also be penalized with lower rates credited to the cash value that serves as collateral.

HOW DOES THE DEATH BENEFIT WORK?

What happens to the money you have in your policy when you die? Your **beneficiary** (the person who receives the proceeds of a policy when the insured dies) will receive the **death benefit**. The "death benefit" is the original amount of money you were insured for (face amount), plus any additional death benefit purchased by the dividends credited to your policy over the years. The additional amounts are called **paid-up additions**.

Most whole life policies are set up so that a portion of the dividends accruing in the policy purchases more insurance.

EXAMPLE:

Using figures from a highly rated life insurance company, the death benefit for a 35-year-old male nonsmoker would grow from the original $50,000 to $132,332 at the end of 20 years, and then to $232,311 when the insured reaches 65 years of age. This means that if he dies today, his beneficiaries will receive $50,000; if he dies in 20 years, they will get $132,332; and if he dies at the age of 65, they will get $232,311.

An important point is that they will get the death benefit, but they will *not* get the cash value or the dividends. The insurance company retains those funds. That's it—case closed.

EXAMPLE:

Let's say a 35-year-old female nonsmoker has a premium of $66.50 a month for the next 20 years on a face amount of $50,000. At the end of 20 years the death benefit has grown to $143,591 (if the dividends are being used to buy more insurance). During that time, the cash value and dividends that have accumulated come to $38,957, but if the insured dies in the twentieth year, they are *not* paid to the beneficiary. The total amount of money the beneficiary receives is the $143,591 death benefit.

HOW DOES CASH VALUE WORK?

Cash value is the money that builds up in your policy while you pay your premiums. This cash value grows at an interest rate the insurer determines. If you get no earnings or dividends at all, the cash value will creep along very slowly and finally close in on the face amount of the policy at age 100.

The cost of a whole life policy is averaged out over the policyholder's lifetime. In order to offer a level, or fixed, premium for life, the insurer charges more for the policy in the early years, which means that it takes several years before the cash value starts to build substantially within the policy. It is important to understand that you take out whole life insurance because of its long-term and not its short-term benefits.

Using the L-100 ordinary life policy ("ordinary life" is another term for whole life) written by the highly rated American Family Life of Madison, WI, we see that a 35-year-old male nonsmoker pays $76.50 a month for a $50,000 policy. The cash values grow as shown in Table 5.1.

Table 5.1 How Cash Value Increases on a Whole Life Policy

Year	Premium	Dividend	Cash Value	Total Cash Value
1	$76.50	$ 6.00	$ 0.00	$ 6.00
2	$76.50	96.00	0.00	102.00
3	$76.50	196.00	500.00	802.00
4	$76.50	272.00	1100.00	1687.00
5	$76.50	366.00	1750.00	2728.00
10	$76.50	982.00	6250.00	11308.00
20	$76.50	2,848.00	14,050.00	43,452.00

You'll notice that in the first several years a whole life policy builds almost nothing for cash value and very little for total cash value (dividends plus cash value). This reflects the fact that the insurance company is taking out the costs of setting up, issuing, and maintaining the policy up front. It's not until the third, fourth, and fifth years that you start seeing a cash buildup; consequently the longer you keep a policy, the more money will accumulate.

IMPORTANT POINT: All cash value is guaranteed! It cannot be lost or used up in the policy. It will always be there for you in case you need it.

How Can I Get Money Out of the Policy?

There are two basic ways to get the cash value out of your policy:

1. You can surrender the policy by not making the premium payments—in other words, cancel the contract entirely. The company will send you whatever cash value has accrued to that point in time. However, the company has the option to use the available cash value to keep the policy in force (they'll keep paying the premiums with the cash value), so make sure you notify them of your intentions to cancel the policy.
2. You can take a policy loan against the cash value. The policy owner has the unquestioned right to borrow any amount up to the full cash value at an interest rate stipulated in the contract.

Rates may vary from 1 percent to 8 percent, making this inexpensive source of loans one of the most attractive features of the policy. Remember that many companies today are charging a variable interest rate (one that fluctuates up and down). Be sure to check before you sign the loan document.

It is important to know that the loan rate is a "true" rate that is computed on the actual outstanding balance of the loan. Suppose the policy owner borrows $1,000 in January at a rate of 6 percent. If none of the loan has been repaid by January of the next year, the policy owner will owe $60 for the use of the money. If the policy owner decides to repay $300 at the end of the first year, the interest payable at the end of the second year will be $42 for the use of the remaining $700 (.06 times $700).

Why Should I Have to Pay Interest to Borrow My Own Money?

I am asked this question quite often. The reason is that the cash value of the policy is not the unrestricted property of the insured. Until the policy is canceled, the policy owner "shares" the property with the company in exchange for the company's guarantee of death benefits.

This requirement isn't really as bad as it may sound. For one thing, the guarantee is still in force even though an amount equal to the cash value has been borrowed, and the guarantee depends upon the insurance company's being able to use the cash reserves for income-producing investments.

For another thing, the cash value you borrow continues to grow even though it's not in the policy anymore. If you borrow $500 at 7.4 percent interest, the insurance company still pays the guaranteed rate of return—in this case 4.9 percent on the $500.

Also, you *never* have to pay a loan back with your own cash if you don't want to. Many people don't look at their cash values as a source of money because they're afraid they'll have to start paying the loan back right away or that the policy will lapse because the loan isn't being repaid. This simply isn't true.

Rather than repaying the loan at all, you can let the death benefit pay the loan back when you die.

EXAMPLE:

Let's say you borrow $5,000 from your policy, which has a death benefit of $100,000, and three years from now you die. The insurance company will subtract the loan amount of $5,000 less the interest from the $100,000 and give your beneficiary the remainder. That's not so bad, is it? It beats trying to pay a loan back out of your income when things are tight.

In days of high interest and scarce money, having the ability to borrow against policy cash values is an extremely valuable resource. Ask anyone old enough to have experienced the Depression where they got money to buy food, pay taxes, and just plain survive. Plenty of people will tell you it came from the cash values of their life insurance policies! Many farms and houses were saved from foreclosure by the cash value in life insurance policies.

HOW DO DIVIDENDS WORK?

If your whole life policy is a **participating** policy, it accumulates and may pay a **dividend**. An insurance "dividend" is a refund of a premium that subsequent experience has shown was too high —that is, more than the company needed to pay death claims and keep adequate reserves. Insurance companies like to protect themselves from the worst and later tell you that things weren't so bad.

Another way to put it is that there are surplus funds that the life insurance company accumulates over a year's time by investing your premiums, and this income is distributed to all eligible owners as dividends. In other words, if the life insurance company makes a profit with its investments (believe me, the good companies always make a profit), they turn around and distribute some of that profit to you.

Some people let their dividends accumulate in the policy, some like getting a check once a year, and some use the dividends to buy more insurance. You can choose the approach that best fits your situation. If you're letting dividends accumulate in the policy or using them to buy more insurance, remember that you have the right to withdraw those funds at any time merely by asking your agent to forward the proper form for you to sign and send in to the company. This is a simple process, and don't let anyone tell you otherwise.

In the 1960s and 1970s dividends were low. But in the 1980s, policyholders received far higher dividends than the companies had earlier projected, making the return on cash value a respectable 7 percent or 8 percent. Dividends of some companies have reached such heights that they can more than pay your entire premium after just 8 or 10 years (the vanishing premium concept).

Note that there are some policies that don't pay dividends. Known as **nonparticipating policies**, they are sold by stock companies and generally have lower premiums. Mutual (participating) companies won't guarantee future dividends, but their dividend projections are based on their anticipation of investment performance and on their mortality experience. The front page of your whole life policy will tell you whether it is "participating" or "nonparticipating."

HOW DO VANISHING, OR DISAPPEARING, PREMIUMS WORK?

For a 25-year-old parent, the prospect of paying life insurance premiums until age 65 is very intimidating. Paying premiums until age 65 used to be the only way to go. Times change however, and, fortunately, so do life insurance products.

We now have the **vanishing premium concept**. This is a plan that allows the consumer to stop making payments out of pocket after five to seven years in some cases; it could be longer.

Here's how the "vanishing" premium works: You have the option to let your dividends pay the premium when they have accumulated sufficiently to do so. How long you pay depends upon your age and how much insurance you buy. Of course, the premium never really "disappears." It still has to be paid, but instead of being drafted out of your checking account, the money to pay it is coming out of the policy itself. If a portion of the dividends is being used to pay the premium, that must mean there will be less dividends building up in the policy. And that's exactly what happens, as Table 5.2 illustrates. Again taking the example of a 35-year-old male nonsmoker paying $76.50 a month for a $50,000 policy, I have omitted years two through five, which are shown in Table 5.1, and picked up the example at year six.

From years one through seven, the premium of $76.50 a month is being paid by the consumer, but in year eight it starts being paid by the dividends. The figures in parentheses beside the figures under "dividends," "cash value," and "total cash value" represent the amounts that would have accrued if the consumer had continued to pay the premium out of pocket.

Note that in the 20th year, if our 35-year-old male had continued paying the premium, he would have built up a total cash

Table 5.2 Effects of Vanishing Premiums on a Whole Life Policy

Year	Premium	Dividends	Cash Value	Total Cash Value
1	$76.50	$ 6	$ 0	$ 36
6	$76.50	475	2,600	4,095
7	$76.50	589	3,450	5,597
8	$ 0.00	672 (712)	4,350 (4,350)	6,332 (7,299)
9	$ 0.00	759 (842)	5,300 (5,300)	7,197 (9,214)
20	$ 0.00	1,960 (2,848)	14,050 (14,050)	22,156 (43,452)
30	$ 0.00	3,448 (5,998)	22,900 (22,900)	54,259 (113,790)

value of $43,452, as opposed to about half that, or $22,156, which he accrued when the dividends paid the premiums for him. In the 30th year (age 65), the difference is far more dramatic—$54,259 under the vanishing premium, as opposed to $113,790 if he had continued to pay.

This difference has to be weighed before you decide to take the disappearing-premium option. The point is for you to be able to make a good decision when the time arrives.

You're not required to say when the policy is taken out whether you'll go the "disappearing" route or not. You can decide when the seven years are up. Maybe you'll decide in favor of the higher investment and keep paying the premium yourself. On the other hand, you might want to remodel the house, and that $76.50 a month could be put toward payments on a home-improvement loan.

Another point to be aware of is that neither the agent nor the company can *guarantee* that the dividend will be able to pay the premium. If the company's investment results are poor, or its life-expectancy projections wrong, you will have to pay longer than you thought before the premiums will "vanish." This isn't a problem as long as you understand the concept.

HOW CAN I GET THE BEST BUY IN WHOLE LIFE INSURANCE?

Premiums

Today's annual premium on a good $100,000 whole life policy at age 35 averages about $1,300 for a nonsmoking man and $1,100 for a woman. For the most part, premiums are much lower than they were a decade ago, reflecting longer life expectancy.

A key point about all whole life insurance is that the policy with the lowest premium won't necessarily be the best choice. Premiums are just one factor in building cash value. The others are investment results, interest-rate guarantees, fees and charges, commissions, and favorable borrowing rules.

Illustrations

Most cash-value policies are sold by **illustrations**. These are number-laden computer printouts that agents work up for you. In buying cash-value insurance, it's imperative, and not impossible, to understand illustrations. One reason to do so is that illustrations can give a dishonest agent the chance to use his or her personal computer to exaggerate the company's authorized interest rates or dividend scales. If discovered, that can get an agent's license revoked in a hurry! Your main concern is not to be swayed by a seller who promises far more than the company can reasonably deliver.

Look for two groups of column or figures. The key words are **current** and **guaranteed**. The company's current interest rates and/or dividends paid to the policyholder should be higher than the guaranteed minimum interest rates, which are generally around 4 percent.

Guarantees are worst-case outcomes—the lowest cash values the company is allowed to credit according to the terms of the policy. Current values are based on the optimistic assumption that rates being earned today by the policy's cash value will continue to be stable long into the future. You may find current and guaranteed values side-by-side, a few columns apart, or anywhere on the page. There's no set format.

Interest can be guaranteed, but dividends cannot! Cash values and increases in death benefits labeled "current" will exceed those marked "guaranteed" only by small amounts in the early years of the policy but possibly by hundreds of dollars in the later years. For a more realistic view, ask the agent to figure future earnings at about 6 percent.

In examining illustrations, remember that dividend projections are based on the company's most recent investment experience, and they are certain to be wrong. Dividends will surely be lower in some years and higher in others. The best advice about dividend illustrations is to use them as a reference point for policy comparisons and to get a ballpark idea of where you might be in 10, 20, or 40 years.

Take each illustration for what it is: a seller's projection into a hazy future of what the company is doing now. These numbers do not bind the insurance company in any way.

Buy for Now or Buy for Later?

Whole life insurance shoppers often face a puzzling choice: Buy a whole life policy with a low annual premium but relatively low cash values, or one that charges more for the same death benefit but projects higher cash surrender values? The question is how soon you expect to cash in the policy, if at all, before you die. You could take the cash-surrender values projected for 10 or 20 years hence and use a calculator to figure the annualized return on your premiums paid. If you pay $900 a year and have cash value of $39,000 in 20 years, that works out to 7.5 percent. So does paying

$1,300 a year for a cash value of $56,000 in 20 years. That's lower than some banks or bonds pay, but you should assign some value to the insurance protection.

Companies

To find good whole life policies, first consider only companies that earn ratings of A+ or A in Best's Insurance Reports, which is available in most public libraries.

Second, go through the list of the top dividend payers for permanent insurance companies published by Best in its *Review* magazine. The magazine is published monthly, and a quick look in the index will set you to the right month to find this information.

Best compared 52 large insurers, both for the highest dividends over the past 20 years and for the lowest actual cost of the policy. The top 10 in descending order were Northwestern Mutual Life, State Farm Life, Guardian Life, Massachusetts Mutual Life, Central Life of Iowa, Principal Mutual Life, Phoenix Mutual Life, Home Life, Sun Life of Canada, and Country Life. These aren't the only sound companies, but their dividend records are superior.

Agents

Talk to several agents or brokers and get several policy illustrations. Insist that the seller produce the most conservative dividend projection for whole life. To help you interpret the illustrations, send for *The Life Insurance Investment Advisor*, by Ben Baldwin and William Drom (Probus Publishing).

Agents may try to overwhelm you with their printouts, facts, and figures. Sometimes the agent starts to explain something but you simply don't understand it. Since you don't want to sound dumb by asking a "stupid" question, you keep nodding your head that you understand. Don't do that! Make the agent explain anything you don't understand until it's clear. If the agent doesn't make it clear, find another agent.

For starters, ask the agent three simple things: (1) how much it costs a month, (2) how much the death benefit is, and (3) how much you get if you live until age 65. If the agent can't tell you these things in a simple, easy-to-understand way, get rid of him or her and find one who can!

Start-up fees on cash-value life insurance, including the agent's commission, can be as much as 125 percent of the first year's premium. Rather than take the entire bite at the outset, insurers can nibble away at your account for as long as 15 years.

When Agents Want to Replace Old Policies

There are many insurance agents who make a living by replacing policies. Be very careful when an agent wants to cash in all your old whole life policies and start you with a new program. Why? Remember, you don't build up much cash value or dividend income in those first few years, while as time goes on the buildup becomes quite rapid. If you get rid of the policy you've had for eight years, you sacrifice all the progress you've made, and you must start all over paying the up-front charges and fees.

If you are approached by an agent from another company, or even by your own agent, about replacing your old policies, listen to him or her, make notes on the advantages of the product, and keep whatever printouts or brochures the person shows you. After the agent leaves, call your present agent or get a referral to another agent. Always get a second opinion from a respected source before making such a serious decision.

Maybe it is a better product, and maybe it isn't. Don't cancel your old policies without thinking about it first. And don't be pressured. Things can happen fast if an agent smells blood in the water. Give yourself a cooling-off period of a week or so before you make any decisions. If you do want to make a switch, never, never, cancel your old policies until the new ones are approved and issued!

Agents are trained to go for the kill the first night at your supper table, so be on your guard. The professional agents who really care will respect your feelings and come back if you call them. The ones out for the quick buck won't, but who needs their kind anyway?

WHAT ARE OTHER FEATURES AND REQUIREMENTS OF A WHOLE LIFE POLICY?

The Accidental-Death Clause

When the death of an insured occurs as a result of accidental injury, this benefit provides for an additional payment that is usually equal to the face amount of the policy. Hence, it has long been referred to as **double indemnity**.

EXAMPLE:

Assume that an insured has a $50,000 policy that includes the accidental-death clause. If he is killed in a car accident, his beneficiaries would be paid double the face amount of the policy, or $100,000.

Costs vary from company to company, but to add accidental-death coverage to a life policy is usually quite affordable. In the care of a 35-year-old male nonsmoker, it would cost an additional $4.50 a month. If you are interested in this option, check out the cost with your agent.

The Suicide Clause

To protect the company against potential suicides who are in the market for life insurance, the suicide clause has been made part of all life insurance contracts. The restriction is valid for two years (one year in some states) from the issue date. Thereafter, an insured who commits suicide and has a whole life, term, universal life, or any other type of policy has full coverage.

But remember that suicide must be verified; there is a legal presumption, substantiated by case law, that people don't kill themselves. When there's doubt, death by suicide must be established to the satisfaction of the court.

If the insured dies from a self-inflicted gunshot wound or kills herself by shutting the garage door and sitting in a running car, suicide is rather simple to prove. It also helps if suicide notes are left behind. On the other hand, if an insured drives off a cliff with her car, suicide is more difficult to prove because of the absence of evidence.

The accidental death benefit (which pays double the face amount) obviously does not cover suicide, since suicide is not accidental.

The Guaranteed Insurability Option (GIO)

The **GIO** allows policyholders to buy certain agreed-upon amounts of insurance at different times of their lives without having to prove their insurability. In most cases, these options are offered at certain ages, or when the insured marries or has children.

Having a condition like high blood pressure, a heart murmur or obesity, or a disease like multiple sclerosis, can make it difficult to find an insurer willing to provide you with a new policy, depending upon the severity of the condition. With the guaranteed insurability clause, your insurer is required to cover you. The actual rules vary from company to company, but the guaranteed-insurability benefit could provide for the following:

- Additional coverage up to the face amount of the policy or original death benefit at several different ages in the life of the insured

- Additional coverage up to the face amount of the policy when the insured gets married
- Additional coverage up to the face amount of the policy when the insured becomes a parent

This is a good feature to have if you have reason to suspect that you might develop a medical condition that would preclude you from getting life insurance—if, for example, several of your family members have developed heart disease in middle age. The GIO feature guarantees that you can purchase more life insurance up to the stated amounts of the policy.

Using a composite of several highly rated life insurance companies, the cost for a 35-year-old male nonsmoker to add an additional $25,000 at different times in his life would run an extra $3 to $4 a month.

The Waiver-of-Premium Benefit

This clause states that the insurance company will waive all premiums coming due during a time when you are totally disabled for six months or more starting after age 5 and continuing to age 60 (this could change with different companies). "Totally disabled" means you can't work at all. If you have the waiver-of-premium benefit and you are disabled—whether for three years or for the rest of your life—the company will keep the policy in force without your having to pay the premium. In essence, they are paying the premium for you.

Normally this benefit is included on the policies that are sold in today's market at *no extra cost*.

Make sure this benefit is included on your policy. The last thing you want to do during a disability period is drop your life policy—especially if it's been building cash values and dividends for the last 15 years. With this clause, you don't ever have to!

The Incontestability Clause

The incontestability clause says that the company has only two years to uncover and prove any improper actions in obtaining the policy on the part of the owner. An example of an improper action would be the concealment of an ailment or physical history that could have affected the insured's acceptability. If the policy is over two years old, the company cannot bring action against the beneficiaries and refuse to pay a death claim.

The only exception to this restraint on the insurance company would be if actual fraud was committed by the applicant in obtaining the policy. In this case, no contract of insurance would be considered to have taken place. However, insurance companies find fraud very difficult to prove, because it's hard to establish beyond doubt the intent of a dead person.

The Grace Period

Most life insurance policies allow a grace period of 30 or 31 days, which means that if the premium is not received in that period the policy is canceled. (Some universal life policies have a grace period of 60 or 61 days.) This isn't a threat, it's a fact. The policy is always canceled the day after the grace period unless you are borrowing from the policy to pay the premium.

The policy can be reinstated up to three years from the date of the lapse, but a new application must be filled out in order for the coverage to begin again. This can pose a major problem if you have developed a medical condition that precludes you from being accepted by the insurance company.

During the grace period, which begins on the date on which the premium is due, the owner can pay the premium and continue uninterrupted coverage. Even if death occurs within the grace period and the premium has not been paid, coverage is afforded by the policy. In that event, the premium due is subtracted from any proceeds payable to the beneficiary.

How Do I Change Beneficiaries?

If you want to change a beneficiary, call your agent and ask for the appropriate form. All you have to do is sign it, send it in, and the change will be made. However, the only one who can change the beneficiary is the owner of the policy.

> **EXAMPLE:**
>
> In divorce cases, it is not uncommon for the wife to call up and ask the agent to make sure her ex-husband doesn't change the beneficiary from her to his new wife. The agent can't help her, because the only one who can instruct the company is the policyowner. The beneficiary can't cash the policy in or borrow against it or do anything else regarding it without the owner's knowledge and signature.

SUMMARY: ADVANTAGES AND DISADVANTAGES OF WHOLE LIFE INSURANCE

Advantages

- You can accumulate cash value and dividends during the life of the policy.

- The premium never increases.
- The death benefit increases if you purchase paid-up additions of life insurance, thus providing a hedge against inflation.
- There are ways to limit the number of years you pay the premium out of your pocket (vanishing-premium concept).
- You can borrow the cash value or withdraw the dividends at any time, which gives you a "living benefit."

Disadvantages

There is only one disadvantage to whole life: It costs more than other plans such as term and universal life at younger ages, but in general it is an excellent plan if you can afford it.

WHAT IS TERM LIFE INSURANCE?

Term life is for someone with great financial responsibilities. It enables you to insure yourself for enormous sums with minimum outlays. A healthy, nonsmoking 35-year-old can buy $500,000 of term insurance for less than $600 a year. Rates per $1,000 often diminish at breakpoints of $100,000, $250,000, $500,000 and $1,000,000. Buying term in small amounts is wasteful. A $10,000 term policy may cost "pennies per day," but if you compute the cost per $1,000 of coverage, it is exorbitant. Some companies and agents won't deal in amounts below $100,000.

This type of life insurance is pure protection. It pays only if you die, and there are no cash value and dividends accumulating in this policy, and there are no living benefits. It's a very popular type of life insurance for young people just starting out in business with families to protect because of its low, affordable price.

VARIETIES OF TERM LIFE INSURANCE

The varieties of term life are annual renewable term, decreasing term, and five-year level term.

Annual Renewable Term (ART)

Annual renewable, or increasing, term is the most common and the simplest. You pay an annual premium and have the right to renew the policy for each succeeding year, but at a higher rate as you grow older. Rates tend to go up only a few cents per $1,000 each year until around age 40, when they accelerate more rapidly. You may find it worthwhile to switch companies every few years, because the rate may be much less for a new policyholder than for an existing policyholder of the same age.

> **EXAMPLE:**
>
> A 40-year-old man in excellent health pays $ .64 per $1,000 (plus an annual $80 policy fee) to buy the lowest-cost term policy from United Investors Life. That means a $1,000,000 policy would cost $640 plus $80, or $720. Two years later his rate rises to $1.44, or about what a 52-year-old pays in his first year with United Investors (yearly cost would be $1520). This is a considerable three-year hike.

National Insurance Consumer Organization advises considering a switch every few years. However, some companies refuse to accept habitual policy jumpers, or else demand three years of premiums in advance if yours is a replacement sale.

Decreasing Term

In decreasing term, the premiums stay the same, but the benefits decrease over time. This form is useful for insuring a declining debt, such as a house mortgage, and is written in terms of 10, 15, 20, 25, or 30 years. If you die, this cheaper insurance can be used to pay off the mortgage loan, leaving your other life insurance untouched. The life insurance should decrease as your loan balance decreases.

Five-Year Level Term

There's also five-year level term, in which the benefits stay the same, but the premium increases every five years. A five-year level term policy is good for those who want the death benefit to stay the same and not decrease. For example, if you know you are going to have a large debt for a short period of time (under five years), this policy would work fine. The rate doesn't change, and the coverage remains constant.

IS TERM INSURANCE A GOOD BUY?

According to Michael Murray, insurance professor at Drake University in Des Moines, Iowa, "Most people buy too little life insurance because they're being sold a cash-value policy when they simply can't afford the insurance they need at the cash-value rates."

Term insurance definitely has its place in today's market. As with any other life insurance product, the key is to understand its strengths and weaknesses.

As indicated, term insurance is inexpensive when you buy it new. Young people who need a lot of insurance, say a doctor starting out in practice, like it because of its price, especially as compared with that of whole life. The fixed annual premium for a typical whole life contract at age 35 runs around 10 to 15 times as much as the first-year premium for a term policy—i.e., for $1,000,000 worth of coverage, you could pay over $7,000, instead of $1,820 for term!

Regardless of what a life insurance agent tells you, and, believe me, they'll give you all kinds of reasons why term life insurance is bad, from the standpoint of *pure protection* it's the best product money can buy. The reason life insurance was developed was to provide money for a family to live on after the main income provider's death and to pay off outstanding debts; if the inexpensive term product allows a consumer to accomplish these goals, so be it.

Besides, you're not locked in. You can start out with term and convert the policy to whole life when you feel able to afford it. Almost all term policies allow for conversion to another product regardless of whether you qualify medically at the time of conversion.

Business people use term insurance to cover large short-term debts.

EXAMPLE:

You borrow $500,000 on a note to be paid back within two years. Instead of taking out a whole life policy, you take the much cheaper term policy and cancel it when the note is paid off. Most banks recommend term insurance to cover their clients' loans for this reason. Term life insurance works great for the short haul!

Remember, regardless of what a life insurance agent may say, you don't have to have the most expensive policy in order to protect your family!

HOW DO I SHOP FOR TERM INSURANCE?

Shopping for term isn't easy. Term is the most basic form of life insurance, but it has varying versions and prices. In a review of 415 policies with a face amount of $1,000,000, the difference in cost between the cheapest plan and the most expensive over 10 years was $42,000—enough to buy a Mercedes-Benz 300! Further, the seemingly least expensive policy, a product known as **reentry**

term, may cost the most in the long run because the insurer can drop you or triple your premium if you get sick.

What Are "Good Value" Rates?

The nonprofit National Insurance Consumer Organization (NICO) publishes guidelines, called good value rates on annual renewable term (ART), the most common variety of term insurance

Table 5.3, compiled by *Changing Times* (April 1988), shows an array of such rates at different ages for female and male nonsmokers. Multiply the rate by each $1,000 of coverage you are considering buying and then add $80 to get the total price for one year. Using the figures from the table, a nonsmoking 35-year-old man would pay $240 a year for a $200,000 policy ($.80 × $2,000 + $80 = $240). NICO says these aren't necessarily the lowest rates around, but for policies of $100,000 or more, they provide a useful benchmark.

What Are Quote Services?

There are consumer-oriented surrogates known as insurance premium quote services. You can call their toll-free numbers and request data on several policies suitable to your age, sex, health, smoking habits, and state of residence.

According to Steve Stark, vice president of marketing for SelectQuote in San Francisco, one of the five services that screen and sell low-cost term insurance, about one-third of the 561 life insurance companies rated tops for financial strength by the A.M. Best Company offer "competitive term products." Stark estimates that of that third, about 25 are likely to be worth checking out for the various combinations of age, sex, health, and amount of

Table 5.3 Good Value Rates on Annual Renewable Term Insurance (for each $1,000 of coverage)

Age	Nonsmoker		Smoker	
	Male	Female	Male	Female
18–30	$0.76	$0.68	$1.05	$1.01
35	0.80	0.74	1.36	1.26
40	1.03	0.95	2.06	1.65
45	1.45	1.20	2.95	2.30
50	2.60	1.76	4.16	3.30

SOURCE: National Insurance Consumer Organization

coverage at the lowest rates. (Mostly as a result of such competition, term prices have been declining for several years. Now the sharpest declines may be over, and some companies have raised rates about 10 percent since 1986 for certain groups of customers.)

A test run by *MONEY Magazine* in 1989 showed that quote services can greatly ease your search for a reliable, low-cost policy, once you learn how to interpret their information.

MONEY asked five firms to supply their best picks for a hypothetical New York State couple in their forties. All of the services turned up satisfactory term policies. *MONEY* also asked four respected insurance agents for their picks. They named either the same policies offered by the quote services or ones that were no bargains. The services, after all quote only term insurance.

Four of the five services are free. They are Insurance-Quote (1-800-972-1104); LifeQuote (1-800-776-7873); SelectQuote (1-800-343-1985); and TermQuote (1-800-444-8376). They make their profits as agents for the insurers they decide are the most competitive. The fifth service, Insurance Information Quote (1-800-472-5800), sells quotes at $50 a report. In *MONEY*'s test, all but one of Insurance Information's best picks were also proposed by the free services.

Evaluating information from the quote services can be tough. It appears on computer printouts in presentations that vary from complicated to incomprehensible. The following steps will help you choose the most suitable and economical policy:

- Check for guaranteed renewability. Stay away from any policy you cannot renew without proof of your continued good health until reentry or at least age 70.
- Compare prices over the number of years you expect to be insured. If you are insuring yourself to protect your family, add up the premiums over your remaining child-rearing years. The first-year expense tells you little about your total cost. The Art policy rises every year. Other policies step up every 5, 10, or 15 years. The cost for some 10-year policies rises more than 150 percent in the eleventh year!
- Be sure you can convert the policy to a cash-value contract with a fixed premium, regardless of your health. Any worthwhile term policy should offer this conversion option until you are at least 60.
- Don't use so-called re-entry premiums to compare policies. Re-entry premiums assume the same health level as before and are at least 50 percent *below* the standard, or current,

premiums after 5 or 10 years. Since your health may have failed by re-entry time, make it absolutely clear to the premium quote services that you want current premiums.

- Ignore guaranteed premiums. Some printouts show a separate schedule for premium increases under the heading "guaranteed." You can be sure of paying current premiums for only one to three years with most policies; after that, insurers have the right to charge the much higher guaranteed premiums. However, few if any insurers are likely to raise the scheduled premiums of existing policyholders.

The more term insurance you buy, the cheaper should be the cost per $1,000. Rates per $1,000 tend to decline at common break points: $100,000, $250,000, $500,000 and $1 million. "In many cases, believe it or not," says Steve Stark from SelectQuote, "it is less expensive to buy a $250,000 policy than one for $220,000."

- Check the policy fees. Most companies add an annual fee —perhaps $50 to $80—no matter what the size of the term policy. That makes buying small amounts of term insurance more expensive.

SUMMARY: ADVANTAGES AND DISADVANTAGES OF TERM LIFE INSURANCE

Advantages
- The monthly premium is initially inexpensive.
- In most cases, the contract guarantees the ability to convert to another product regardless of your health.

Disadvantages
- There are absolutely no cash values or dividends accumulating in a term policy for the insured to use as a "living benefit."
- The premiums start out cheap but increase as time goes on. A $250,000 death benefit that costs $300 a year in your early thirties (more for smokers) might cost $750 at age 45 and more than $1,000 by your early fifties.

WHAT ARE UNIVERSAL LIFE AND VARIABLE LIFE INSURANCE?

UNIVERSAL LIFE
Universal life, also known as "flexible-premium adjustable life", is one of the most popular cash-value policies. This form of in-

surance suits couples with up-and-down incomes or uncertain insurance needs—precisely because of its flexibility: They can change both the premiums and the face amount from year to year. It is billed as the cash-value policy for the buyer who can't afford whole life.

Universal life is essentially a combination of term insurance and a savings account, on which the insurer is required by law to pay a minimum interest rate. The interest rate credited to your cash account can go up or down as the insurer decides in contrast with straight whole life. You, in turn, may vary your premium payments (usually after two years), sending extra money when rates are high or skipping payments when you're short of cash. You can make lump-sum deposits, just as you can with a savings account, and you can build up tax-deferred cash values.

Be sure, though, that your accumulated cash value is enough to cover the monthly deductions for death protection and policy expenses. If you skip too many payments or pay too little on them, the monthly charges can exhaust your cash value, making your policy worthless. Some states require the insurer to warn you of this in advance (the company should be sending you regular statements in any case).

While universal policies don't pay dividends, the insurer sweetens the pot by raising interest rates credited to the investment portion or by cutting monthly charges. Because the insurer can transfer its investment risks to you by controlling interest rates and by guaranteeing only a low return (typically between 4 percent and 4.5 percent), it can charge lower premiums than those of whole life policies.

Recently, this plan has worked less smoothly than insurers expected. Many universal life policies were sold in the early 1980s when market interest rates were running at 12 percent a year. Today, companies are experiencing "negative good will," because current market rates allow them to pay only 8 percent or 9 percent on their investment accounts. Consequently, some purchasers have had to pay higher premiums to keep their insurance coverage intact.

Considering the absence of dividends and the uncertainties of financial markets, however, universal life may not end up the better choice later on. There are some aspects of the universal life product that can be a problem and that you should be aware of: Examine the agent's printout closely, and find out what happens if you cancel the policy after one year, three years, or ten years. What money can you lose?

When universal life first came out, most of the policies were "front-end loaded," meaning that service fees and administration costs were taken out up front, as in whole life, and cash values built up slowly.

The majority of universal life products are now "rear-end loaded"—that is, the company encourages you to stay with the policy for at least 10 years by the way they handle a cancellation or cash surrender. Table 5.4 illustrates this concept with the example of a 35-year-old male nonsmoker who has taken out a $50,000 universal life policy:

You can see that the cash-value column is higher than the surrender-value column up until the eleventh year. At that time, the cash value and the surrender value become the same. Therefore, if you keep the policy for at least 10 years, you will not have paid any charges. You are charged only if you cancel the policy before the 10 years is up.

It's a product worth considering. Remember that you're looking for the most protection for the period of time that suits your needs, at a price you can afford.

SUMMARY: ADVANTAGES AND DISADVANTAGES OF UNIVERSAL LIFE INSURANCE

Advantages

- It's cheaper than whole life, and in the past the interest credited on the account has fluctuated between a high of 15 percent and a rate of 8 percent to 10 percent today.

Table 5.4 Effect of Time Held on Charges in a Universal Life Policy

Year	Cash Value	Surrender Value
1	$ 274	$ 0
2	568	66
3	882	422
4	1,216	798
5	1,572	1,195
6	1,950	1,614
7	2,352	2,055
8	2,779	2,521
9	3,233	3,012
10	3,716	3,531
11	4,256	4,256

- It's flexible. After the first two years, the premiums usually can be raised, lowered, or skipped, and you can make lump-sum deposits into it at any time.

Disadvantages

- A comparison between whole life and universal life shows that whole life's overall investment worth, through its cash value and dividends, is much, much greater over the years.
- Because the interest rate that insurance companies pay on this product is tied to stocks and securities, the risk is higher for a loss than with traditional whole life.

VARIABLE LIFE

Straight whole life and universal life policies have interest rates based on fixed-income investments. **Variable life** lets you direct some or all of the cash value into securities markets, commonly through mutual funds. Variable is thus sold by prospectus and offers the most extensive disclosure of costs, terms, and alternative investment scenarios.

Conservative financial advisers say variable is inappropriate as your primary life insurance because so much of its value hinges on investment performance. Not just your cash value but your death benefit also can fall as well as rise. A variable policy can have a death benefit of $300,000 one year and $250,000 the next. There is a minimum guaranteed death benefit, but you pay much more for this protection than you would with universal, whole life, or term.

The attraction is all on the investment side. Earnings in stock, bonds, or real estate are tax-deferred as long as they are not withdrawn; there is no tax on interest and dividends.

WHAT IS BUSINESS LIFE INSURANCE?

This is one of the most neglected ways of protecting one's family and business. The same types of life insurance are used in this area—it's just the way they are used that's different.

Business life insurance is primarily a funding vehicle. It provides money for solutions to problems caused by death. If the problem is, say, loss of profits when an owner or other key employee dies, and if the solution is to have money on hand to offset lost profits and hire a replacement, then life insurance answers the question "Where will the money come from?" Most death-related business problems have solutions that require money.

WHAT HAPPENS WHEN A BUSINESS OWNER DIES?

Sole Proprietorship

When a sole proprietor dies, the business is almost certain to die with the owner unless there is someone in the family who can step in and keep it running. The reason is that the creditors of the business line up right away to collect their money. The beneficiaries are put under tremendous pressure to settle all accounts payable immediately.

The problem this creates is that the business then must be sold, and quickly. Whenever it is necessary to sell quickly, the potential buyer is in a strong bargaining position, and the sellers can see their asset greatly diminish. In most cases, the buyer won't offer nearly what the business is worth, and the shrinkage could be as high as 50 percent.

Joint Partnership

The death of a partner *automatically* dissolves the partnership. Without advance planning, the surviving partner virtually has no control in seeing that the business continues. He might try to get the deceased's spouse or other heirs to sell out to him, but that decision is theirs, not his.

If nothing has been done while both partners are still living to make sure the business can continue despite the death of either of them, here is what the surviving partner will be forced to do:

- Complete all unfinished contracts. If there is a loss, it's his alone, and if there's a profit, he must share it with the estate of the deceased partner.
- Collect all accounts receivables.
- Pay all business debts.
- Convert all remaining assets into cash at the best price obtainable.
- Share any cash balance with the estate of the deceased partner.

What does all this mean? It means that the business can go down the tubes real quick! A forced liquidation of the business is usually a disaster. Here's why:

1. There can be as high as a 50 percent or more financial loss to the surviving partner and the heirs of the deceased partner. Everyone wants a good "buy" out there today, and a forced sale of a business brings out the bargain

hunters. The business you and your partner worked so hard to build up could go for literally nothing.

2. Liquidation means a loss of business and position, often permanent, to the surviving partner. The surviving partner's dreams are shattered, and he is looking at losing the business.

3. When liquidation begins, business income stops. All receipts must be held in trust for distribution as a part of the business interest. It's not a very happy prospect.

BUSINESS INSURANCE REMEDIES

What can you do to avoid the above scenarios? Have insurance!

Buy-Sell Insurance

Insurance is often taken out on the life of each partner by the other partner for the purpose of purchasing his business interests from the estate at death. If one partner dies, a **buy-sell agreement** provides that the other partner would have the life insurance proceeds to buy out this deceased partner's interest in the business. The buy-sell agreement is "funded" with the life insurance policies.

An attorney usually draws up the buy-sell agreement after you calculate the value of the business and what it would take financially to buy each other's interest out. This arrangement can be applied to any form of business—a sole proprietorship, partnership, or corporation. It is a must if you want to protect the business in case of the untimely death of one of the owners.

Key Man, or Key Employee, Insurance

A **key man** is a productive member of a business team who occupies so important a position that the employee's untimely death would seriously impair the profitable operation of the business.

If you have an employee who is indispensable to the smooth running of your business, you can take a life insurance policy out on him or her in case of an untimely death. This money would pay to keep the business from going under while you search for another key person.

OTHER IMPORTANT QUESTIONS

HOW MUCH LIFE INSURANCE DO I NEED?

In 1988, reports the American Council of Life Insurance, the average insured household owned $108,200 worth of coverage.

This may sound substantial, but if you were to take $108,200 and place it in a money market fund earning 7 percent, it would produce only $7,574 a year. That's not only below minimum wage, but it's taxable, too.

Even adding other income your survivors could expect, such as social security benefits and pension checks, the amount would still be below what your household lives on now. If your survivors were to then draw on the principal, taking out $1,000 a month, the entire $108,200 would be eaten up in just over nine years. No wonder insurance experts believe that most families, especially those living comfortably, are underinsured.

Insurance brokers once used imprecise guidelines to estimate need, like the "multiple-of-income" approach, which called for insurance equal to four or five times your salary in order to protect your family's living standards. The problem with such shortcuts, says Virginia Bevington, senior financial planner for APEX Advisory Services in Cambridge, Massachusetts, is "that they are not based on anyone's exact situation, so they end up understating or overstating the need."

Ideally, your insurance payout, invested at a reasonable rate of return, should generate the income your beneficiaries need to fill the gap between their other financial resources and their cash needs.

What Is a Financial-Needs Analysis?

To figure the amount of insurance a family needs, insurance brokers and financial planners perform what's called a **capital-needs analysis**, or **financial-needs analysis**. It's a straightforward process that estimates the coverage necessary to provide sufficient income. Using this method, you can also compare the effects of different approaches, such as providing an extra lump sum to pay off the mortgage immediately versus providing a high enough income to keep up the payments.

You should start by estimating your "income objective," expressed in today's dollars. Based on current spending patterns and financial obligations—i.e., that which your income covers at present, plus your debts—how much gross income will your family need? $35,000 a year? $60,000 a year?

Next, list other financial resources your survivors could tap:

- Current liquid assets—What counts is cash and securities that can be used to pay expenses or generate income after death. The more you have, the less insurance you need.

- Other insurance proceeds—You can count insurance provided by your employer, such as group term insurance, with the proviso that if you ever leave the company or get fired, you will probably lose this benefit. Your estate also may have rights to a lump-sum payment from your pension plan. Include Social Security benefits payable to spouse and children. By completing Form SSA 7004, Request for Statement of Earnings, you can learn what benefits you and your survivors have coming. (To get this form, call 1-800-234-5772.) In 1988, the maximum monthly Social Security payout to a surviving spouse was $838; to a family, $1,834.
- Survivor's earning power—The more your spouse can earn in the years ahead, the less insurance you need. Make a conservative estimate in today's dollars, allowing for only small raises beyond inflation unless you know that a lucrative new job or promotion is in the cards.

The shortfall between your other financial resources and your income objective equals your life insurance needs.

EXAMPLE:

Say your income objective is $60,000 a year. Your spouse earns $20,000; Social Security is good for $13,000; and other investments will generate $2,000, for a total of $35,000. Thus, insurance has to contribute about $25,000 to make up the difference.

That's this year. What about succeeding years? It takes a mountain of cash to create that much income for decades to come. To earn $25,000 a year from 9 percent Treasury bonds, you need $277,778 worth. And that's just for income; you would have to provide separately for any lump sums you want to set aside to pay off the mortgage or send your kids to college.

Another approach to figuring how much life insurance you need adds in the large, lump-sum expenses. The worksheet in Table 5.5 will help you figure out how much life insurance you need to generate enough income after you die to help your family avoid a financial catastrophe. Under this method, you would make sure you had enough to do the following:

- Pay off the house in case of the death of either spouse. Many families today live on incomes of both the husband and the wife, so if one of these incomes is suddenly taken

away, disaster occurs because there's not enough money for house payments.
- Pay off major bills such as credit cards, car loans, and other installment debt—anything that has a monthly payment.
- Have enough money for a decent funeral ($5,000 to $10,000).

If the surviving spouse can pay off the house, all installment debt, and the funeral expense, the family has a chance to survive.

But Can I Afford That?

Now comes the hard part. You know what you need, but the amount seems beyond reach. One possibility is to wait. Plenty of people do just that. If you're single or your death wouldn't visit financial hardship on anyone, life insurance is a luxury. Benefits from your group policy at work should more than suffice.

To me, it really starts with how much money you can comfortably spend per month for life insurance. Don't let the agent get carried away with your money. If we all bought enough life insurance to pay our debts, educate our children, and provide an income for our spouse until age 65, we'd be broke.

There's no doubt that large amounts of life insurance are required to satisfy what most financial-needs analyses show that a young family would require. The FNA works great in figuring what you need, but how many people can afford this much? Some can and some can't. It's now the job of the agent to help you get the most for the money you *can* spend.

I always feel more comfortable when people tell me honestly how much money they can budget monthly for life insurance. This helps me plan a program that does a couple of things: (1) accomplishes at least the most important of their goals, whether it's paying off their house, providing an education for their children, or replacing the deceased spouse's income; and (2) keeps them happy by staying within their budget.

Instead of ignoring the issue and not buying any insurance, if you know how much you need and have a family, or a tremendous amount of debt to cover, or both, you need to look at term, universal life, whole life, and variable life and pick what's best for you. Figure the amount of money you can spend comfortably on life insurance every month. No more, no less. You can grow into a program as your income increases and your financial situation improves.

Table 5.5 How Much Life Insurance Do You Need?

1. Enter funeral and estate-tax expenses. (Use $2,200 if your net worth, including real estate, is less than $20,000; $5,000 if it is between $20,000 and $200,000, and $10,000 if it exceeds $200,000.) $_____

2. Enter total family debts (except home mortgage). $_____

3. Enter twice your monthly take-home pay as an emergency fund. $_____

4. Enter future college expenses (the current averages are $14,100 per year per child for private school and $6,600 per year for public school). $_____

5. Figure total family annual living expenses, including mortgage payments or rent, costs of food, clothing, insurance, child care, etc. $_____

6. Enter surviving spouse's income sources:
   a. Spouse's annual after-tax pay. $_____
   b. Spouse's annual Social Security benefits ($3,000 if you have no children, $4,000 if you have one child or $5,000 for two or more minors). $_____
   c. Add a and b. $_____

7. Enter net annual-income needs (5 minus 6c). $_____

8. Enter investment-rate factor (from table below). _____

9. Enter total net-income needs (multiply 7 by 8). $_____

10. Enter total monetary needs (add 1, 2, 3, 4 and 9). $_____

11. Enter total investment assets. $_____

12. Your life-insurance needs (10 minus 11). $_____

Your investment-rate factor

How much annual income your life-insurance benefits will generate depends on whether you're the cautious passbook-account type or a more daring stock, bonds and real-estate player. To complete step 8, above, go to the line that matches the number of years until your spouse turns 90 and then choose the "rate factor" that best describes your family's approach.

Note: The conservative factor assumes 2 percent real annual growth, after inflation. Aggressive factor assumes 4 percent.

Years until spouse is 90	Rate factor	
	Conservative	Aggressive
25	20	16
30	22	17
35	25	19
40	27	20
45	30	21
50	31	21
55	33	22
60	35	23

SOURCE: *U.S. News and World Report* (July 1989). Copyright 1989 by Bailard, Biehl, & Kaiser, Inc. Reprinted by permission.

DO BOTH SPOUSES NEED LIFE INSURANCE?

Today, there are more and more households with two working spouses; in fact, it's seldom that I see anything else. It's quite evident that if either spouse's income ceases, the household is seriously threatened. Having life insurance to pay off major debts like the house and car loan would eliminate a considerable amount of pressure and upheaval, as well as potential economic disaster.

And what about child care? Whether one spouse was at home with the children, or one income was already covering child care, with only one income remaining, child care will be an enormous burden. It could run $500 to $1,000 a month to hire someone to take care of the kids. Where's that money going to come from? Life insurance would allow the surviving parent to continue to work without undue worry and stress.

SHOULD THE CHILDREN HAVE LIFE INSURANCE?

People ask me this question quite often. One reason to have a life insurance policy on your children is strictly for a death benefit. A small policy in the amount of $4,000 to $5,000 costs only $4 to $5 a month and would assure you the money for a proper burial.

There are a couple of other reasons to consider buying a policy for your child: (1) You can save him or her money for later, and (2) to provide guaranteed insurability.

First, the average cost for a $25,000 whole life policy on an eight-year-old female is about $18.75 monthly, while the same policy would cost a 30-year-old, if she didn't smoke, an average of $34.50 a month. Remember that whole life comes with a fixed rate. You could give your daughter a great savings for when she's an adult. She would have a $25,000 whole life policy that's inexpensive compared with buying it at age 30. The younger the child is when you buy the policy, the cheaper it is.

The other advantage is that you can guarantee your child the ability to purchase more life insurance as she grows older without worrying about showing proof of health. If she develops high blood pressure, a heart murmur, or other problems, she may find herself either unable to purchase life insurance or able to purchase it only at very high rated-up premiums.

WHAT ABOUT PAYING FOR COLLEGE?

You hear a lot about buying a policy on your child when he is young so that he will have money to go to college. I don't believe that works as well today as it did 20 years ago. College education costs are escalating so fast (they've doubled in the last 10 years) that there is virtually no way for the small premium you pay for a child's policy to provide the cash values and dividends necessary to pay for college costs *now*, let alone 20 years from now.

If you want to have money to send your kids to college, you need insurance on one of the adults instead of on the children. Table 5.6 shows how this works out.

EXAMPLE:

If a 35-year-old male nonsmoker buys a $50,000 whole life policy on himself today, in 15 years, when his three-year-old daughter is ready to attend college, he could have $23,781 in the whole life policy, as compared with $4,639 in the daughter's policy (see Table 5.6).

It's very difficult for a middle-class family—one that owns a home and makes over $25,000 a year—to obtain student-loan financing these days. What will it be like when your kids are ready to go to college 10 to 15 years from now? My advice is to keep a small policy on your child that has the guaranteed-insurability clause, but if you want to build up a considerable amount of cash value and dividends for a college education, you should both take policies out on yourselves.

WHAT ARE THE TAX CONSEQUENCES OF LIFE INSURANCE?

A great feature of life insurance that has investment value (whole life and universal life) is that the monies accruing in it are tax-deferred. The insurance companies always pay a very acceptable interest rate on their policies, which you can protect from the tax collector for a long time.

If you're taking $60 a month out of your check and putting it in your savings account, you're probably earning less than 6

Table 5.6 Comparison of Policies for Saving for Child's College Education

Policy	Cash Value	Premiums Paid
Adult Whole Life	$23,781	$13,770
Adult Universal	$ 6,763	$ 8,122
Child's Whole Life	$ 4,639	$ 810

percent interest on the money. Right? Not only is that a poor return, but you're forced to pay taxes on it, which makes it even poorer. Remember the 1099 form you get at the end of each year that shows how much interest you've earned?

Instead, you could take out a life insurance policy for whatever amount $60 a month would buy, let the interest accrue tax-deferred, and have a death benefit besides.

When Do You Pay Tax on the Proceeds from a Life Insurance Policy?

You pay when you cash the policy in, but not on the whole cash value.

> **EXAMPLE:**
>
> If you cash in your policy and take $100,000, this is not all treated as income for the IRS. You are taxed on the *difference* between the premium you paid over the years, let's say $75,000, and the amount of cash value removed ($100,000). Therefore, the amount considered to be taxable income would be $25,000. This amount is taxed as "earned income," not as a capital gain. Because dividends are considered to be an "overpayment of premium dollars," you would not pay income tax on any dividend accumulations. For example, if you cash in a policy that has $50,000 cash value and $25,000 dividends, only the cash value of $50,000 less the total premium paid will be considered for tax purposes.

Does the Beneficiary Have to Pay Tax?

When you die, the life insurance death benefit goes to your beneficiary completely tax-free. It's not considered income to the beneficiary, and it has no tax consequences whatsoever.

CAN I USE MY LIFE INSURANCE TO HELP SUPPLEMENT MY RETIREMENT INCOME?

If you have a whole life or universal life policy that builds cash value and dividends, you can use those monies to supplement your retirement.

When you are close to retirement, ask your agent how much money you have in your policy and then do one of two things: (1) cash the policy in and take all the money (don't forget, you do have to pay taxes on the difference between the cash value and the premiums you paid in), or (2) withdraw the dividends and borrow the cash value.

It's possible to set up a monthly, quarterly, semiannual, or annual method of disbursement for the funds that would dovetail nicely with your other retirement monies.

WHAT ABOUT PHYSICALS?

The requirement for physicals depends upon your age, your present physical condition, the amount of life insurance you're applying for, and the company you're dealing with. A number of things can happen when you apply for life insurance:

- You will not be required to do anything.
- You will be asked to have a ParaMedical I exam. This includes filling out a medical history form; having your height, weight, pulse, and blood pressure recorded; having a urinalysis; and possibly having a blood test for AIDS. This information would be taken by a licensed ParaMedical nurse at your home or at work. If you think you might have been exposed to the AIDS virus, you should find out before you get a blood test whether the results will be given to your employer.
- You could be asked to have a ParaMedical II done, which is the same as the ParaMedical I with the addition of an electrocardiogram.
- You could be asked to have a complete physical exam, to be done by your own doctor.

It varies from company to company, but the testing is usually paid for by the insurance company. The ParaMed I and ParaMed II can run anywhere from $20 to $75, and a full physical can run from $200 to $1,000. When you're shopping for insurance, ask the agent if any of these are going to be required and who's going to pay for them, so there's no confusion.

LIFE INSURANCE CHECKLIST

Review your life policy to see what it contains. Call your agent if you have any questions.

☐ Do you have whole life insurance? What is your cash value? What is your loan value? How much has accumulated so far in dividends? Can you "disappear" your premiums?

☐ Do you have term insurance? Is it level term, decreasing term, or increasing term? Is your term insurance convertible? Is it renewable?

☐ Do you have universal life or variable life insurance? What is your cash value? What is your surrender value? What is the current interest the policy is paying? Can you add to or reduce your premium upon request?

☐ What special features do you have? Do you have accidental death? Waiver of premium? Guaranteed insurability option?

☐ Do you need to change or update the beneficiaries listed on your policy?

☐ Have you sat down with your agent and looked at whether you have enough insurance? Have you told him or her what you want insurance to do for you and your family?

☐ If you do not currently have life insurance, keep these tips in mind:

- Know what you want your insurance to do.
- Talk to several different agents and have them explain whole life, term, and universal life.
- Take some time to reflect and then decide what kind of policy you want.
- Check out features, options, and coverages comparing the costs and the benefits on all three.
- Go to the public library and make sure the company you want to deal with is rated A+ or A. You can find the information in A.M. Best's Insurance Reports.

CHAPTER SIX

Down on the Farm:
Farm and Ranch Insurance

WHAT IS FARM OR RANCH INSURANCE?

Compared with the more common auto and house insurance policies, a farm policy is more complex. The reason is that there is more to cover. For example, farm or ranch property is defined as dwellings, barns, granaries, outbuildings and other structures, and their contents. It also includes livestock, hay and grain in stacks, and machinery and farm implements if they are situated on land that is used for poultry, truck, fruit, livestock, dairy, or other farming or ranching purposes.

If you think your farm buildings are automatically covered on a farm policy, you may or may not be right. Some policies will automatically include them, others won't unless they're specifically listed. This is just one of many points an experienced agent will know and be able to explain to you.

It is imperative that you have an agent who is very knowledgeable regarding farm insurance and has had considerable experience writing farm policies. Inexperience on the agent's part could cost you lots of money.

PACKAGING

Almost all insurance companies **package** their policies. "Packaging" consists of several programs of coverage in one written contract for one premium. The advantage is in dealing with only one agent and one company, and in paying only one premium. In most cases, you get more coverage for your money.

COMPONENTS OF A FARM CONTRACT

Companies vary as to how they package their coverages, but you will discover, when you shop around, that most insurance companies provide the same basic program.

Farm policy contracts generally consist of the following four coverage components:

- Dwelling, personal property, and loss of use
- Farm personal property
- Outbuildings
- Liability and medical expense

These will be considered in turn.

WHAT COVERAGES ARE THERE FOR THE DWELLING AND PERSONAL PROPERTY?

THE TYPES OF CONTRACTS

As with homeowners contracts, you can choose among several coverages for the house you live in plus its contents: basic form 1, broad form 2, and comprehensive form 3.

Basic Form 1

This policy provides protection against accidental physical loss to property by fire, theft, and the perils grouped under extended coverages. Extended coverages are windstorm and hail, explosion, riot or civil commotion, aircraft, vehicles, smoke, vandalism, and malicious mischief.

As its name indicates, this is a *basic* policy. Like the homeowners form 1 (HO-1), it covers fewer named perils than the form 2 or form 3 contracts. Some of the catastrophes not covered by the form 1 are falling objects, including trees; weight of ice, sleet, and snow; bursting of heating system or freezing of pipes; and sudden damage from artificially generated electrical current.

If you live in the southern United States, it's not a high priority to have coverage against damage from weight of ice, sleet, or snow. Of course, you still could have problems with lightning, falling objects, and bursting of a heating system.

You can save up to 15 percent on the premium by purchasing form 1, but be sure you know what coverages you're sacrificing.

Broad Form 2

This policy is similar to the form 1 except that it includes the perils the form 1 did not cover, which creates a "broader" policy. Since the cost for the broad form 2 is virtually the same as for the form 3 with most major farm insurers, it's not a good buy to take the broad form 2 unless you can't qualify for form 3.

The insurance company decides that according to the age of the dwelling and its condition. If the structure is older, the paint is peeling, and the roof is 20 years old or more, you may not qualify for a form 3 and will have to go with the broad form 2.

Comprehensive Form 3

If you want the most perils covered, and your property qualifies, it's best to take the comprehensive form 3 policy. Both the broad form 2 and the form 3 cost 15 percent to 20 percent more than the basic form 1. As with the HO-3 (see Chapter 1), the 17 perils you are covered for with the comprehensive form 3 are as follows:

- Fire or lightning
- Windstorm or hail
- Explosion
- Riot or civil commotion
- Damage from aircraft
- Smoke
- Vandalism and malicious mischief
- Theft from and away from the premises
- Damage by any vehicle
- Breakage of glass
- Falling objects
- Weight of ice, sleet, and snow
- Bursting or tearing of heating system
- Accidental discharge or overflow of water system
- Damage from freezing of plumbing
- Damage from electrical current to appliances
- Damage from rain seepage

WHY DO RATES VARY?

First of all, rates vary from state to state. While coverages for liability, farm buildings, and machinery vary only slightly from company to company, the cost to insure the farm dwelling can be considerably different from state to state.

Coverage on a $50,000 frame dwelling with a $250 deductible could range from a low of $200 in Colorado to a high of $350 in Kansas.

Apart from state-by-state differences, all companies calculate a policy's cost in the same basic way. As with homeowners insurance, they consider the following:

- The location within a state. The closer the insured property is to a town with a fire department, the lower the premium.
- Whether the structure is made of frame or brick. Most companies charge around 5 percent to 10 percent more to insure houses made of wood because they tend to suffer more damage in storms, fires, and other disasters.
- The fire-protection class of the area. Every town in the United States has been assigned a fire-protection class by the Insurance Services Offices (ISO), an industry group in New York City. The classification is based on the quality of fire-protection service in the town closest to your farm —that is, whether there is a full-time fire department, how extensively the firefighters are trained, and what the distance is from your house to the closest source of water.

WHAT ADDITIONAL COVERAGES SHOULD I LOOK AT?

You may need to buy additional coverages depending on (1) the amount of premium you can afford, and (2) how much and what kind of insurance you want that's not on the basic policy. Here are several coverages you might look at:

Coverage against Earthquake Damage

Under this endorsement, your house is protected from direct loss caused by earthquake or volcanic eruption. Naturally, the premium is relatively inexpensive in places like Nebraska ($.20 per $1,000 of coverage), where the chance of an earthquake's occurring is almost zero. But if you live in California, the insurance company might charge as much as $1.32 per $1,000 of coverage.

Extended Coverage on Jewelry, Watches, and Furs

As with the HO-3 homeowners policy, the form 3 farm policy carries only $500 in coverage on jewelry, watches, and furs. If you don't have this much in jewelry or other items, there's no sense paying the extra premium. If you have a considerable amount of valuables, you may want to get a quote for extra coverage.

This endorsement is an all-risks coverage for the specific amount you need, as opposed to a named-peril coverage. "All-risks" means that the policy protects against calamities such as losing a diamond from its setting or having a ring disappear down the garbage disposal. These events are far more common than fire and theft losses, which are the only ones covered in the standard policy.

You will probably be asked to provide a written appraisal that is no more than two years old on the items you want to endorse, or schedule. To "endorse" or "schedule" something to the policy means to add it on specifically. Most appraisals are not free, but they're worth the price. Here's a tip. If possible, take your jewelry back to the store where you originally purchased it to get the appraisal. They may do it for free or for a reduced fee because you're one of their customers.

The average cost for this endorsement runs around $10 per $1,000 of coverage, so that if you wanted to cover $10,000 worth of jewelry, it would cost $100 annually, in addition to your normal premium.

Personal-Computer and Electronic-Equipment Endorsement

The only reason to pay the extra premium for this endorsement is that, with most policies, it has a $50 deductible. This means that if you have a $500 or $1,000 deductible on your policy and your personal computer is stolen, you only have $50 to worry about in deductible. Another worry with computers is lightning losses, but if the equipment has a surge protector, you probably don't have to be too concerned.

This endorsement is not inexpensive, averaging around $5 per $1,000 of coverage. If you have $2,000 worth of computer equipment, it would cost approximately $10 annually to schedule it on the policy.

Outdoor-Antenna Endorsement

Outdoor "dish" antennas are quite popular today in farming communities. Most farm policies come with anywhere from $500 to $1,000 for coverage of outdoor antennas, which is usually sufficient. The only item you may need to insure with an endorsement is the dish itself, if it costs significantly more than $500, as the receiver and equipment in the house are covered as personal property. The cost averages around $4 per $1,000 of coverage.

Personal-Property Replacement-Cost Endorsement

This endorsement states that the insurance company will pay to replace the damaged item with an item of similar quality or to fix the damaged item, whichever is less.

EXAMPLE:

If you have a five-year-old television set that cost $600 new and lightning destroys it, without the replacement-cost endorsement the claim will be figured like this: $600 original cost − ($200 depreciation + $250 deductible) = $150 check to you.

Not only do you get next to nothing for the television, but you still have to go out and buy another one.

What happens if you *do* have the replacement-cost endorsement? The claim will be figured like this: $650 replacement cost − $250 deductible = $450 check to you.

The figures speak for themselves. The extra cost for this endorsement runs around $10 to $25 a year. If you can't afford it right now, consider adding it at a later date.

Scheduled Personal Property

If you feel that the basic coverage for certain items such as guns, silverware, artworks, etc., isn't enough, you can increase the coverage by paying extra premium. Be cautious, however, because insuring items with an endorsement, or "floater," can be expensive —running into hundreds of dollars a year. Make sure you know how much the policy automatically covers before adding on.

Here is a list of items that can be endorsed, and the approximate annual cost per $1,000 of coverage to do it:

- Jewelry—$10
- Furs—$3.50
- Cameras—$15
- Musical instruments—$6
- Silverware—$3.50
- Golf equipment—$15
- Fine arts—$4
- Guns—$20
- Portable tools—$25

If you have a valuable collection of any one of these items, consult your agent about extending the coverage.

WHAT COVERAGES ARE THERE FOR FARM PERSONAL PROPERTY?

Farm personal property refers to the equipment, livestock, feed, etc., specifically relating to the operation of the farm or ranch. It does not refer to the personal property in the farmhouse or any other structure used for living, as this property is covered with the dwelling. It also doesn't include automobiles and trucks, which must be insured with an auto policy.

BLANKET OR SCHEDULED COVERAGE

In most cases, farm personal property may be written as either a **blanket** or a **scheduled** coverage. Let's take a look at both:

Blanket

"Blanket" coverage is when all of your farm personal property is grouped together and totaled, rather than being listed item by item, as in a "scheduled" policy. If the total worth of your farm personal property was $175,000, the blanket would be written for that amount, and the specific items covered would not be listed on the policy.

The most important point is that *all* farm personal property must be included in determining the total value of the blanket, or you won't get full coverage on any specific loss.

EXAMPLE:

A fire in one of your quonsets burns up the $75,000 tractor you just purchased. When the claims representative arrives to adjust the loss the first thing he or she will do is inventory the total amount of farm equipment you own. If this inventory totals $450,000 but your blanket is only for $225,000, I guarantee that you won't be happy with what happens next!

The amount for which you will be covered will be in a proportion of the stated to the actual worth of the inventory. Let's say you have $450,000 worth of property, but only $225,000 is stated on the farm policy—a proportion of 50 percent. Thus, on the loss of the $75,000 tractor, you will receive only 50 percent, or $37,500.

If I had to pick the biggest pitfall regarding insurance coverage for a farmer, this would be it! To save some premium, you don't have to insure for 100 percent of the value of your machinery, but you should insure for at least 80 percent.

Sit down with your agent and go over your blanket coverage. Make sure you understand it, so that if a loss occurs you will be happy with the settlement. Insurance companies have inventory forms to fill out that establish the value of your blanket. It's worth it to take the time and do a thorough job.

Normally, blanket policies have a minimum amount of $20,000 coverage, so if you have farm personal property valued at less than that, you would probably have to schedule the items.

Schedule

Sometimes, but not very often, the insured selects scheduled instead of blanket coverage. "Scheduling" is when the insured lists and describes each specific item to be covered—including make, model, year, and the specific dollar amount to apply to each item.

This works out well if the farm is a small operation and there just isn't enough property to allow for blanket coverage. Costs vary, but scheduling farm machinery should average $4 to $6 per $1,000 of coverage.

WHAT COVERAGES ARE PROVIDED UNDER THE BLANKET?

The following perils are covered:

- Fire or lightning
- Windstorm or hail
- Explosion
- Riot or civil commotion
- Aircraft
- Vehicles
- Smoke
- Electrocution

In addition to these, the most important coverages to consider are theft, vandalism, and malicious mischief; overturn or collision; and additional livestock perils.

Theft, Vandalism, and Malicious Mischief

The possibility that someone will get on your tractor and ride into the sunset with it is rather remote, but things can happen to the smaller items you insure under the blanket. If someone gets into your quonset that is several miles away from the main buildings and steals all of your tools, you're out of luck without this endorsement.

Overturn or Collision

This is good coverage if you farm hilly ground, on which there is a risk of overturn, or have to transport tractors and combines from one field to another on public roads, so that there is a risk of collision. Any damages you sustain in such accidents will only be covered if you have the overturn or collision endorsement.

IMPORTANT NOTE: The collision coverage will only protect for damage to tires if the damage occurs at the same time as the overturn or collision. Curiously enough, if you strike a large rock while combining and it causes your machine to overturn, the damage isn't covered! In order to get this further protection, you can endorse an "all-risks" option to the machinery for an added premium.

Additional Livestock Perils

This option covers livestock such as cattle, horses, mules, and swine over 30 days old against loss due to drownings, attack by dogs or wild animals, collapse of buildings, and accidental shootings.

> **EXAMPLE:**
>
> Thirty head of cattle belonging to one of my clients drifted aimlessly during a blizzard and ended up on one of the property's ponds. The ice broke and several of the animals drowned. We paid for the loss the client sustained because he had this coverage.

OTHER QUESTIONS REGARDING FARM PERSONAL PROPERTY

How Do I Cover Communication Devices?

Most farmers have citizens-band radios in their trucks to communicate with the home base back at the farmhouse. CBs are a prime target for theft. Most farm policies require that CBs be scheduled on the policy rather than covering them automatically.

Premiums vary from company to company, but an average price is $36 per $1,000 of coverage. If you have $5,000 worth of equipment, the annual premium would run $180.

How Do I Cover My Irrigation Equipment?

If you have either an irrigation pipe or a pivot irrigation system, you should know that some policies include your irrigation equipment under the blanket, while other companies require you to schedule it. It is to your advantage to have it included in the blanket because of the cost savings. Scheduling the equipment could be twice as expensive as paying under the blanket. Make sure you have it completely covered one way or the other, however.

If I Borrow My Neighbor's Combine, Am I Covered?

What happens if you're driving your neighbor's combine and you slip off the road into a ditch? Any farmer will tell you this can be a major problem!

Before you make the arrangements to use a neighbor's equipment, call your agent and ask what you need to do to cover yourself. The agent will tell you either you're covered or you need to get an endorsement for "borrowed machinery." In the insurance business, it's always better to be safe than sorry.

If My Hogs Smother or Freeze to Death, Are They Covered?

Two of the more common causes of death in livestock—freezing and smothering—are not automatically covered with most blanket policies. If you have livestock and you live in an area of the country that gets quite cold, you should definitely check your coverage regarding these possibilities.

You also have to be careful in knowing what the endorsement covers. In many cases, it only covers the livestock for freezing and smothering in blizzards, and not, for example, if a sow rolls over on top of her piglets. Also check whether losses are covered outside *and* inside farm buildings. Freezing and smothering inside buildings usually are not covered.

You can get the endorsement for $1 to $2 per $1,000 of coverage, with no deductibles taken in case of a loss.

Are the Windows on My Tractor and Combine Covered for Glass Breakage?

Some farm policies include what is referred to as "farm equipment glass" in the blanket, while others require you to add an endorsement. This would be a question to ask your agent.

WHAT IS CROP-HAIL INSURANCE?

The first crop policy was issued more than a century ago, with hail as its basic peril. Currently, it is available in all states and is sold by private insurance companies with competition from the Federal Crop Insurance Corporation, an agency of the U.S. Department of Agriculture. It is completely separate from the farmowner's policy. Although it can be sold by your existing agent, the company he or she places the business with specializes in writing crop-hail insurance.

A number of crop-hail policies are available, each with its own set of coverages and exclusions. While the Crop-Hail Association has produced a simplified standard policy, coverages vary from state to state and are tailored to take into account differences in climate and other environmental factors.

What these policies have in common is that the coverage becomes effective once the crop is above the ground, and it expires when the crop is harvested. Also, the limits of coverage are expressed in terms of acreage rather than in total value of the crop.

Until 1980, private insurers protected only against the perils of fire, lightning, hail, and wind (if accompanied by hail that destroys at least 5 percent of the crop). The federal government, however, offered broader coverage on a limited geographical basis. The broad policy, in effect, protects crops against such additional perils as insects, excessive moisture, drought, and other perils not specifically excluded.

WHAT COVERAGES ARE THERE FOR OUTBUILDINGS?

In contrast with a homeowners policy, all outbuildings or structures not attached to the dwelling must be scheduled for coverage. Normally each outbuilding or structure will be classified individually. The following are considered to be outbuildings: grain bins, swimming pools, barns, milk houses, quonsets, granary or feed-handling buildings, shop and machinery storage buildings, farrowing houses, hog confinement barns, silos, corncribs and hay sheds, grain-handling complexes, and garages.

The covered perils on outbuildings are as follows:

- Fire or lightning
- Windstorm or hail
- Explosion
- Riot or civil commotion
- Aircraft
- Vehicle
- Smoke
- Vandalism and malicious mischief
- Theft

Make sure you understand that the outbuildings you have on your farmstead are in most cases insured as a separate part of your policy. That coverage has nothing to do with the house you live in. Another point to remember is that it covers the structure only, not the contents. The contents are covered under the blanket or scheduled part of the policy for farm personal property.

WHAT LIABILITY AND MEDICAL COVERAGES DO I HAVE?

Liability and medical-expense coverage are perhaps the most important aspects of insurance protection, no matter what the specific type of insurance, if *you* could be held liable for anyone else's injury or property damage. (Obviously, it doesn't apply to health insurance for you and your family or to life insurance.)

Liability applies in cases of bodily injury or property damage on or off your premises, *if your negligence caused the problem*. **Medical-expense coverage** generally applies to injuries sustained by others on your premises *regardless* of negligence.

WHAT IS MY LIABILITY PROTECTION?

This is critical coverage for the farmer to have. If you are negligent and someone either is injured on your land or has his or her property ruined, you can be sued for thousands of dollars. You can even lose your farm if you're not covered.

> **EXAMPLE:**
>
> One windy Saturday morning several years ago, a client of mine was burning corn stubble. As a safety precaution, he plowed a firebreak around the stubble patch. Several hours later a big gust of wind caused the fire to jump completely over the plowed ground. Before the farmer knew it, the fire had burned up his neighbor's (Neighbor A's) fence and started on Neighbor A's pivot irrigation system, which was valued at $40,000. Luckily, only a couple of the pivot's tires were damaged.
>
> Later, my insured learned that the fire totally destroyed another neighbor's alfalfa field. Because Neighbor B relied on the alfalfa to feed his cattle, he would be forced to buy feed, which would be very expensive.
>
> My client was covered, and we paid for the damaged pivot tires, the fence, and the monetary loss sustained by Neighbor B—a total of about $15,000. Where would a young farmer come up with that amount of money on his own?

Make sure you have an adequate liability limit—minimally $100,000, and better, to $1,000,000, on your policy. If it's less than $100,000, you might want to call your agent and find out the cost to increase it. Most people are surprised at how inexpensive the increase turns out to be. Premiums vary, but going from

$100,000 liability to $1,000,000 can cost as little as 1 percent or less of the entire policy premium.

Do I Need to Tell My Agent all of the Land I Own or Rent?

You better believe it! Tell your agent *all* of the land you own, and double-check the legal descriptions for accuracy.

Why is this so important? If someone is injured on a piece of your land, but that ground is not specifically listed on the policy, you could find yourself unprotected. The insurance company will not pay for a loss that happened on ground they didn't insure in the first place.

By the same token, if you own land, but you don't have any buildings or machinery on it, you need only a straight liability policy. The cost is based on the number of acres owned. One large farm insurer quotes a price of $.65 an acre for $300,000 liability coverage.

What About Doing Custom Work for Neighbors?

Custom work is defined as "farming operations performed by the insured for others for a fee." Many policies exclude operations you might perform while working for your neighbor. These exclusions include the following:

- Blasting
- Ditching or trenching
- Excavating
- Logging
- Weed spraying
- Wood sawing
- Insecticide application, including spraying and fogging
- Anhydrous ammonia application and related operations

EXAMPLE:

One of my clients was applying fertilizer to his neighbor's field for a fee. The plastic sprayer tank, with a gasoline pump and several cardboard boxes that held the containers of fertilizer, were in my insured's truck. The pump got hot and set fire to the cardboard boxes causing the whole truck to go up in flames. The fertilizer eventually made its way onto the open ground, polluting the soil.

Since applying fertilizer is excluded from the liability coverages, we didn't pay for any of the damages—not for the fertilizer that the neighbor had purchased for my insured to apply, and not for the cleanup of the ground. We didn't pay for the insured's truck either because he didn't have comprehensive coverage on his vehicle insurance.

You can add an endorsement for custom work. Normally, the premium is figured on how much money you receive for doing the work. One company figures that, starting at $1,000, for every $500 you make working for someone, you pay an additional $8 a year in premium. Thus, if you made $2,000 plowing your neighbor's field, it would cost an extra $24 in premium to protect your liability exposure ($8 × the three extra $500 sums). Make sure you review your policy at least once a year with your agent in order to keep current on your coverage.

What If a Friend Rides One of My Horses, Falls Off, and Is Severely Injured?

You would have coverage under the liability limits of your policy as long as all the horses you own are listed—that is, as long as your insurance company knows you have the horses in the first place. If you only allow your immediate family to ride the horses, there is no extra charge, but if you allow other people to ride, the insurance company will ask for extra premium because of the added risk involved with riding horses.

The cost is normally figured per horse, donkey, mule, or pony. This additional liability coverage averages $7 to $10 a year per animal.

If you train or rent horses or run a stud service, you should ask your agent how your farm policy would cover these activities, if at all.

WHAT MEDICAL-EXPENSE COVERAGE IS THERE ON A FARM POLICY?

As with the homeowner's policy, this coverage pays medical expenses to people who are injured on your property. You *do not* have to be considered negligent for it to pay. Normal limits on a policy are from $500 to $1,000, which are generally adequate.

You should be aware that there is an optional medical coverage that is called "medical insurance to the named insured." This allows you to cover yourself, your spouse and children, and any hired help for a stated amount of insurance limit, normally between $500 and $1,000, if they are injured in a farm-related activity.

Farmers are in the top five professions for suffering work-related accidents. A farm is a high-risk environment because of the machinery being used, so that having some extra coverage in this area is well worth the cost.

Remember that it has to be a farm-related injury before the company pays! If you cut yourself on barbed wire or fall off the tractor, you'll have coverage. If you have a heart attack, get cancer, or break your leg in a car accident, this coverage doesn't apply.

I recommend this coverage even if you have health insurance because it could eliminate the deductible that most certainly will be charged by your health insurance carrier in case of an accident.

EXAMPLE:

The normal limits you can apply for under this coverage range from $500 to $5,000. Assume that you have a $1,000 deductible and a straight 80/20 coinsurance clause on your regular health policy. On a $10,000 bill, therefore, you would have to pay the first $3,000 ($1,000 deductible plus 20 percent × $10,000, or $2,000 for the coinsurance). (See Chapter 3 for more about coinsurance.) By having the maximum coverage under medical insurance to the named insured on your farm policy, you would be reimbursed the $3,000 that is not paid by your regular health policy, so you would have 100 percent coverage!

Again, the accident has to be farm-related. An average cost is $20 per person for $500 coverage and $42 per person for $5,000 coverage. In cases like this, I feel the premium is justified.

HOW CAN I CUT PREMIUM COSTS?

The average cost for a complete farm policy, obtained from a leading farm policy writer, ranged from a low of $429 in Illinois to a high of $791 in Wisconsin. In most farm states, the rate was between $500 and $600.

FACTORS THAT AFFECT THE PREMIUM

Some companies offer credits if it's evident that you take excellent care of your farm—that is, if the buildings aren't in need of major repairs or paint and if the general housekeeping is above average. It does pay to take care of your buildings. I have seen discounts of as much as 20 percent to 25 percent depending upon the following factors:

- Premises and operations—This takes in housekeeping, maintenance of buildings and equipment, and condition and adequacy of fences. What is the overall estimation of the risk?

- Location—What is the proximity to neighbors, proximity and quality of the primary responding fire department? How are road conditions? What is the exposure to wind damage?
- Building features—What is the condition and maintenance of buildings; condition and adequacy of wiring and heating?
- Farm personal property—Is there proper storage for equipment and hazardous materials? What is the age, condition, and maintenance of machinery? Are safety guards in their proper place on all machinery, and are there fire extinguishers on highly valued machinery?
- Large-loss potential—Takes in distribution of the property to minimize a major loss. How close are buildings to each other and how likely is it that a fire would destroy all of them at one time?
- Fire protection—Are there smoke-alarm and fire-alarm systems in major buildings? Is there fire-fighting equipment on hand? Are there "No Smoking" signs?
- Management—What is management's loss experience, number of years in farming/ranching, indebtedness, attitude toward safety, and cooperation in completing forms? What type of overall operation is it (profitable or unprofitable)?

These categories are used to rate the risk so that the company can determine how many credits to allow. Reducing your risk in these areas can be an excellent way to drop your premium!

SHOPPING TIPS

To cut premiums, try the following:

- Shop around. Prices vary between companies, so check them out.
- Shop within the same company. The parent company may lower its rates while your agent automatically renews you at the old rate, so compare rates every few years. If there's only a 5 percent difference and you're happy with the service, there's probably no reason to switch. But if there is a 20 percent difference between companies, check it out.

- Buy all your policies from one agent or company. Many companies that write auto and farm owner's policies offer a discount of 5 percent to 20 percent if you agree to keep all of your business with them.
- Get a high deductible. All companies offer discounts for deductibles higher than the basic $250. You usually can get a 10 percent discount for selecting a $500 deductible, a 15 percent discount for a $1,000 deductible, and a 25 percent discount for a $2,500 deductible (if available).

FARM INSURANCE CHECKLIST

If you own a farm or a ranch, look at your insurance policy.

Dwelling and Personal Property

☐ Check what type of farm policy you have. Is it a basic form 1, a broad form 2, or a comprehensive form 3?

☐ Is there enough insurance on the house itself?

☐ Do you have enough coverage on your personal property within the house, such as furniture, appliances, clothing, and carpeting?

☐ Will you be assured of receiving a new item at today's prices in case of a loss, or will the company deduct for depreciation before paying the claim?

☐ Do you have any expensive extra items or collections, such as guns, jewelry, art, dish antennas, or computers that need to be endorsed?

☐ Are there any endorsements you should know about that you don't have right now?

Farm Personal Property and Outbuildings

☐ Do you have a "scheduled" or a "blanket" policy?

☐ If it's a scheduled policy, are all the items you want covered listed on the policy?

☐ If it's a blanket policy, is the total coverage up to date and accurate?

☐ Are there any endorsements you need to be concerned with that deal with this part of the policy?

☐ Are all the buildings you want insured listed on the policy at the right limits of insurance?

☐ Have you asked for any credits the company may be able to give?

Liability

☐ Do you have all the land you own listed on the policy and are the legal descriptions correct?

☐ Do you need to raise or lower the amount of coverage?

☐ Do you have horses or mules that need to be endorsed to the policy?

☐ Are you interested in having medical coverage for you or members of your family in case of an accident directly related to farm activities?

CHAPTER SEVEN

When I'm 65:
Medicare Supplement Insurance

THE LIMITATIONS OF MEDICARE

When President Lyndon Johnson signed the Medicare Act in the summer of 1965, he promised that older Americans would never be denied "the healing miracle of modern medicine," nor would "illness crush and destroy the savings they had so carefully put away."

For the last quarter of the century the federal government has struggled to keep that promise, spending ever-increasing sums to subsidize health care for people 65 and older. The government spent only $3.1 billion on Medicare in 1967, the first full year that benefits were paid; by 1988 the bill came to nearly $86 billion.

In the last five years, Medicare's costs for doctors alone have doubled, growing 40 percent faster than the economy as a whole. To add insult to injury, physicians may charge patients more than Medicare's allowable fees, up to certain government-regulated percentages that are being phased in over the next several years.

About a quarter of all Medicare claims involve some excess charges, and these charges continue to mount. In 1975, excess charges cost Medicare beneficiaries $500 million. By 1987, the cost had risen to $2.7 billion. This excess in physicians' fees today represents one of the biggest gaps in Medicare coverage—coverage that was not designed to pay for everything.

Medicare beneficiaries also pay deductibles and copayments.

Knowing how these work is the key to understanding coverage under Medicare—and the key to choosing a supplement insurance policy, known as medigap, that takes up Medicare's slack.

THE APPEAL OF MEDIGAP

The less money you have, the more appealing medigap insurance may look, especially if you expect to be faced with high out-of-pocket medical costs. There is a danger here. You may already be covered for much of what these high-cost policies provide.

The medigap market suffers from an image problem because of the charge that some medigap policies are overpriced, with duplicate coverage being sold to the unwary by means of scare tactics and high pressure. There is no doubt that unscrupulous insurance agents take advantage of the elderly every day in this country when dealing in the medigap market. According to Price Waterhouse actuary Ron Becker, "There are a lot of unnecessary extras on some medigap policies." However, true medigap policies *cannot* duplicate Medicare coverage.

This chapter is intended to give you enough information to make intelligent and sound economic decisions when looking for a good medigap policy.

HOW MEDICARE WORKS

Medicare is divided into two parts—hospital insurance (Part A), and physician and other provider services (Part B). Medicare does not pay the entire cost for all services covered by the program. You and your insurance company must pay certain **deductibles** and **copayments**. A "deductible" is an initial dollar amount that Medicare does not pay. A "copayment" is your share of expenses for covered services after you have paid the deductible.

Besides having deductibles and copayments, another coverage gap is created by Medicare's establishment of allowable limits in cost for the various services included under its purview.

TWO IMPORTANT TERMS: APPROVED AMOUNT AND ASSIGNMENT

What Does "Approved Amount" Mean?

Medicare each year reviews the usual charges of doctors or suppliers for each covered service and the charges of other doctors and suppliers in the area for the same service to decide on an **approved amount**. The amount approved in payment for a claim is often lower than the actual charge made by the doctor or supplier.

Medicare gives doctors the option of accepting the allowable charge as payment in full or requiring the patient to pay the difference between the allowable and the actual charge. That gap is the excess charge.

Many doctors bill excess charges. According to a June 1989 article in a leading consumer magazine, such charges averaged 37 percent more than Medicare's allowable charge in late 1988.

Even if you have Medicare supplement insurance, you might not get 100 percent coverage for your Part B bills, because not all medigap policies pay excess charges.

EXAMPLE:

Suppose your doctor charges $4,000 for an operation, but the amount Medicare has approved for that operation is $3,000. Assuming you have already met the annual $75 Part B deductible, Medicare would pay 80 percent of the $3,000 approved amount, or $2,400. Many supplement insurance policies will pay your 20 percent share of the $3,000 approved amount, or $600, but not the excess charge. That would leave a balance of $1,000 that you would have to pay out of your own pocket.

What Does "Assignment" Mean?

You can avoid having to pay more than the Medicare-approved amount by using doctors and medical suppliers who accept **assignment**. "Assignment" means that the doctor or supplier accepts Medicare's approved amount as full payment and cannot legally bill you for anything above that amount. All physicians and qualified laboratories *must* accept assignment for covered clinical diagnostic laboratory tests.

Only about one-third of all doctors accept assignment regularly. The rest may accept assignment only when they believe a patient cannot pay the extra charges. In effect, the doctors are free to provide their own tests to patients, accepting the allowable fee for some and billing others at a higher rate.

Whether your doctor accepts assignment depends in part on where you live, the doctor's specialty, and your age. Massachusetts requires all medical doctors to accept the Medicare allowable charge as payment in full. Wyoming doesn't have this requirement, and in that state only 18 percent of physicians accept assignment.

Psychiatrists and nephrologists are more likely to accept assignment than anesthesiologists, surgeons, and general practitioners. Doctors are also more likely to take assignments from patients closer to 85 than from those who are 65.

How Do I Find Doctors Who Will Accept Assignment?

Because you can't tell in advance whether the approved amount and the actual charge for covered services and supplies will be the same, always ask your doctors or medical suppliers, such as laboratories and therapists, if they accept assignment of Medicare benefits.

You can also consult a directory. Some doctors and suppliers have agreed to participate in Medicare and accept assignment on all Medicare claims. Their names and addresses are listed in The Medicare Participating Physician/Supplier Directory that is distributed to senior-citizen organizations, all local Social Security and Railroad Retirement offices, all hospitals, and all state and area offices of the Administration on Aging.

WHAT EXPENSES ARE NOT COVERED BY MEDICARE?

In addition to the gaps left by deductibles, copayments, and excess physicians' charges, there are also services and supplies not covered by Medicare. Among them are the following:

- Private room in a hospital
- Private-duty nursing
- Skilled nursing-home care beyond 100 days per benefit period
- Custodial nursing-home care
- Intermediate nursing-home care
- Most outpatient prescription drugs
- Care received outside the United States, except under limited circumstances in Canada and Mexico
- Dental care or dentures, checkups, most routine immunizations, cosmetic surgery, routine foot care, eye examinations and the cost of eyeglasses or hearing aids
- Any services that Medicare does not consider medically necessary

WHAT DO MEDICARE SUPPLEMENT POLICIES COVER?

Medicare supplement, or medigap, policies fill in at least some of the gaps created by Medicare's deductibles and limits. Because these gaps leave you with responsibility for a portion of your medical costs, you may want to purchase such a supplement policy.

Some policies pay only for items allowed by Medicare; others pay for out-of-hospital prescription drugs, medical appliances, and equipment. They may also pay for hospital days beyond the Medicare limit and cover the copayments for a long stay in a nursing home.

The supplement policy is split into two areas, Medicare Part A and Medicare Part B, just like the Medicare coverage itself. For the various allowances and benefits under each part, we'll look at where Medicare stops and what medigap picks up.

MEDICARE PART A: HOSPITAL COVERAGE, SERVICES, AND SUPPLIES
Hospitalization
Medicare coverage pays for medically necessary inpatient care in a hospital, consisting of a semiprivate room and board, general nursing care, and miscellaneous hospital services and supplies. The benefits include special-care units, drugs, laboratory tests, diagnostic X-rays, medical supplies, operating- and recovery-room time, and anesthesia and rehabilitation services.

Medicare measures the services it covers according to a benefit period, which begins when you are hospitalized and ends after you have been out of the hospital or other approved facility for 60 days in a row. If you go into the hospital again, you start another benefit period, and all Part A benefits are renewed. There is no limit on how many benefit periods you can have, with the exception of hospice care—the limit on that is 210 days a year.

Effective January 1, 1990, Medicare pays the following:

- First 60 days—all but $592
- 61st to 90th day—all but $148 a day
- 91st to 150th day—all but $296, plus a 60-day, once-in-a-lifetime reserve at $296 per day
- Beyond 150th day—nothing

Good Medicare supplement policies will pay the $592, the $148 per day, and the $296 per day that Medicare does not pay. Most Medicare supplement policies will not pay after the 150th day. (See Table 7.1.)

Blood
Medicare pays all costs except nonreplacement fees (blood deductible) for the first three pints of blood for each benefit period.

Table 7.1   Typical Medigap Policy

SERVICE	BENEFIT	MEDICARE PAYS	THIS POLICY PAYS	YOU PAY CHARGES NOT EL-IGIBLE UNDER MEDICARE &
HOSPITALIZATION . . . Semiprivate room and board, general nursing and miscellaneous hospital services and supplies.	First 60 days	All but $592.00	☐ The $592 Deductible OR ☐ Nothing	The deductible, if any.
Includes meals, special care units, drugs, lab tests, diagnostic X-rays, medical supplies, operating and recovery room, anesthesia and rehabilitation services.	61st to 90th day	All but $148.00 a Day	$148.00 a Day	NONE
	91st to 150th day	All but $296.00 a Day	$296.00 a Day	NONE
	Beyond 150 days	Nothing	All Eligible Expenses* for an additional 365 day lifetime maximum.	All charges after the 365 days lifetime maximum.
POSTHOSPITAL SKILLED NURSING CARE . . . In a facility approved by, Medicare. You must have been in a hospital for at least three days and enter the facility within 30 days after hospital discharge.	First 20 days	100% of costs	No Coverage	NONE
	Additional 80 days	All but $74.00 a Day	$74.00 a Day	NONE
	Beyond 100 days	Nothing	Nothing	Expenses incurred beyond 100 days.
MEDICAL EXPENSE	Physician's services, inpatient and outpatient medical services and supplies at a hospital; physical and speech therapy; and ambulance	80% of reasonable charge (After $75.00 deductible)	20% of Eligible Expenses* after a deductible of ☐ $75 (for Outpatient care only) OR ☐ $200 (for Both Out-patient and Inpatient care)	The calendar year deductible, if any as well as any charges for which benefits are not provided by this policy.

These figures are for 1990 and are subject to change each year. The policy benefits change when Medicare benefits change.

The chart summarizing Medicare benefits only briefly described such benefits. For additional details or limitations of Medicare, contact the Health Care Financing Administration or its Medicare Publications.

VALUABLE BENEFITS

Medicare does not pay for the first 3 pints of blood under Part A or Part B. This policy pays for the first 3 pints of blood.

The total policy benefits payable by us is $250,000 per lifetime.

*Eligible expense is a health care expense determined to be eligible for benefits by Medicare. Any expenses or portion of expenses that Medicare considers unreasonable or unnecessary or in excess of customary or prevailing charges is not an eligible expense.

EXCLUSIONS

No benefits are provided for:

1. Eligible expenses incurred while your policy is not in force.
2. Any expenses or portion of expense that Medicare considers unreasonable or unnecessary.
3. Any expense or portion of expense not covered by Medicare except as noted in the benefits section of this policy.
4. Outpatient treatment for mental illness.
5. Private duty nursing.
6. Custodial or intermediate nursing care.
7. Self-administered drugs or biologicals.
8. Care received outside the U.S.A. unless charges are approved by Medicare or OPTIONAL COVERAGE is purchased.
9. Charges for the care, treatment, filling, removal, or replacement of teeth or structures directly supporting the teeth.
10. Expenses for routine physical examinations and directly related tests, eye glasses or eye examinations for the purpose of prescribing, fitting or changing eye glasses, or hearing aids.
11. Charges for cosmetic surgery, except if required for the prompt repair of accidental injury or for the improvement of the functioning of a malformed part of the body.
12. Charges for routine foot care, orthopedic shoes or supportive devices of the feet.
13. Charges which neither you nor another party on your behalf has a legal obligation to pay.
14. Charge paid directly or indirectly by any governmental agency.
15. War or any act of war.
16. Personal comfort items.
17. People under age 65 or if you're over 65 and not eligible for or covered by Medicare Part A and Part B.
18. The extent that payment has been made, or can reasonably be expected to be made, under a worker's compensation law or plan of the United States or a state.
19. Charges imposed by your immediate relatives or members of your household.
20. Home health care above the number of visits covered by Medicare.
21. Skilled nursing home care costs and intermediate nursing homecare costs, (beyond what is covered by Medicare).

(continued)

Table 7.1 *(continued)*

WAITING PERIOD FOR PREEXISTING CONDITIONS

An injury or sickness you had before the Policy Effective Date is not covered until your policy has been in force for six months. This applies to any injury or sickness for which medical advice was given or treatment was recommended by or received from a physician within six months before the Policy Effective Date. You are not eligible for benefits resulting from any such injury or sickness unless the medical expense is incurred more than six months after the Policy Effective Date.

We will not consider taking prescribed medication as receiving treatment from a physician UNLESS medical advice regarding the prescription or the treated condition was given by a physician within the six month period before the Policy Effective Date.

RENEWAL TERMS - RENEWAL MAY BE REFUSED AS STATED BELOW

You have the right to keep the policy in force during your lifetime by the payment in advance or during the grace period of the premium rate then in effect, subject to our right to refuse renewal as stated below.

We may refuse to renew your policy if we refuse to renew all policies issued on this form in your state where you live.

OPTIONAL COVERAGE (Check if applied for)

☐ Foreign Travel Medical Emergency Treatment Coverage – We'll pay 80% of those services and supplies that Medicare would have covered in the U.S.A. up to a maximum of $2,500 for each medical emergency. A medical emergency is an acute condition occurring more than 60 days after the effective date of this coverage for a sickness or injury occurring spontaneously and unexpectedly and demanding immediate attention.

PREMIUMS

As you get older, your renewal premium will increase periodically. Premiums may also change because of changes in policy benefits resulting from changes in Medicare. Your renewal premium may also be changed if we change the premium for all policies of this form and class in the state where you live.

Premium (at the time of application)

$ _____ Annual; $ _____ Semi–Annual;

$ _____ Quarterly; $ _____ AmPlan*

*Does not include the additional AmPlan monthly premium charge.

Your Medicare supplement policy would pay for the first three pints of blood.

Skilled-Nursing-Facility Care

Medicare imposes strict eligibility requirements for skilled-nursing benefits. Skilled-nursing care is defined as daily nursing and rehabilitative care that can be performed only by, or under the supervision of, skilled medical personnel. Care must be based on doctor's orders. Care must be provided in a Medicare-approved facility (a nursing home that is licensed by the state or certified by Medicare or medicaid to provide skilled care; it may also provide intermediate and custodial care), and a doctor must certify that such care is needed daily.

During a benefit period, Part A can help pay for up to 100 days of extended care services in a skilled nursing facility. *All* approved amounts for the first 20 days of care are fully paid by Medicare (after a consecutive three-day hospital confinement— not counting the discharge day). The next 80 days require a daily copayment of $74 (the 1990 amount), which is the patient's responsibility.

The typical Medicare supplement policy picks up the $74-a-day copayment for the 21st to the 100th day, but it does not pay any charges beyond the 100th day.

Home-Health Care

There are also strict eligibility rules for home-health benefits. Part A pays the cost of medically necessary intermittent home visits up to three weeks per illness, five days per week. Coverage includes the intermittent services of a skilled nurse and the services of physical and speech therapists when furnished through a Medicare-certified home-health agency.

If you are confined to your home and are under the care of a physician, Part A can also cover reasonable and necessary part-time home-health and skilled-nursing services, occupational therapy, medical social services, medical supplies, and a portion of the cost of durable medical equipment.

Part A does not cover full-time nursing care, drugs, meals delivered to your home, or homemaker services. **Home-health-care services are covered under most medigap policies. Medicare pays 80 percent of the eligible reasonable charges after a $75 deductible; the medigap policy pays the other 20 percent of the charges.**

Hospice Care

For terminally ill patients who choose care in a Medicare-certified hospice program, Medicare pays all expenses for nursing and doctor services, supplies, appliances, social services, counseling, home-health and homemaker services. It also pays for pain-relief drugs, but the patient must pay either 5 percent of the cost or $5.

Part A will pay for hospice care for two 90-day benefit periods and one 30-day period, for a total of 210 days of care. **Most Medicare supplement policies do not pay for hospice coverage.**

MEDICARE PART B: MEDICAL SERVICES AND SUPPLIES

Medicare Part B helps pay for physicians' services and various other medical services and supplies. You are automatically enrolled in Part B when you enroll in Part A unless you state that you don't want it.

You do not have to purchase Part B, but it is an excellent buy because the federal government pays about 75 percent of the actual cost. If you don't have Part B coverage and you want it, you may enroll during the general enrollment period from January 1 through March 31 each year.

If you are covered under your own or your spouse's employer group-health plan, you may enroll in Part B when the employment on which this coverage is based comes to an end, or when the plan is terminated, whichever occurs first.

When you use your Part B benefits, you will be required to pay the first $75 (the annual deductible) of charges approved by Medicare. After that, Medicare Part B generally pays 80 percent and you pay 20 percent of the approved amount for covered services you receive for the rest of the year.

Doctors' Services

Part B covers physicians' and surgeons' services whether you receive them at home, in the doctor's office, or in a clinic or hospital—that is, both inpatient and outpatient treatment. Services include anesthesia, radiology, pathology, surgery, psychiatry, some podiatric treatment, second-opinion consultations, and dental care if it involves jaw surgery or setting a broken jaw or facial bones. (Routine physical exams are not covered.)

Psychiatric services require a special note. In 1989, the limit on total, lifetime, inpatient psychiatric hospital days was raised to 190. Outpatient psychiatric services are covered by Medicare also, but only to a total of $1,100 per year.

In addition to the 20 percent coinsurance, beneficiaries are responsible for any excess charges. As for these charges, doctors are paid in a way that is confusing to beneficiaries and costly to the program. Here's how Medicare determines allowable charges for most Part B claims:

The insurance companies that process claims for Medicare compare each bill submitted by a doctor with the doctor's customary charge for that particular service. The lowest of three such fees becomes the allowable charge on which Medicare bases its payment. Allowable charges for the same service may be different for each beneficiary, depending on the doctor's location and his or her billing practice.

Figuring the doctor's customary charge and the prevailing charge (the common charge for that market) is a mind-boggling exercise. For example, Empire Blue Cross and Blue Shield processes about 25 million pieces of information in its computers to determine allowable charges for doctors in 16 counties of New York.

While supplement policies vary as to payment of excess charges, most medigap policies pay at least the 20 percent not covered by Medicare on reasonable charges for physicians' services. (See Table 7.1.)

Prescription Drugs

Medicare pays for inpatient prescription drugs. Prescription drugs are also furnished for hospice enrollees; Medicare pays 80 percent for immunosuppressives provided during the first year after an organ transplant.

The Medicare supplement policy will pay the other 20 percent in the case of an organ transplant.

Other Medical Services and Supplies

Medicare pays for outpatient hospital services, X-rays and laboratory tests, certain ambulance services, and the purchase or rental of durable medical equipment, such as wheelchairs. Medicare pays 100 percent of the allowable charge for clinical diagnostic tests performed in independent labs certified by Medicare. If you have tests done in a noncertified lab, you'll have to pay for them yourself.

Most medigap policies try to pay what Medicare does not. In this case, Medicare pays 80 percent of the reasonable charges after a $75 deductible is taken. Most medigap policies pay the other 20 percent of eligible expenses in this area.

DO I NEED PRIVATE HEALTH INSURANCE IN ADDITION TO MEDICARE?

If you are a Medicare beneficiary enrolled in a prepayment plan such as a health maintenance organization (HMO), or a competitive medical plan (CMP), which has a contract with Medicare, you may not need a Medicare supplement policy.

Low-income people who are eligible for medicaid don't need a Medicare supplement policy; medicaid pays the bills. Limited financial assistance is available through medicaid for paying a share of acute care costs for certain low-income elderly and disabled Medicare beneficiaries.

If your annual income is below the national poverty level and you do not have access to many financial resources, you may qualify for some government assistance in paying Medicare monthly premiums and the Medicare deductibles and copayments. In 1989, the national poverty level was $5,890 for an individual and

$8,020 for a married couple. If you think you qualify, contact your state or local social-service agency.

Whether you need health insurance to supplement Medicare is a matter you will want to discuss with someone who understands both insurance and your financial situation. The best time to do this is *before* you reach 65.

HOW DO THE AVAILABLE POLICIES COMPARE?

A leading consumer magazine (*Consumer Reports*, June 1989) rated the best medigap policies as of spring 1989. They asked 53 major companies to send information about their policies written to supplement Medicare. Twenty-five companies, representing 80 percent of the market, responded and sent their most popular plans.

Since coverage for excess charges is so important, the magazine also rated special excess-coverage policies available from AARP (American Association of Retired Persons), Mutual of Omaha, and Blue Cross and Blue Shield of Florida, even though they might not be heavily sold.

The magazine determined a number of features that a good policy should have and assigned points to each, giving the most weight to how well the plans filled the Part A and Part B gaps.

They judged whether policies had too many exclusions and limitations, whether they were renewable for life, and whether their preexisting-conditions clauses were particularly bad. They also noted rejection rates, lapse rates, the clarity of the policy language, and any major state reinforcement actions against companies.

The plans in the top ratings group all offer excellent coverage. The 10 top-rated companies in the survey are Bankers Life and Casualty; Pioneer Life; Standard Life and Accident; Golden Rule; Prudential, AARP (the Comprehensive Medicare Supplement, not the Supplement Plus policy, which is much cheaper); Pyramid Life; Colonial Penn; First National Life; National Home Life; and Equitable Life and Casualty.

The medigap policies of these companies provide generous benefits for excess physicians' charges, leaving between $75 and $775 of expenses uncovered for the sample claim that was used. The eighth-ranked policy, sold by First National Life, offers the best coverage for excess physicians' charges.

Policies lower in the ratings offer less generous basic coverage and tend to be more restrictive once a policy is issued. Many don't pay the $75 Part B deductible.

The policies from Golden Rule (fourth-ranked) and National Home Life (ninth-ranked) merited "Best Buy" ratings, offering policyholders excellent coverage at an attractive price. Golden Rule keeps its price down in several ways. First, it does not pay its agents high commissions to sell the policies (a good idea). Less desirable from the consumer's point of view is its practice of selling only to healthy people. Golden Rule may simply refuse to sell you a policy if it suspects you are in poor health, and it won't promise to renew your policy even if it accepts you as a customer.

While AARP's best-selling regular Medicare Supplement Plus policy got only a mediocre rating, the same cannot be said for its excess-charges policy, the Comprehensive Medicare Supplement. This plan offers benefits for excess physicians' charges that are as generous as the first-ranked Bankers Life and Casualty policy. But its $110.50 monthly premium makes it the highest-priced policy in the survey. No wonder only 3 percent of AARP's members have bought it. Perhaps AARP's Supplement Plus was the best-selling policy in part because its monthly premium at the time of the survey was only $48.60, one of the lowest. This policy does not pay excess medical charges or the Part B deductible. However, it is fairly liberal in its exclusions and limitations.

Many companies don't require a physical examination or a doctor's statement before issuing the coverage. In fact, about half of the companies in the survey, mostly Blue Cross organizations and AARP, take all comers, no questions asked. They also charge everyone the same rate. Their best-selling policies didn't provide the coverage the magazine felt was the most important, however. A policy that's readily available and cheap is no bargain if it doesn't also cover the most important risks.

Many buyers have few choices other than the local Blue Cross plan, since the best plans are not universally available. Many of the high-rated companies (Bankers Life, Golden Rule, Pioneer Life, and Colonial Penn) do not sell policies in New York, where Blue Cross plans dominate the market.

Other companies are choosier than Blue Cross and AARP, requiring applicants to meet certain standards. Rejection rates vary. Colonial Penn rejects less than 1 percent of all applicants, while National Home Life turns down between 10 percent and 15 percent.

The older you are, the higher the premium. No matter what the premium is when you buy the policy, it's likely to increase. A few state regulators have begun to take a hard look at premiums to see if they're too high. They are looking at loss ratios, a rough measure of a policy's premiums in relation to the benefits paid out.

Eleven of the policies in the study cannot be canceled; in effect, they are guaranteed renewable for the life of the policy-holder. They are Bankers Life and Casualty, Pioneer Life, Standard Life and Accident, Pyramid Life, Colonial Penn, First National Life, National Home Life, Equitable Life and Casualty, Blue Cross and Blue Shield of North Carolina, Community Mutual Blue Cross (Cincinnati), and United American.

A few companies can cancel any individual's policy without regard to whether all of the company's policies are canceled, the rule for most companies. California Blue Cross can cancel any policy with 30 days' notice. This is something you should check on before buying a policy.

HOW CAN I GET THE BEST SUPPLEMENT POLICY?

The following are some tips in shopping for a Medicare supplement policy:

1. Shop carefully before you buy. Policies differ widely as to coverage and cost, and companies differ as to service. Shop around and find several companies with which to compare price and coverages.

2. Don't buy more than you need. The Health Insurance Association of America, an industry trade group, estimates that almost one-fifth of all Medicare supplement policyholders own more than one policy. There's no coordination of benefits among these policies, meaning that all will pay, but buying more than one is a waste of money! For example, there is no need to buy policies that pay only for dread diseases and specific coverages. One good policy will cost less and do the job of several inadequate ones.

Federal criminal and civil penalties can be imposed against any company or agent who knowingly sells you a health insurance policy that substantially duplicates coverage you already have. If you believe this has happened to you, call 1-800-638-6833 or 1-800-492-6603.

3. Consider alternatives. Depending on your health-care needs and finances, you may prefer the group coverage where you previously worked—an HMO, a CMP, or other prepayment plan. The amount you would pay for HMO services could be less than the price of a good supplemental policy.

4. Check for exclusion of preexisting conditions. Preexisting con-

ditions are those conditions for which medical advice was given by a doctor or treatment was received before the effective date of the policy. Many policies do not cover health problems that you have at the time of purchase.

Most policies also require a waiting period before they will cover you, and they prescribe how long you must have had the condition for the waiting period to apply. Some define a preexisting condition as any ailment diagnosed within the last six months; others cut this to the last three months. The waiting period before coverage begins is usually after one to six months.

Other companies guarantee acceptance regardless of preexisting conditions as long as you have not been hospitalized within six months of the effective date of the policy. Most state laws require Medicare supplement policies to cover these conditions after the policy has been in effect for six months.

5. Check for exclusions of mental and emotional disorders. Many policies exclude coverage for mental and nervous disorders, although some are fussier than others. Pyramid Life excludes coverage for mental or emotional disorders, alcoholism, and drug addiction. AARP's plan is more liberal, excluding hospital coverage for mental, psychoneurotic, and personality disorders unless Medicare covers them.

6. Beware of replacing existing coverage. Be suspicious of a suggestion that you give up your policy and buy a replacement. The new policy may impose waiting periods or have exclusions or waiting periods for preexisting conditions. On the other hand, don't keep inadequate policies simply because you have had them a long time.

7. Be aware of maximum benefits. Most policies have some type of limit on benefits. They may restrict either the dollar amount that will be paid for treatment of a condition or the number of days of care for which payment will be made.

8. Check your right to renew. Beware of policies that let the company refuse to renew your policy on an individual basis except for the failure to pay the premium. Most policies cannot be canceled by the company unless *all* policies of that type are canceled in the state. Therefore, these policies cannot be canceled because of claims or disputes. Some policies are guaranteed renewable for life.

9. Be aware that policies to supplement Medicare are always private. Medicare supplements are not sold or serviced by the state or federal government. State insurance departments approve policies sold by insurance companies, but approval only means that the company and policy meet the requirements of state law. Do not believe any claims that insurance to supplement Medicare is a government-sponsored program! Report any person trying to sell you an insurance policy and claiming to be a government representative to your state insurance department or federal authorities.

10. Look for coverage for excess charges. If your current Medicare supplement does not provide coverage for excess charges, ask your carrier if it offers another plan that does. Compare its cost with some of the highest-rated plans in the magazine survey reported above.

11. Consider a company that charges everyone the same rate. If you're older or in poor health, you'll want a liberal company— one that does not scrutinize every health problem you may have. While your premiums are likely to be lower, be sure the coverage is adequate. On the other hand, if you've just turned 65 and are in good health, a company that charges lower premiums for younger people or one that carefully checks a person's health status may be the one you want.

12. Know with whom you're dealing. One of the biggest reasons why the elderly are taken advantage of when buying Medicare supplement policies is that they deal with people they don't know—agents who don't care what happens to them. Try to buy the policy from someone local, who has a good reputation in the area. Take your time and pick the best agent. Keep your agent's name, address, and telephone number on hand in case you need it.

13. Make sure you're dealing with a licensed agent. Agents must be licensed by their state and may be required to carry official identification, showing their names and the companies they represent. If an agent cannot verify that he or she is licensed, do not buy from that person.

14. Take your time. Do not be pressured into buying a policy because an agent tells you there is a limited enrollment period. The good and honest agents will not rush you!

You *must* be given a clearly worded summary of the policy. Read it carefully. If you are uncertain whether a program is worthy, ask the salesperson to explain it to a friend or a relative whose judgment you respect.

15. Complete the application carefully. Some companies ask for detailed medical information. If they do and you leave out any of the medical information requested, coverage could be refused for a period of time for a medical condition you neglected to mention. Do not believe anyone who tells you that your medical history on an application is not important!

16. *Never pay cash.* Pay by check, money order, or bank draft made payable to the *insurance company*, not to the agent!

17. *Expect prompt policy delivery and refunds.* The insurance company should deliver a policy within 30 days. If it does not, contact the company and obtain in writing the reason for the delay. If 60 days go by without information, contact your state insurance department.

18. *Ask about the "free-look" provision.* Insurance companies are *required* to give you at least 30 days to review a Medicare supplement policy. If you decide you don't want the policy, send it back to the agent or company within 30 days of receiving it and you will be entitled to a refund of all premiums you paid.

MEDICARE SUPPLEMENT CHECKLIST

Look at the policy you have or the ones you're considering. Does the policy cover the following:

☐ Medicare Part A hospital deductible?

☐ Medicare Part A hospital daily copayments?

☐ Hospital care beyond Medicare's limits?

☐ Medicare B annual deductible?

☐ Medicare B copayments?

☐ Medicare blood deductibles?

☐ Private hospital room?

☐ Private hospital nurses?

☐ Medical appliances such as eyeglasses and hearing aids?

☐ Custodial nursing-home care?

☐ Can the company cancel or renew the policy?

☐ What are the policy limits for covered services?

☐ What health conditions are excluded under the policy?

☐ How often can the company raise the premium?

☐ How long before existing health problems are covered?

☐ Does the policy have a waiting period? How long?

☐ Do you need more information? To learn more about Medicare and medigap coverage, send for these free booklets:

- *Medicare Catastrophic Protection and Other New Benefits,* Consumer Information Center, Department 65, Pueblo, CO 81009
- *Catastrophic Coverage Under Medicare: New Healthcare Protection for Older Americans,* D13299 AARP Fulfillment, 1909 K St., N.W., Washington, DC
- *Health Insurance Association of America Booklet,* HIAA Box 41455, Washington, DC 20018

If you have questions about changes in Medicare coverage, call the Department of Health and Human Services at 1-800-888-1770.

CHAPTER EIGHT

Something Happened— Now What?

Filing a Claim

*T*his chapter will help you do the right thing when it comes time to make a claim to your insurance company. There are certain steps you should follow in order to maximize your chances of being treated fairly and, equally important, to minimize your frustration and anger. Included are four major lines of insurance that involve claims—auto, homeowners, health, and business—as examples.

AUTO INSURANCE CLAIMS

A typical driver will be involved in an auto accident only once in nine years. Therefore, the need to make a claim rarely presents itself. The odds are therefore pretty good that you're going to be angry, frustrated, confused, and generally overwhelmed when it *is* necessary to file a claim, because it doesn't happen often enough for you to become an expert.

Making a claim for any type of insurance is often a headache, but car claims can be especially frustrating. It's an inconvenience if your vehicle is going to be in the shop for a week. It's also frustrating if the other company turns down your claim and you don't have collision coverage. That's one of the main reasons you have an agent. The true colors of both the insurance company and the agent are revealed when there's a claim. Some do a good job, and some don't.

CONSUMER SATISFACTION AND DISSATISFACTION

In its October 1988 issue, *Consumer Reports* magazine reported the results of its survey of the handling of auto claims. The key question asked in this survey was how would consumers rate the claims service they received. Were they completely satisfied, very satisfied, somewhat satisfied, fairly well satisfied, or completely dissatisfied? Over 50 companies were rated, whose coverage represents 75 percent of the automobile insurance sold.

The results were that insurance companies overall handle auto claims to the complete satisfaction of consumers 60 percent of the time. What are some of the problems that were found?

Delays

Of the claimants surveyed, 45 percent said they received payment within seven days of filing a claim, and 89 percent received payment within 30 days.

It should be understood that some types of claims take longer to handle than others. Nevertheless, virtually every state has some sort of unfair-claims-practice act that sets minimum response standards for companies to follow when settling claims. These laws usually require companies to contact insureds within 30 days of being notified of the claim. Some laws also specify that payment be made within a set period, generally 60 days after the company substantiates the claim. A few states, like Michigan, even add a penalty to the amount the insurance company owes if payment isn't made on time.

Insurance companies themselves usually impose tougher deadlines than those required by the unfair-claims-practice acts. Allstate, for example, says that most collision and comprehensive claims (the easiest to handle) should be settled within five days of being reported.

Disputes over Damage Claimed

In the survey, most of the claims involved collision, theft, or vandalism, and more than 90 percent were settled for less than $5,000. Only a small percentage involved bodily injuries.

If there is disagreement over the amount of the settlement, it usually centers on two issues—how much the car should be valued at when there's a total loss, and whether damage was caused by the accident or existed before the accident.

A disagreement over the value of the car is especially frustrating when an insurance company offers you less than what you need in order to pay off the outstanding balance on a loan. An expensive car financed over a long period of time could depreciate faster than the loan is being repaid.

EXAMPLE:

In Atlanta a doctor insured with Aetna bought a 1987 Jeep Cherokee, financing the entire $23,000 purchase with a five-year loan. Nine months later the car was totaled in a head-on collision, and Aetna's adjuster valued the car at $21,000. The doctor carried a $500 deductible on his collision coverage, so he received a check for $20,500. He still owed $23,000 on the loan, so he had to pay the rest out of his own pocket.

Deciding Who's at Fault

Disputes frequently arise over who's at fault in the accident and to what extent. Almost 7 percent of the policyholders at the Erie Insurance company reported disagreement with their company over whether they were at fault, while only 0.5 percent of the insureds at TransAmerica had such disagreements.

There are three statutes that may apply in this area:

1. Pure comparative negligence—Under the pure-comparative-negligence law, injured parties may collect up to the amount of their damages minus the percentage by which they are at fault. Suppose a driver failed to sound her horn or brake to avoid a collision with a car that had run a stop sign. The insurance company may decide she was 20 percent at fault. If her damages are $1,000, she can collect only $800 from the other driver's carrier.

2. Modified comparative negligence—Under the modified comparative-negligence law, which is on the books in most states, drivers can collect from the other party's carrier only if they are at fault less than a set percentage, usually 49 percent or 50 percent (and only in that percentage of the damages). Thus, a driver who is 51 percent or more responsible cannot collect anything.

3. Contributory negligence—In a few states, such as Alabama and Indiana, which have a contributory-negligence law, parties cannot collect at all if they are as much as 1 percent at fault!

Assessing the percentage of fault is the job of the company claims representative or a jury if the case goes to court. Fixing the percentage usually leads to disputes because few drivers believe they were to blame at all in an accident in which the other driver was primarily at fault.

COLLISION

What Do I Do in a One-Car Accident?

Making a claim for a one-car accident is usually much simpler than for a two-car accident. Some examples of one-car accidents are (1) you're driving home from work on an icy street, lose control of the vehicle, and slam into a telephone pole; or (2) you're backing out of a service station and accidentally hit a light pole. The accident involves only your car.

Here are five steps you should follow:

Step 1. How you respond initially depends on where the accident takes place and the amount of damage to the car. If it happens on someone's property, inform the owner and leave your name and address and the name of your insurance company. Call your agent when you get home.

If the accident happens on a street or highway, take note of the approximate location, proceed to your destination, and then call your agent. It's not imperative to report it immediately, but your immediate contact with the agent should expedite the handling of the claim. The agent will record the information on a "loss report."

Step 2. The next step is to obtain at least two estimates for the damage to your vehicle. Some companies require three. If the damage is under $1,000, most insurance companies will not require an adjuster to look at the vehicle. If the estimates seem to be in line with current costs for that type of repair, the company will generally issue a check in the amount of the lowest bid.

If the repair shop of your choice gives the higher of the two bids, you still can have the work done there, but you'll have to pay the difference.

A common question claimants ask is, "Can I have the claim check made out in my name only?" Sometimes the insurance company will make the check out to both the claimant *and* the repair shop, or to the claimant and a lien holder, if there is one. If there isn't a loan on the vehicle, most insurance companies will issue a check the way you want it. If you choose not to have the damage fixed and use the money for something else, so be it. Keep in mind, however, that if you should have an accident in the future that involves the same part of the vehicle, the insurance company won't pay another dime for that repair.

What happens if the body shop finds that it was off in its initial estimate because of a mistake in addition or because of pricing a part incorrectly, or it finds more damage to the vehicle after getting into the actual repair work? This shouldn't be a problem as long as the additional item or repair is legitimate—that is, as long as it relates to the original accident. Have the repair shop contact your agent in such a case.

Step 3. Once your agent receives the information about the accident and the estimates, allow a couple of days for him or her to write the report and send all of the paperwork to the insurance company's claims office. If it's determined that no field adjuster is required, you should have a check in 10 to 14 days from the date of the accident. Remember, if you don't report the accident to your agent and get the estimates in right away, the whole claims process will be delayed. If you haven't heard anything within a week, call your agent to make sure the forms were received. It's always better to check on a claim than assume everything is all right.

Normally you are in a hurry to have your car fixed, especially if you need a car to get to work or to get the kids to school. If the damages are minimal enough that there isn't a need for a field adjuster, you might be able to tell the repair shop to proceed with ordering the parts and even schedule the car for the actual repairs. This depends upon the repair shop—some won't do any work without a check in hand. Call your agent first to see if it would be all right to proceed on this basis to save time.

Step 4. If the damage is over $1,000, the insurance company usually wants to inspect the vehicle. The company may have a "drive-in" claims office, which is very convenient, or an adjuster will be sent over to inspect your vehicle. Sometimes the adjuster pays the claim immediately, and sometimes not. If there is a liability question involved, or if there is a problem with the estimates, or if he or she just doesn't have time, you may not be issued a check on the spot.

Step 5. If the vehicle is considered a total loss—a loss in which the amount of damage exceeds the value of the vehicle—new problems can enter the picture. Most insureds shudder at the thought of having their vehicles "totaled." Why? They fear that the insurance company is going to cheat them out of the full value of their car on the final settlement. This can and does happen, but there are ways to keep it from happening to you:

- Ask your agent how the company figures the **fair-market value**—this is the value of the vehicle on today's market.

- Call local used-car lots and ask what a car like yours would sell for if they had it on the lot. Tell them how many miles it has, whether the vehicle has new tires, what kind of shape the interior is in, if the engine has been recently overhauled, and anything else that would help establish the fair market value of that vehicle.
- Also, call the bank or claims office and ask for the vehicle's **book value**. "Book value" takes into consideration low mileage, accessories, and age of the vehicle. Although this figure will no doubt be lower than the "market value," the combination of the two figures will give you an idea of what the vehicle is actually worth.
- You can negotiate with the adjuster. The adjuster will ask, "What do you think the car is worth?" If you've done your homework, you should be able to state a figure that's realistic. If your figure and the adjuster's don't agree and the adjuster won't budge, refuse the settlement and say that you will contact your agent.

  A good agent will take your information and discuss it with the adjuster. That's not to say that the agent can wave a magic wand and get you whatever you want, but if your agent won't check into it any further, find out who the manager is and call that person. Hopefully, the problem will be resolved at this point, but even if it is, you've lost confidence in your agent. Find another one!
- Above all else, try to keep calm when you're talking to the claims adjuster. If he or she senses hostility on your part, it could work against you. Irritating the person who writes the checks is not a good policy.

What Do I Do in a Two-Car Accident?

These are more complicated because two insurance companies are involved. Here are seven steps to follow:

Step 1. If you're involved in an accident with another vehicle, no matter how insignificant the damage may seem, no matter what the other person says or pleads, call the police! Here's why:

The police will take statements from both parties; they will take pictures if necessary, measure skid marks, etc. The police report then helps the claims adjuster establish who's at fault. It also allows the accident to become a public record and verifies who's involved in the accident, which could be valuable in case you have to go to court.

Step 2. As soon as possible after the accident, contact your agent. He or she should give you instructions on how to proceed.

One thing you will probably have to do is fill out a Proof of Financial Responsibility form, which must be mailed to the Department of Insurance within 10 days of the accident. This form is similar to the local police report or highway patrol report filled out at the scene of the accident, and most states require it. It asks for complete insurance information, and it's a way for the states that require a minimum liability coverage on every vehicle to make sure the law is being followed. If they don't receive the form within 10 days of the accident, they can start proceedings to take your license.

This form is a little involved, so if you need help with it, ask your agent.

Step 3. Let your insurance company handle any correspondence with the other party. If the other party calls and wants to know what's happening, say you've notified your agent and your agent will be getting in touch with them. The insurance companies decide who's at fault in an accident. The claims representatives deal with hundreds of thousands of accidents every year, and are very experienced at discovering who's at fault.

Step 4. If you're at fault, your company will pay up to the policy limits for whatever property and damages the other party sustained. Avoid getting involved with what your company is paying the other party. Concern yourself with making sure that you are reimbursed fairly for the damages to *your* vehicle.

Step 5. If you're injured in the accident, forward all medical bills to your agent immediately, or better yet, have the bills mailed directly to your agent.

Step 6. If the other party was clearly at fault, and if you have collision coverage on your vehicle, you have two choices as to what to do next:

- You can turn in the two or three damage estimates required to the other insurance company and wait for someone to get in touch with you.
- You can have *your* insurance company pay for the damages minus your collision deductible, and then your company will collect from the other company and, hopefully, reimburse the deductible.

The second approach is called **subrogation**, and I recommend it highly. The reason is, you don't know how long it will take the other company to handle the claim. It may be slow, and your agent can't do much to pressure another company into moving faster. On the other hand, your agent *can* affect how fast your own company handles the claim.

Are you likely to get back your deductible? After paying the loss, your insurance company will submit the entire bill to the other company for reimbursement. If the other company agrees that its insured was at fault, it will reimburse your company in full, which, in turn, should send you back the deductible.

Step 7. What happens if neither side is considered to be at fault? Or both are? This happens most commonly when the accident takes place in an unmarked intersection (no Stop signs). It's quite common for insurance companies to acknowledge both parties to be guilty of a certain degree of negligence. This means that each one takes care of its own insured vehicle, denying the claims of the other. If you have collision coverage, you're all right. If you don't, your only alternative is to take the other party to small claims court.

No-Fault

In the late 1960s, when auto insurance premiums began their upward rise, a proposal to reform the way auto accident victims were compensated was written into the insurance laws of the various states. The basic premise of no-fault insurance was to have each driver's insurance coverage pay for his or her injuries, regardless who was at fault in an accident. In theory, this would eliminate the need to sue the other driver, and premium dollars that used to go toward attorney's fees would be redirected to accident victims.

The premise was appealing. However, trial lawyers, who had the most to lose from this consumer-orientated initiative, succeeded either in defeating no-fault laws or weakening them to the point at which lawsuits continued as before. In state after state, no-fault laws became useless in controlling premiums. In New Jersey, which has no-fault but still allows lawsuits for minor injuries, premiums in 1986 averaged 25 percent higher than in Michigan, which has the best no-fault law in the country. (See Chapter 2.)

No-fault laws vary from state to state. Remember that if you're the victim, no-fault insurance permits you to recover from your own insurance company such losses as medical and hospital expenses, lost income, and other unavoidable expenses resulting from accident-related injuries.

One aspect of no-fault insurance to keep in mind is that,

except in Michigan, it doesn't apply to property damage. The damage you cause to other people's property with an automobile can be insured only under property-damage-liability insurance, which is mandatory coverage in most states. Damage to your own vehicle comes under your collision and comprehensive coverages.

Don't make the mistake of one driver who failed to collect information from the other motorist in an accident because he thought each person's no-fault would cover his own damages, regardless of who was at fault. Damage to his car was paid for by his collision coverage but he lost his deductible because his insurer was unable to recoup the money from the other driver's insurer.

What If the Other Company Won't Pay?

What happens if you don't have collision coverage and you're involved in an accident that is the other person's fault? The other company may deny the claim, stating the opinion that *you* were at fault. If the damage to your vehicle is under $1,500 (the usual minimum limit before a claim can be settled in regular district court), consider taking the case to small claims court. Here are the steps:

Step 1. Tell your agent the other company denied the claim and won't pay a dime. Ask the agent to call your company's claims office and review the accident report and circumstances. Does your company think you'd have a very good chance of winning a small claims action against the other driver? If they sound positive, proceed to the next step. If they don't think you'd have a good chance, rethink it.

Step 2. If you've decided to go ahead, you have to initiate the action by filing at the county courthouse. This is a very simple process, requiring you to fill out a one-page form telling the court who was involved, when the accident occurred, and what happened. The clerk will set a court date anywhere from a month to three months in the future, depending on the court's schedule. The clerk also will ask if you want the summons notifying the **respondent** (the other party) mailed or delivered in person by the county sheriff. It costs slightly more to have it delivered, but it's worth it, since a personal visit from the sheriff generally gets their attention. It can cost anywhere from $26 to $75 to initiate an action in small claims court.

Step 3. Prepare for the trial by getting estimates of the damage, a copy of the police report, and the agreement to testify of any witnesses you can locate, including the police officer who filled out the original accident report.

Step 4. You go to court on the appointed day. There is no reason for a lawyer to accompany you if you have a good agent. It's such a simple process. If the other party fails to appear, you automatically win the suit, and a judgment is entered against the respondent. That judgment will have to be satisfied before the respondent can apply for a house loan and, in some cases, even a library card.

If the other party appears, the judge simply asks both parties to tell their sides of the accident. No lawyers or insurance agents are allowed to speak—no one but you as the plaintiff, the other party as respondent, and any witnesses. The judge reviews all the information and makes a decision. If it's in your favor, the respondent is ordered to pay for court costs in addition to damages sustained to your vehicle.

Step 5. The first thing to do if you win the case is to contact your agent—if he or she hasn't gone with you to court. The agent should immediately send the evidence of the judgment to the other insurance company and request that the claim be paid. Once the other company receives notice that their client lost a small claims court action, they pay the bill! If they don't pay the bill, their client all of a sudden becomes *personally* responsible for the damages.

Since I've been an agent, I've helped close to 20 clients take someone to small claims court in order to recover a monetary loss sustained as a result of a car accident. We've won all of these cases, and my insureds have been reimbursed money they normally would not have seen. The last one was a judgment of almost $1,200 that the other company paid immediately after I sent them the proof of the judgment in my client's favor!

WHAT CLAIMS CAN BE MADE UNDER THE COMPREHENSIVE PORTION OF MY POLICY?

Windshield Loss

If a rock strikes the windshield and pits it, call your agent before a crack develops and spreads. He or she will know if a "repair" job will suffice as opposed to replacing the entire windshield.

Why is this important? If you have a deductible, most insurance companies will waive it and pay for the whole repair job. This is a purely economical decision on the insurance company's part. They would much rather pay $50 for a repair job than $300 for a new windshield. If the repair job isn't satisfactory, you can then have the windshield replaced. In this case, call your agent first. The company should pay for a new windshield minus your deductible, if applicable.

Vandalism or Theft Loss

Call the police! Many insurance companies won't process a claim if you don't contact the local authorities and file a loss report. Companies require this so that if the guilty party is caught, they can begin proceedings to get their money back.

Hail Loss

This is one of the most common comprehensive losses across the country. If your car has been damaged in a hail storm, make a claim. The agent will fill out a loss report and if the damage is significant (over $1,000), an adjuster will probably come to inspect the car.

The adjuster gives you a choice of payment method:

- You can get the exact amount needed to repair the damage to your vehicle.
- You can get what is known as an **appearance loss**. This means that if the vehicle is too old to be worth repairing the adjuster offers an amount to cover the loss of value to the car because of the hail damage. This is always a flat cash settlement.

How you and the adjuster arrive at this "loss-of-value" figure is rather like old-fashioned horse trading. My experience has been that the adjuster usually offers a fair price, but not always! Remember, the adjuster works for the insurance company and it wants to settle as low as it can. What should you do?

If you're uneasy with how much is offered, say you want to think about it. Buy some time. Ask your friends about their settlements. Call your agent and discuss the offer. See if he or she thinks it's a fair amount. Put pressure on the agent to agree or disagree.

Contact the adjuster and explain your position. Remain calm and polite. If your arguments have a sound economic basis, and you don't alienate the adjuster by displaying a belligerent attitude, you just might get the price you want!

If there's a lien holder on the vehicle, the check will be issued in both your names. If your loan balance is minimal, or if you have other collateral at the bank, the bank may not require the check to be in both names. Ask your banker about this.

AUTO MEDICAL CLAIMS

Regardless of who's at fault in an accident, your medical coverage (if you have it) will pay the bills up to the limit stated on the policy. If you or anyone riding in your vehicle is injured in an accident, take the necessary precaution of getting checked by a doctor. If the injuries are slight, just bumps and bruises, indicate as much to your agent. If they're more serious, make sure you receive treatment.

The adjuster should work closely with you and make sure the claim is handled properly, especially if the other party was at fault and the adjuster represents their interests.

If you're in an accident in which the other driver is at fault and he or she has insurance, it's very likely the other company will try to hurry you into a settlement. Small injuries can turn into huge lawsuits very quickly, so most adjusters want to settle and have you waive all rights to further recourse against the company before the claim escalates. Where the claim can escalate is not in the area of property damage or for medical bills; it's usually for what's known as **pain and suffering**. "Pain and suffering" losses are usually compensatory monetary awards given to people who have been injured in car accidents. The money is to help compensate for the pain and inconvenience they have experienced as a result of their injuries.

Let's face it, a great many people in the United States are wealthy today because of settlements they have received for car accidents. Some of these were legitimate claims and some were for the stereotypical "whiplash" injuries, which are difficult to disprove in a court of law.

You don't need to run out and obtain the services of an attorney immediately after an accident. Consider that approximately a third to a half of whatever you collect from the insurance company will go to your lawyer. Let the claims adjusters handle the claim first, offering you what they think is a fair settlement. They will usually pay for the property damage and medical expenses immediately.

If you think what they have offered you is unfair, call your agent to find out what settlements are being made for similar accidents. Let your insurance company have an opportunity to settle the claim to your satisfaction first! If you're still unhappy and feel that you're being treated unfairly, consider these steps: (1) Call your agent's district manager and voice your complaint; (2) call your insurance company's main claims office and voice your objections; and (3) contact the state department of insurance and file a formal complaint.

If, after pursuing these avenues, you still have not received satisfaction, call an attorney.

RESIDENTIAL PROPERTY CLAIMS

When you buy homeowners, renter's, or farm owner's insurance, you may think that you're buying peace of mind. You pay hundreds, maybe thousands of dollars a year in the belief that you will be fully satisfied if you file a claim. Depending upon the company you choose, you may be in for a surprise.

In its October 1988 issue, *Consumer Reports* magazine reported the results of its survey of over 260,000 people in 1988 that focused on 23,000 respondents who filed homeowners claims during the previous three years. Some companies proved worthy of their customer's trust; others left as many as one in five homeowners dissatisfied with the way their claims were handled.

One of the most important factors was the amount of the final settlement or how much money insureds actually collected on their claims. Although homeowners insurance is often advertised as protection against catastrophic loss, most of the respondents filed claims for relatively small amounts. More than a third of the claims were for $500 or less; only about one in ten were for more than $3,000. The average claim was $800.

The respondents received an average of about 87 cents for every dollar claimed. Nearly 33 percent received full compensation, and about 3 percent actually recovered more than they claimed. Only about one in ten respondents reported that the final amount of settlement was too small for their claim.

Here are some tips to make sure your claim is settled to your satisfaction.

FIRE AND TORNADO

Ask anyone who's had a fire in his home and he can tell you just how terrible it is. A tornado can be even worse, leaving virtually nothing left of a house caught in its path.

Inventory

Most agents suggest that you fill out an inventory of property in case a fire or a tornado completely destroys your home. This means going through the residence room by room, writing down everything in it and what its original cost was. Filling out an inventory is a time-consuming and easy-to-put-off task, but having one available when a disaster strikes gives you an advantage. Why?

First, your claim is handled faster and more accurately. Second, to try and rely on memory alone for this information is less than ideal because you may miss certain items and cost yourself money.

Photos

Besides an inventory, if you have pictures of each room, that's better yet. These can be Polaroids or any type of snapshot. It stands to reason that the claims adjuster will handle the easiest claims first, which means you get your money faster.

Living Expenses

If you have to move into a motel or hotel while your home is being repaired, be sure to keep an itemized list of all extra expenses you incur. This would include the cost of your motel room and food. You need to be specific so you can get exact reimbursement from the insurance company.

HAIL LOSS

This is a very common peril throughout much of the United States, and you should know what to expect when an adjuster comes to look at your hail-damaged home.

If the roof is a total loss and you have a replacement-cost policy, the claim will be settled as follows: You'll be paid a price per square of shingles for labor to remove the old shingles and replace them with new ones, as well as for the felt undercovering and the shingles themselves. IMPORTANT NOTE: The insurance company is only obligated to pay for removing and replacing *one* layer of shingles. If your roof has been shingled over several times, which is common, you're responsible for the cost above replacing the single layer.

Companies differ in the way they reimburse you, but here are a couple of ways it can be done:

EXAMPLE:

The adjuster figures the number of squares it takes to reshingle the house and garage (let's say 22 squares) and multiplies that by the going rate per square (say, $95 per square). Thus, 22 × $95 = $2,090. Subtract the $100 deductible, and your check comes to $1,990.

EXAMPLE:

The company may pay you an initial sum for depreciated value, or present-day value, of the roof, which takes into account its condition and age. If the company determines that to be $1,500, the adjuster will give you a check for $1,500 less the $100 deductible, or $1,400.

Wait a minute, you say to the agent. You told me this was a replacement-cost policy when I bought it from you! Where's the rest of my money? The company will pay you that *after* you replace the roof. If you don't replace the roof, the $1,400 is all the money you're going to get. The insurance company is anticipating that you could avoid putting on a new roof, eventually change companies, and put in another claim at the other company.

What happens if you don't have the replacement-cost feature on your home policy?

EXAMPLE:

Using the same example, the most money you'd collect is the depreciated figure of $1,500 less the $100 deductible, or $1,400. If the roof's badly damaged and you have to get it fixed no matter what, you're going to be considerably short of having the full $2,090 to do it.

To avoid this problem, I recommend that you make sure your house policy includes replacement cost for the roof.

THEFT

Call the local authorities any time something is stolen from your premises. Get a police report on file. The insurance company will have an easier time handling the claim, and in the long run this may lower your rates. If the culprits are caught and they make restitution, it should help the insurance company keep the rates down.

Here are some other ideas: Write down the serial number, make, and model of such items as your VCR, televisions, stereos, guns, and tools. This will be an invaluable aid when the police try to find your property. Some people also have their name and address permanently inscribed on these items. This might make the items harder to "fence" and easier to recover.

EARTHQUAKE AND FLOOD

These disasters are called **catastrophic losses**, and insurance companies dispatch whole teams of adjusters to the disaster site almost immediately. They should be working within hours after the loss taking care of their clients. Companies are very much aware of how much business can be lost through sloppy, slow claims work following a disaster, so your claim should be handled quickly and fairly.

How much can you actually recover if your house is a total loss? You will receive up to the policy limits for the dwelling and personal property.

MEDICAL

Whenever anyone other than a member of your immediate family is hurt on your premises, you have protection under the medical-payments-to-others part of your homeowners policy.

EXAMPLE:

While you're babysitting for your grandchild, she falls out of bed and cuts her head. Your daughter's not going to sue you, but there are doctor's bills and the emergency-room bill to pay, or at least a deductible. Your medical payments to others will pay those bills up to the limits stated in the policy. Tell your daughter to send you the bills so you can forward them to your agent. They should be paid in full with no deductible to you. Insurance companies consider this a simple claim.

LIABILITY

Whenever anything happens on your premises involving an injury to anyone other than your immediate family, call your agent immediately. Don't wait! It's possible that the individual won't make an issue out of what happened, but he or she may also see dollar signs and want to sue you for negligence.

After the accident don't say anything to the claimant about what happened, except to assure him or her you have called your agent and passed on all the information. If the claimant wants the name of your agent, supply it. Consult your agent about what you should say if a lawyer representing the other party contacts you and wants you to give a statement. You don't want to say or do something that may jeopardize your case if it goes to court.

The steps to keep in mind are the following:

Step 1. Give prompt notice to your agent, including (1) the time, place, and circumstances of the accident or occurrence; and (2) the names and addresses of any claimants and witnesses.

Step 2. Submit to any tape-recorded or written statements the company might request.

Step 3. Forward any notice, demand, or legal paper relating to the accident.

Step 4. Assist the company in making settlement and cooperating in matters concerning the suit.

HEALTH CLAIMS

INDIVIDUAL (FEE-FOR-SERVICE) HEALTH INSURANCE

Health claims tend to take longer than most other types of insurance claims because of the number of different people (and bills) to be dealt with. Radiologists, anesthesiologists, surgeons, the hospital, and your regular doctor can become involved in a major health claim.

How Soon Will I Be Reimbursed?

The first rule is, Try to be patient! This doesn't mean you can't check with your agent to see how things are progressing, however. In fact, you *should* check about once a week.

How Should I Send Bills In?

The best way to send your bills in for payment is to accumulate them and mail or deliver the lot to the agent's office, or mail directly to the claims office if you don't have an agent. If you don't know where that is, call the company and find out. Accumulating bills rather than sending them in one at a time helps avoid confusion on your end as well as the insurance company's; you know for sure what has been submitted. Make sure that you keep copies of the bills just in case they get lost in the mail, or for reference in case of questions. Payment should take two to three weeks.

In many states the hospital automatically sends its bill directly to your insurance company, especially if the company is one they deal with on a regular basis.

What Does "Over Reasonable and Customary" Mean?

One of the biggest headaches in health claims is getting back a statement that includes the phrase, "over reasonable and customary." In other words, your insurance company only paid so much on a claim because the amount billed was over the "reasonable and customary" amount for that service (see Chapter 3). You get stuck for the difference!

Is it the insurance company's fault that you've got this problem? Are their "reasonable and customary" limits too low? Most insurance companies pay claims based on the 85th to 90th percentile of what a particular procedure costs. This means that if you had 100 surgeons doing the same exact surgery, the insurance company pays what 90 of the surgeons would have charged.

This is all well and good, but while the insurance company is trying to decide what's reasonable and customary and is not paying the bill, you're getting nasty notices from the surgeon. In fact, she's turned you over to the local credit collection agency! Now what do you do?

If you're lucky to have an insurance company that pays "over reasonable and customary" costs, but the bill is being questioned by the insurance company, very few collection agencies will press the issue. They can, but they run the risk of being countersued for harassment; consequently, they are reluctant to pursue it. That doesn't mean the hospital or surgeon still won't try to intimidate you into paying right away.

Your insurance company will be attempting to establish communication with the surgeon, trying to find out why the bill is $200 higher than the normal charge. If they find that it's higher because of medical complications, that's no problem! The insurance company should pay right away. But if the surgeon is just expensive, the insurance company will try to negotiate until (1) the surgeon drops the difference, (2) they split the difference, or (3) the insurance company pays the difference.

If your insurance company doesn't pay "over reasonable and customary" costs, *you* have the problem. The first thing to do is check with your agent to find out on what percentile the company is basing its limits. Armed with that information, talk to the doctor and calmly point out that you want to pay the bill but at the same time you want to pay what's fair. Could the doctor explain to you why her bill is so much higher than the reasonable and customary charge? Were there complications? Does she realize the percentile in which her bill falls in the overall surgeons' scale?

If nothing is done, you might tell the doctor that you have no intention of paying the difference and to communicate with your attorney. This may convince her to reconsider and be satisfied with the money already collected from the insurance company. If that doesn't work, consult your attorney.

Do I Need to Check My Bills?

Get in the habit of double-checking every bill, especially the hospital bill. Look for errors in addition and subtraction, double charges, and inflated costs. You'd be surprised how much of that happens. I know of one major midwestern insurance company that saved over $2,000,000 in "mistakes and overbillings" in one year by having a Medical Services Review staff person go over bills for errors. It's a sad commentary on the system, but it's reality.

MEDICARE SUPPLEMENT CLAIMS

The procedure for filing a claim if you have Medicare supplement insurance is fairly simple:

Step 1. The proper procedure for the doctor, the hospital, or other billing parties is for their billing department to send the bill directly to Medicare.

Step 2. Medicare will process it and send you the **Explanation of Benefits (EOB)** sheet, along with a check for what they are responsible to pay. The EOB will show the date of service, the amount charged, the name of the medical provider, and the total amount approved by Medicare.

Step 3. Take or send your EOB to your Medicare supplement insurance agent, who will forward it to the insurance company. Ask your agent if you need to include an itemized list of the bills in addition to the EOB. Some companies require it and some don't. If yours does, request it from the billing department of the medical service. Your medigap insurance will pay you what Medicare didn't. This is a very simple process, and you should receive your check quickly.

Excess Charges

It's in your best interests to check prior to purchasing a Medicare supplement policy how it deals with extra charges, meaning those above the "assignment" of benefits. (See Chapter 7.) Medical providers who take assignment accept whatever charge Medicare approves. If their bill to you is $750 and Medicare approves $600, they write off the difference and don't ask you for it. If they don't accept assignment, you'll have to pay the extra charges, if there are any, yourself. The assignment process is not usually decided on a case-by-case basis. The doctors you go to either accept assignment or they don't. It still can happen, however, that a doctor accepts the assignment and yet bills out an excess charge to the patient.

BUSINESS CLAIMS

PROPERTY CLAIMS

In the case of a property loss under the business owner's policy here's what you should do:

Step 1. If a law has been broken—if there's been a robbery, break-in, or act of vandalism—contact the appropriate authorities. This makes processing the claim easier and may lead to recovering the items.

Step 2. Call your agent as soon as possible and tell him or her what happened. Don't wait. Give the agent the time and place of the event, a description of the property, and the names and addresses of any witnesses.

Step 3. Do what is reasonable and necessary to protect covered property from further damage and keep a record of your expenses. This is *very* important. If someone breaks a window, get it fixed right away. If rain seeps in around that window because of another problem, damaging more property, you run the risk of being denied payment for the new damage, unless you can show you responded to the earlier problem. If temporary repairs need to be made, don't wait for permission from your insurance company! Get the repairs made, keep a record of what it costs, and give it to the company. The insurance company will be appreciative of your efforts to minimize the damage.

Step 4. If it is feasible, separate the damaged property from the undamaged and make an inventory of the damaged items. Do the best job you can under the circumstances. The insurance company realizes that you still need to run your business and your time is limited.

Step 5. Cooperate with the insurance company during the investigation and settlement of the claim. Show them the damaged property and any records pertaining to your loss that they reasonably request. Also, permit the insurance company to take samples of the damaged property for inspection, testing, and analysis.

Step 6. The insurance company may want to question you under oath with regard to losses resulting from theft and fraud. You should consult your attorney about this, but if you don't have anything to hide, it shouldn't be a problem.

Step 7. If someone is injured or there is some possibility of a liability claim against you, you should first, notify the police if a law may have been broken; and second, tell your agent what happened as soon as possible. Do this even though no claim has been made, but you or another protected person is aware of having done something that may later result in a claim. This notice should include the following:

- The time and place of the event
- The name of the protected person involved
- The specific nature of the incident, including the type of claim that may result
- The names and addresses of any witnesses and injured people

Step 8. Send your agent copies of all demands or legal documents if someone makes a claim or starts a lawsuit.

Step 9. Cooperate and assist the company in securing and giving evidence, attending hearings and trials, and obtaining the attendance of witnesses.

Step 10. Never assume any financial obligation or pay out any money without the company's consent. This rule doesn't apply to first aid given to others at the time of an accident.

WORKER'S COMPENSATION CLAIMS

If an injury occurs in your business, take the following steps:

Step 1. Provide for immediate medical and other services required for the injured employee at the accident scene.

Step 2. Give your agent the names and addresses of the injured persons and of any witnesses, and any other information needed.

Step 3. Forward to your agent all notices, demands, and legal papers related to the injury, claim, proceeding, or lawsuit.

Step 4. Cooperate with the insurance company and assist in the investigation, settlement, or defense of any claim.

Step 5. Don't do anything after an injury occurs that would interfere with the insurance company's right to recover payments from others.

Step 6. Don't voluntarily make payments, assume obligations, or incur expenses, except at your own cost.

Step 7. Fill out a worker's compensation claim form. You should have a supply of these forms available. Normally, the agent fills out an insurance claim form, but the worker's compensation form is a little different. It asks specific questions about the employee, such as starting date of employment, wages, and length of absence from work, and the majority of the form needs to be filled out by you. If you have any questions on the form itself, the agent can help you. However, it's your responsibility to complete the form and send it to the agent as soon as possible.

INSURANCE CLAIMS CHECKLIST

When you have to make a claim, go through this list and check off the following items:

Auto Claims

☐ Did you call the police department?

☐ Did you notify your agent?

☐ Did you get two estimates?

☐ Did you make sure the Proof of Financial Responsibility form was filled in, signed, and mailed to the Department of Motor Vehicles?

☐ Have you kept on top of the claim by double-checking that your agent has all the information he or she needs?

Homeowners Claims

☐ Have you notified your agent of the loss?

☐ Have you taken steps to prevent further loss?

☐ Do you have an inventory list of your personal property and pictures of each room in the house?

☐ Have you kept records of any major purchases such as TVs, VCRs, guns, etc.?

☐ Did you identify and mark all major items in the house or apartment in case of theft?

Health and Medicare Supplement Claims

☐ Have you notified your agent of the claim?

☐ Have you accumulated all of the bills and checked them for accuracy?

☐ Have you made sure the agent has all the information he or she needs in order for the claim to be paid?

☐ Have you or your doctor, hospital, etc., sent the claim to Medicare?

☐ Have you presented the Explanation of Benefits form provided by Medicare to your medigap carrier for payment?

Business Claims

☐ Have you notified your agent of the loss?

☐ Have you taken steps to prevent further loss?

☐ Do you have an inventory of all business personal property?

☐ Do you have worker's compensation claim forms in your place of business?

☐ Did you notify your agent immediately after any of your employees were injured?

☐ Have you called the police department in case of a suspected theft?

APPENDIX A

Consumer Resources

If you have any remaining questions about your insurance coverage or want to learn more about insurance-related matters, the following organizations and publications can help you get started.

ORGANIZATIONS

Consumer Group

National Insurance Consumer Organization (NICO)
344 Commerce Street
Alexandria, VA 22314

Insurer Groups

Health Insurance

Health Insurance Association of America (HIAA)
P.O. Box 41455
Washington, DC 20018

Residential and Auto Insurance

Insurance Information Institute (IIL)
110 William Street
New York, NY 10038

Life Insurance

American Council of Life Insurance (ACLI)
1001 Pennsylvania Ave., N.W.
Washington, DC 20004

These three organizations have a free consumer hotline: 1-800-942-4242.

PUBLICATIONS

Best's Aggregates & Averages, Property-Casualty. A.M. Best Company, Oldwick, NJ 08858. Annual. Gives statistics by companies and by aggregates for stock, mutual, reciprocal, and Lloyds organizations.

Best's Insurance Reports, Property-Casualty. A.M. Best Company, Oldwick, NJ 08858. Annual. Reports on and rates the financial position, history, and transactions of insurers in the United States and Canada.

Insurance Facts: Property/Casualty Fact Book. Insurance Information Institute, 110 William Street, New York, NY 10038. Annual. A comprehensive statistical yearbook giving data about property/casualty insurance.

Also from the Insurance Information Institute, two free pamphlets: *Home Insurance Basics* and *Sharing the Risk.*

State Insurance Commissioners

The majority of state commissioners are appointed by state governors and serve at their pleasure. Eleven states, designated with an asterisk (*), presently elect insurance commissioners to four-year terms. California (**) will elect its insurance commissioner for the first time in November 1990 to a four-year term commencing January 1, 1991.

Alabama Mike Weaver, Commissioner of Insurance, 135 South Union St., #181, Montgomery, AL 36130-3401. Tel. 205-269-3550.

Alaska Jim Jordan, Acting Director of Insurance, P.O. Box "D," Juneau, AK 99811. Tel. 907-465-2515.

American Samoa Afa Roberts, Insurance Commissioner, Office of the Governor, Pago Pago, AS 96797. Tel. 684-633-4116.

Arizona Susan Gallinger, Director of Insurance, 3030 North 3rd St., Suite 1100, Phoenix, AZ 85012. Tel. 602-255-5400.

Arkansas Ron Taylor, Insurance Commissioner, 400 University Tower Building, 12th and University Streets, Little Rock, AR 72204. Tel. 501-371-1325.

*California*** Roxani Gillespie, Commissioner of Insurance, 100 Van Ness Ave., San Francisco, CA 94102. Tel. 415-557-9624; 800-233-9045.

Colorado Joanne Hill, Commissioner of Insurance, 303 W. Colfax Ave., 5th Floor, Denver, CO 80204. Tel. 303-620-4300.

Connecticut Peter F. Kelly, Insurance Commissioner, 165 Capitol Ave., State Office Bldg., Hartford, CT 06106. Tel. 203-297-3800.

Reprinted by permission from *1990 Property/Casualty Insurance Facts*, published by the Insurance Information Institute. Copyright © 1990 Insurance Information Institute. All rights reserved.

Delaware* David N. Levinson, Insurance Commissioner, 841 Silver Lake Blvd., Dover, DE 19901. Tel. 302-736-4251; 800-282-8611.

District of Columbia Margurite C. Stokes, Superintendent of Insurance, 613 G St., NW, 6th Floor, Washington, DC 20001. Tel. 202-727-7424.

Florida* Tom Gallagher, Insurance Commissioner, State Capitol, Plaza Level 11, Tallahassee, FL 32399-0300. Tel. 904-488-3440; 800-342-2762.

Georgia* Warren D. Evans, Insurance Commissioner, 2 Martin L. King, Jr. Dr., Floyd Memorial Building, 716 West Tower, Atlanta, GA 30334. Tel. 404-656-2056.

Guam Joaquin G. Blaz, Acting Insurance Commissioner, P.O. Box 2796, Agana, GU 96910. Tel. 011-671-477-1040.

Hawaii Robin Campaniano, Insurance Commissioner, P.O. Box 3614, Honolulu, HA 96811. Tel. 808-548-5450; 800-548-5450.

Idaho Anthony Fagiano, Director of Insurance, 500 S. 10th St., Boise, ID 83720. Tel. 208-334-2250.

Illinois Zack Stamp, Director of Insurance, 320 W. Washington St., 4th Floor, Springfield, IL 62767. Tel. 217-782-4515.

Indiana John J. Dillon III, Commissioner of Insurance, 311 West Washington St., Suite 300, Indianapolis, IN 46204-2787. Tel. 317-232-2386; 800-622-4461.

Iowa William D. Hager, Commissioner of Insurance, Lucas State Office Building, 6th Floor, Des Moines, IA 50319. Tel. 515-281-5705.

Kansas* Fletcher Bell, Commissioner of Insurance, 420 South West Ninth St., Topeka, KS 66612. Tel. 913-296-7801; 800-432-2484.

Kentucky Leroy L. Morgan, Insurance Commissioner, 229 West Maine St., P.O. Box 517, Frankfort, KY 40602. Tel. 502-564-3630.

Louisiana* Doug Green, Commissioner of Insurance, 950 North 5th St., Baton Rouge, LA 70802. Tel. 504-342-5328.

Maine Joseph A. Edwards, Superintendent of Insurance, State House, Station 34, Augusta, ME 04333. Tel. 207-582-8707.

Maryland John A. Donaho, Insurance Commissioner, 501 St. Paul Pl., 7th Floor South, Baltimore, MD 21202. Tel. 301-333-2520; 800-492-6116.

Massachusetts Timothy Gailey, Commissioner of Insurance, 280 Friend St., Boston, MA 02114. Tel. 617-727-7189.

Michigan Dhiraj Shah, Acting Insurance Commissioner, 611 West Ottawa St., 2nd floor, Lansing, MI 48933. Tel. 517-373-9273.

Minnesota Michael A. Hatch, Commissioner of Commerce, 500 Metro Square Building, 5th Floor, St. Paul, MN 55101. Tel. 612-296-6848; 800-652-9747.

Mississippi* George Dale, Commissioner of Insurance, 1804 Walter Sillers Building, Jackson, MS 39201 (P.O. Box 79, Jackson, MS 39205). Tel. 601-359-3569.

Missouri Lew Melahn, Director of Insurance, 301 W. High St. 6 North, P.O. Box 690, Jefferson City, MO 65102-0690. Tel. 314-751-2451.

Montana* Andrea Bennett, Commissioner of Insurance, 126 North Sanders, Mitchell Building, Rm. 270, Helena, MT 59620 (P.O. Box 4009, Helena, MT 59604). Tel. 406-444-2040; 800-332-6148.

Nebraska William H. McCartney, Director of Insurance, Terminal Bldg., 941 O St., Suite 400, Lincoln, NE 68508. Tel. 402-471-2201.

Nevada David A. Gates, Commissioner of Insurance, Nye Building, 201 South Fall St., Carson City, NV 89710. Tel. 702-885-4270; 800-992-0900.

New Hampshire Louis E. Bergeron, Insurance Commissioner, 169 Manchester St., Concord, NH 03301. Tel. 603-271-2261; 800-852-3416.

New Jersey Kenneth D. Merin, Commissioner of Insurance, 20 West State St., Trenton, NJ 08625. Tel. 609-292-5363.

New Mexico Fabian Chavez, Superintendent of Insurance, Department of Insurance, P.O. Drawer 1269, Santa Fe, NM 87504-1269. Tel. 505-827-4500.

New York James P. Corcoran, Superintendent of Insurance, 160 W. Broadway, New York, NY 10013. Tel. 212-602-0429; 800-522-4370.

North Carolina* James E. Long, Commissioner of Insurance, Dobbs Building, P.O. Box 26387, Raleigh, NC 27611. Tel. 919-733-7349; 800-662-7777.

North Dakota* Earl R. Pomeroy, Commissioner of Insurance, Capitol Building, Fifth Floor, 600 East Blvd., Bismarck, ND 58505-0320. Tel. 701-224-2440; 800-247-0560.

Ohio George Fabe, Director of Insurance, 2100 Stella Court, Columbus, OH 43266-0566. Tel. 614-644-2658; 800-282-4658.

Oklahoma* Gerald Grimes, Insurance Commissioner, 1901 N. Walnut St., Oklahoma City, OK 73105. Tel. 405-521-2828.

Oregon Theodore R. Kulongoski, Insurance Commissioner, 21 Labor and Industries Bldg., Salem, OR 97310. Tel. 503-378-4271.

Pennsylvania Constance B. Foster, Insurance Commissioner, 1326 Strawberry Square, 13th Floor, Harrisburg, PA 17120. Tel. 717-787-5173.

Puerto Rico Miguel Villafane, Commissioner of Insurance, Fernandez Juncos Station, P.O. Box 8330, Santurce, PR 00910. Tel. 809-722-8686.

Rhode Island Robert J. Janes, Insurance Commissioner, 233 Richmond St., Providence, RI 02903-4233. Tel. 401-277-2246.

South Carolina John G. Richards, Chief Insurance Commissioner, 1612 Marion St., P.O. Box 100105, Columbia, SC 29202-3105. Tel. 803-737-6117.

South Dakota Mary Jane Cleary, Director of Insurance, Insurance Building, 910 E. Sioux Ave., Pierre, SD 57501. Tel. 605-773-3563.

Tennessee Elaine A. McReynolds, Commissioner of Insurance, 500 James Robertson Pkwy., 5th Floor, Nashville, TN 37243-0565. Tel. 615-741-2241; 800-342-4029.

Texas A. W. Pogue, Commissioner of Insurance, 1110 San Jacinto Blvd., Austin, TX 78701-1998. MC001-0. Tel. 512-463-6464.

Utah Harold C. Yancey, Commissioner of Insurance, 160 E. Third St., 300 South, Salt Lake City, UT 84111. Tel. 801-530-6400.

Vermont Gretchen Babcock, Commissioner of Insurance, State Office Building, 120 State St., Montpelier, VT 05602. Tel. 802-828-3301.

Virgin Islands Derek M. Hodge, Commissioner of Insurance, Kongens Gade #18, St. Thomas, VI 00801. Tel. 809-774-2991.

Virginia Steven T. Foster, Commissioner of Insurance, 700 Jefferson Building, Richmond, VA 23219 (P.O. Box 1157, Richmond, VA 23209). Tel. 804-786-3741; 800-552-7945.

Washington* Richard G. Marquardt, Insurance Commissioner, Insurance Building, AQ21, Olympia, WA 98504. Tel. 206-753-7301; 800-562-6900.

West Virginia Hanley Clark, Insurance Commissioner, 2019 Washington St., East, Charleston, WV 25305. Tel. 304-348-3394; 800-642-9004.

Wisconsin Robert D. Haase, Commissioner of Insurance, 123 W. Washington Ave., Madison, WI 53702. Tel. 608-266-0102.

Wyoming Gordon W. Taylor, Insurance Commissioner, Herschler Building, 122 W. 25th St., Cheyenne, WY 82002. Tel. 307-777-7401.

Glossary

accident An event or occurrence that is not foreseen and is unintended.

accidental bodily injury Injury to the body as the result of an accident.

accidental-death clause A clause in a life insurance policy covering what happens when the owner dies as a result of an accident. *See* "double indemnity."

actual cash value The cost of repairing or replacing damaged property with property of the same kind and quality and in the same physical condition; commonly defined as "replacement cost less depreciation."

actuary An accredited technical expert in life insurance. This person, who is professionally trained in mathematics, applies the theory of probability to the business of calculating insurance premiums, policy reserves, and other values.

additional living expense The extra, above-normal costs of food, lodging, and other expenses incurred while a home damaged by an insured peril is being repaired. These additional costs are covered in all forms of the homeowners policy.

adjuster A person who seeks to determine the amount of loss suffered when an insurance claim is submitted and who attempts to settle the claim.

agent Anyone except a duly licensed broker who solicits insurance or aids in the placing of risks, delivery of policies, or collection of premiums on behalf of an insurance company. The "independent" agent usually represents two or more insurance companies under contract in a sales and service capacity and is paid on a commission basis. The "exclusive" agent represents only one company, usually on a commission basis. The "direct writer," or "captive" agent, is the salaried or commissioned employee of a single company.

allied lines A term for forms of insurance allied with fire insurance, covering such perils as sprinkler leakage, water damage, and earthquake.

appearance loss An insurance settlement that pays for the degree of damage from a covered loss when the car or other item is not worth repairing. Also called "loss of value."

appraisal A survey to determine a property's insurable value or the amount of loss.

allowable charge The amount Medicare considers a reasonable charge for medical services or supplies based on the normal and customary charges for a given area.

all-risks coverage Insurance that covers property damage from all perils except those not stated in the policy.

application A form that must be completed by a party who is seeking insurance coverage. This form provides the insurance company with information relevant to its decision to accept or reject the risk.

appurtenant structures Buildings on the same premises as the main building insured under a property insurance policy.

arbitration The binding procedure to settle a claim dispute between insurance company and policyholder. Settlement is determined by two appraisers (one appointed by each party) and a third, neutral party selected by the appraisers.

arson The willful and malicious burning or attempted burning of any structure or other property, often with criminal or fraudulent intent.

assignment The amount of charge Medicare approves for a covered service performed by a doctor or other medical provider.

bail bond A bond that guarantees the appearance of a person in court. It is subject to forfeiture if the person violates the provisions of the bond.

bailee One who has temporary possession of property belonging to another.

basic form A package insurance policy providing coverage against a limited number of specified perils.

blanket coverage Insurance covering more than one item of property at a single location or two or more items of property at different locations.

beneficiary The person(s) designated to receive group-life or accidental-death benefits upon the death of an insured.

benefits The amount payable by the insurance company to a claimant, assignee, or beneficiary under each coverage.

Blue Cross An independent, nonprofit, membership corporation providing protection on a service basis against the cost of hospital care in a limited geographical area.

Blue Shield An independent, nonprofit, membership corporation providing protection on a service basis against the cost of surgery and medical care in a limited geographical area.

bodily-injury-liability coverage Protection for the policyholder in the event that he or she is held financially responsible for another person's bodily injury, sickness, or death.

book value On auto insurance, refers to an average retail price of vehicle.

broad form A package policy providing coverage for the same perils covered in the basic form, plus specified additional perils.

broker A state-licensed person who places business with several insurers and who represents the insurance buyer rather than the insurance company, even though he or she is paid commission by the insurer.

burglary The breaking into of another person's property with felonious intent.

business-income insurance Protection for a business owner against losses resulting from a temporary shutdown because of fire or other insured perils. The insurance provides reimbursement for lost net profits and necessary continuing expenses.

buy-sell agreement An arrangement in a business partnership in which life insurance is taken out by each partner with the other partner as beneficiary, so that if one owner dies, the other can buy the deceased's share in the business with the insurance proceeds.

captive agent *See* agent.

cash value The amount available in cash if a policyholder surrenders or borrows from a policy (usually whole life).

claim Notice to an insurance company that you have suffered a loss and that payment is due under the policy.

coinsurance The arrangement by which the insurer and the insured each pay a percentage of covered losses after the deductible is met.

collision coverage An automobile coverage against damage to the policyholder's vehicle caused by collision with another car or object, or by upset.

commercial lines Insurance for businesses, organizations, institutions, governmental agencies, or other establishments.

comprehensive coverage Coverage against loss or damage to a car from a number of perils, including fire, theft, windstorm, flood, and vandalism.

compulsory insurance Any form of insurance that is required by law.

consequential loss A loss resulting from, but not caused directly by, an insured peril—for example, any spoilage of contents resulting from the loss of refrigeration, which was itself caused by a fire.

consultant An independent insurance expert who does not sell products.

conversion privilege The right given to the insured to change group-life and medical-care coverages to a form of individual insurance without medical examination. The conditions under which conversion can be made are defined in the master policy.

copayment Under Medicare, the insured's share of expenses after the deductible is taken.

current interest rate In life insurance, a term used in contrast with "guaranteed interest rate," which is lower and is considered a worst-case outcome.

custom work On a farm policy, the performance of work by the insured for others for a fee.

death benefit The amount of money the beneficiary stands to receive when the owner of a life insurance policy dies.

deductible The amount a policyholder agrees to pay, per claim or per accident, toward the total amount of an insured loss. Insurance is written at reduced rates depending on how high the deductible is.

depreciation A decrease in the value of property because of wear and tear or obsolescence.

dividend An amount returned to a policyholder by an insurance company out of its earnings. Also, in capital stock companies, a share of the profits distributed to stockholders.

double indemnity A policy provision offered for injury or death that doubles the payment of benefits when accidents occur under designated circumstances.

earned premium The part of the premium that has gone for coverage already provided and that the insurer has, therefore, "earned."

earnings In business insurance, refers to actual net profit, plus payroll expenses, taxes, rents, and other operating expenses normally charged in your business.

effective date The date on which the insurance under a policy begins.

elimination period A specific period of time, beginning at the onset of a disability, that must pass before any policy benefits will be paid. Also known as the "waiting period."

endorsement A form attached to any insurance policy to add to, alter, or vary its provisions.

excess charges The amount of a doctor's or hospital's bill above what Medicare allows and approves under "assignment."

exclusion A provision in an insurance policy that denies coverage for certain perils, persons, property, or location.

experience modification A term in worker's compensation insurance referring to an employer's record of past losses. By having a good record, the employer can earn a discount on the worker's compensation premium.

expiration date The date indicated in an insurance contract as its termination date.

explanation of benefits (EOB) form The form Medicare sends a subscriber, along with a check, to show what Medicare covers.

extended coverages Protection against property damage caused by windstorm, hail, smoke, explosion, riot or civil commotion, vehicle, and aircraft.

fair-market value The price that other items of this type bring on the open market; what an item can be sold for.

financial-needs analysis (FNA) A procedure performed to find out how much life insurance a family needs. Also called a "capital-needs analysis."

financial planner A generalist who can advise a client on the purchase of insurance within the context of an overall financial picture.

financial-responsibility law A law under which a person involved in an automobile accident may be required to furnish security up to certain minimum dollar limits.

fire insurance Coverage for losses caused by fire and lightning, for the removal of property from endangered premises, and for damage caused by smoke and water.

floater A form of insurance that applies to movable property, whatever its location, within the territorial limits imposed by the contract. The coverage "floats" with the property.

flood insurance Coverage against loss resulting from the flood peril.

fraud A deception or strategy used to deceive or cheat, including misrepresentation or concealment.

general liability insurance A form of coverage that pertains, for the most part, to claims arising out of the insured's liability for injuries or damage caused by ownership of property, manufacturing operations, contracting operations, or sale or distribution of products.

glass insurance Protection for loss of or damage to glass and its appurtenances.

group insurance Any insurance plan that covers a number of persons and their dependents under a single policy that is issued to their employer or to an association with which they are affiliated, with individual certificates given to each insured person.

grace period A specified amount of time (often 30 or 31 days) after a premium payment is due in which the policyholder may make such payment without incurring a penalty or loss of coverage.

guaranteed insurability option (GIO) The guarantee that life insurance will be provided under certain conditions or at certain times.

guaranteed renewable contract A contract that the insurer has no right to change unilaterally as long as the policy is in force, other than to make a change in the premium rate for classes of policyholders.

hazard A condition that creates or increases the risk of property damage, bodily injury, or loss of life.

health insurance Insurance against financial losses resulting from sickness or bodily injury.

health maintenance organization (HMO) A prepaid, comprehensive health insurance plan, with fixed rates being paid for services by specified medical providers.

homeowners policy Insurance ranging from coverage for fire and other specified perils, theft, and personal liability, to coverage for all perils except those specifically excluded.

hospice A health-care facility providing medical care and support services to terminally ill persons.

incontestable clause An optional clause (which may be used in guaranteed renewable health insurance contracts) that prevents the insurer from contesting the validity of the contract after it has been in force for two, and sometimes three, years.

independent agent *See* agent.

inland marine coverage A broad type of insurance, generally covering articles that may be transported from one place to another.

insurable risk The conditions that make a risk insurable, such as the following: (1) the peril insured against must produce a definite loss not under the control of the insured; (2) there must be a large number of homogeneous exposures subject to the same perils; (3) the loss must be calculable, and the cost of insuring it must be economically feasible; (4) the peril must be unlikely to affect all insureds simultaneously; and (5) the loss produced by a risk must be definite and have the potential to be financially serious.

insurance Protection by written contract against the financial hazards of specified happenings or fortuitous events.

insurance company Any corporation primarily engaged in the business of selling insurance protection to the public.

key-man or *key-person insurance* An individual policy designed to protect a firm against the loss of income resulting from the death or disability of a highly important employee.

lapse Termination of a policy upon the policyholder's failure to pay the premium within the time required.

liability Any legally enforceable obligation or its cost.

limit The maximum amount of benefits that an insurer agrees to pay in the event of a loss.

loss The amount of insurance or benefits for which the insurer becomes liable when the event insured against occurs.

loss of use A homeowners coverage for having to live outside your house while it is being fixed because of a covered loss.

major medical insurance Health insurance to finance the expense of major illness and injury, characterized by large benefit maximums ranging up to $250,000 or no limit. After an initial deductible, the insurance reimburses the major part of all charges for the hospital, doctors, private nurses, medical appliances, prescribed out-of-hospital treatments, drugs, and medicines. The insured person pays the remainder as coinsurer.

malicious mischief Damage or destruction willfully inflicted on another person's property.

maximum benefit In health insurance, the maximum amount of money the insurance company will pay for a covered illness or injury.

Medicaid A state-funded program of public assistance available to qualifying persons whose income and resources are insufficient to pay for health care.

medical-expense insurance A liability coverage in which the insurer agrees to reimburse the insured and others for medical or funeral expenses incurred under specified conditions without regard for the insured's liability.

Medicare The hospital insurance system and supplementary medical insurance for the aged created by the 1965 amendments to the Social Security Act.

medigap A term sometimes applied to private insurance products that supplement Medicare insurance benefits.

miscellaneous expenses A category of expenses under hospital insurance, such as for X-rays, drugs, and laboratory tests—i.e., charges other than room and board.

named perils Perils specified in a policy as those against which the policyholder is insured.

negligence Failure to use the degree of care that a person of reasonable prudence would use under given or similar circumstances.

no-fault auto insurance A form of insurance by which certain financial losses resulting from an automobile accident, such as medical expenses and loss of income, are paid by a person's own insurance company without regard to fault.

nonparticipating life insurance Life insurance policies that do not pay dividends.

packaging The combining of several insurance programs under one policy for one premium.

pain and suffering award An amount of cash paid to compensate the victim of an automobile accident for the pain and inconvenience involved.

participating policy A whole life insurance policy that expects to pay dividends.

peril The cause of a loss against which protection is provided.

policy A legal contract that sets forth the rights and obligations of both the policyholder and the insurance company.

policyholder The legal entity (employer, union, trustee, creditor) to whom an insurer issues a contract.

policy term The period for which an insurance policy provides coverage.

preexisting conditions A physical or mental condition of an insured that manifested itself prior to the issuance of his or her policy, or a condition that existed prior to issuance for which treatment was received.

preferred provider organization (PPO) An arrangement whereby a third-party payor contracts with a group of medical-care providers who furnish services at fees lower than usual in return for prompt payment and a certain volume of patients.

premium The periodic payment required to keep a policy in force.

professional liability insurance Coverage for a practitioner such as a doctor or lawyer against liability claims for alleged improper care or treatment of the insured. Often called "malpractice" insurance.

property-damage-liability insurance Protection for when you are at fault in an accident that damages someone else's property.

rate The cost of a given unit of insurance on which a premium is based.

rate-up An increase in premium on a health insurance policy based on a preexisting condition.

reasonable and customary A charge for health care that is consistent with the going rate or charge in a certain geographical area for identical or similar services.

reentry policy In term life you must qualify medically in a number of years or pay extra to continue coverage.

reinstatement The resumption of coverage under a policy that has lapsed.

renewal An offer and acceptance of a premium for a new policy term.

rents In business insurance, it is differentiated from earnings in that it is strictly the rent money collected each month.

replacement cost The cost to replace your damaged property at today's prices.

respondent The party being sued.

risk The probable amount of loss foreseen by an insurer in issuing a contract.

salvage Property taken over by an insurer after paying a claim to reduce its loss.

schedule A list of individual items or groups of items not ordinarily covered in an insurance policy that adds them to the policy.

self-insurance A group insurance program whose benefits are financed entirely through the internal means of the policyholder; an alternative to purchasing coverage from a commercial carrier.

standard risk A person classified by an insurance company as being entitled to protection without extra rating or special restriction.

state insurance department A department of a state government whose duty it is to regulate the business of insurance and give the public information on insurance.

stop-loss provision A term indicating the amount of a health insurance claim that is subject to coinsurance. It is also thought of as the maximum amount paid out of pocket, after which the insurance company pays 100 percent.

subrogation A procedure for collecting on an automobile claim when the other driver was at fault by collecting from your insurance company, minus the deductible, and then letting your insurance collect from the other driver's insurance, hopefully recovering your deductible for you.

substandard insurance Insurance issued with an extra premium or special restriction to persons with higher than average mortality rates.

substandard risk An individual who, because of health history or driving record, does not measure up to the underwriting criteria of a standard risk.

term life insurance Insurance that covers you for a specified amount of time with no provisions for accumulating cash value.

theft The taking of something that is not one's own.

time limit The period of time during which notice of claim or proof of loss must be filed.

umbrella liability A form of protection against losses in excess of the amount covered by other liability insurance policies. It also protects against many situations not covered by the usual liability policies.

underinsured-motorist coverage Insurance that pays the insured's losses when the driver at fault has inadequate liability coverage.

underwriter A term that applies to any of the following: (1) a company that receives premiums and accepts responsibility for the fulfillment of the policy contract; (2) a company employee who decides whether the company should assume a particular risk; (3) the agent who sells the policy.

unearned premium That portion of the paid premium applying to the remaining policy term, or that portion of the paid premium for which protection has not been received.

uninsurable risk One deemed not acceptable for insurance because of excessive risk.

uninsured-motorist coverage Insurance that pays for your losses when the other driver is at fault but is uninsured or can't be found.

universal life insurance Lifetime insurance that exhibits a term price for the cost of the insurance while the remainder of the premium goes into an interest-building account.

vandalism The malicious, often random, destruction or spoilage of another person's property.

vanishing premium In whole life insurance, an option to stop paying premiums after a certain number of years and let the dividends pay the premium. Also called "disappearing premium."

variable life insurance An investment instrument sold by prospectus, in which some or all of the cash value is directed into the securities market, commonly through mutual funds. The death benefit "varies" with the success of the investments.

waiting period The length of time an employee must wait from his or her date of employment for insurance coverage to be effective.

waiver The voluntary surrender of a right or privilege known to exist.

waiver of premium A provision that a person's insurance will be kept in full force by the insurer without further payment of the premium in the event of certain circumstances.

whole life insurance Insurance that protects you for your lifetime and accumulates cash values. These can be taken at any time or used to borrow against the policy.

workers' compensation Insurance against liability imposed on certain employers to pay benefits and furnish care to employees who are injured, and to pay benefits to dependents of employees who die as a result of their employment.

Bibliography

Books

Chasen, Nancy H. *Policy Wise*. Glenview, IL: Scott, Foresman and Company, Lifelong Learning Division, 1983.

Edwards, Paul and Sarah. *Working from Home*. Los Angeles, CA: Jeremy P. Tarcher, Inc., 1985. New York: distributed by St. Martin's Press, 1985.

Golonka, Nancy. *How to Protect What's Yours*. Washington, DC: Acropolis Books Ltd., 1983.

Insurance Facts: Property/Casualty Fact Book (Annual). New York: Insurance Information Institute, 1990.

Kuehl, Charles R. *Small Business Planning and Management*. New York: The Dryden Press, 1987.

Smith, Randy Baca. *Setting Up Shop*. New York: McGraw-Hill Book Co., 1982.

Bulletins and Pamphlets

Average Auto Premiums By State—1988. Oldwick, NJ: Best Insurance Management Reports Release No. 4. A. M. Best Company, 1990.

Gabel, Jon; DiCarlo, Steven; Fink, Steven; and de Lissovoy, Gregory. *Research Bulletin—The Health Insurance Picture in 1988*. Health Insurance Association of America, P.O. Box 41455, Washington, DC 20018.

Guide to Health Insurance for People with Medicare. National Association of Insurance Commissioners and the Health Care Financing Administration of the U.S. Department of Health and Human Services, Washington, DC, January 1990.

Sharing the Risk. 3d ed. rev. New York: Insurance Information Institute, 1989.

Source Book of Health Insurance Data 1989. Health Insurance Association of America, P.O. Box 41455, Washington, DC 20018.

Magazines

"Auto Insurance." *Consumer Reports* (October 1988).

"Beyond Medicare." *Consumer Reports* (June 1989).

Bladen, Ashby. "Life Insurance: One of Your Best Investments." *Forbes* (26 June 1989).

Blease, Roger and Pallay, Gary S. "Annual Renewable Term Policy Comparison." *Best's Review* (December 1989).

Bussewitz, Walter. "New Marketing Options in Healthcare." *Life* Association News (January 1988).

"Claims." *Consumer Reports* (October 1988).

"Do You Have Enough Property Insurance?" *Consumer's Research* (August 1989).

Godwin, Philip. "Health Insurance: What You Need, What You Get." *Changing Times* (April 1988).

"Home Insurance: Protecting Almost Everything You Own." *Changing Times* (June 1988).

"How You Can Save on Car Insurance." *Reader's Digest* (May 1989).

"Insuring Your Home." *Consumer Reports* (September 1989).

Klein, Robert J. "A Shopper's Guide to Buying the Best Term Policy." *Money* (August 1989).

Kosnett, Jeff. "Best Buys in Life Insurance." *Changing Times* (April 1988).

Kosnett, Jeff. "Life Insurance after 40." *Changing Times* (May 1989).

Kosnett, Jeff. "The Facts of Life Insurance." *Changing Times* (March 1988).

Marshman, Frances C. "What You Need to Know About Medicare." *Money Guide* (1989).

Pallay, Gary S. "Participating Whole Life Policy Comparison." *Best's Review* (August 1989).

Quinn, Jane Bryant. "The Health Policy Crunch." *Newsweek* (6 November 1989).

Reid, Jeanne L. "Shopping for Health Insurance." *Money* (June 1988).

Rowland, Mary. "Life Insurance." *Working Woman* (June 1988).

Schaeffer, Charles. "Medigap—Costs More, Covers Less." *Changing Times* (April 1989).

Smith, Marguerite T. "Why You Might Go for a Cash-Value Policy." *Money* (December 1988).

Taub, J. S. "Finding Help for a Health Plan Search.' *Independent Business* (March/April 1990).

Walbert, Laura R. "Shopping for Life." *Forbes* (22 February 1988).

Index